BUILDING NEIGHBORHOODS:

JACKSON COUNTY, TENNESSEE

PRIOR TO 1820

Abstractions from Record Group 50, Early Land Records,
Tennessee State Library and Archives

By

BETTY HUFF BRYANT

JANAWAY PUBLISHING, INC.
Santa Maria, California
2014

Building Neighborhoods:
Jackson County, Tennessee, Prior to 1820

Copyright © 1992 by Betty Huff Bryant
All rights reserved.

Originally published,
1992

Reprinted by

Janaway Publishing, Inc.
732 Kelsey Ct.
Santa Maria, California 93454
(805) 925-1038
www.JanawayGenealogy.com

2014

Library of Congress Control Number: 2014940468

ISBN: 978-1-59641-329-0

Made in the United States of America

Acknowledgements:

    Staff of Tennessee State Library and Archives, Manuscript Section. I can not name them all because there are so many of them, and I have worked on this project so long, many of them are now "out of place." That quotation is from a document dated 1817 in Jackson County. The document had not been properly registered, original witnesses were "out of place," and the document had to be re-executed. Library staff members especially patient and helpful are Ann Alley, Ann Bomar, Wayne Moore, Vince McGrath, and Robert DePriest.

    Friends and supporters, members of Upper Cumberland Genealogical Association, Inc., Cookeville, TN. Especially Maurine Ensor Patton and Jane Kirkpatrick Wall who encouraged and sustained me.

    The Jackson County Historical Society, Gainesboro, TN, especially Moldon Tayse.

    Dedicated volunteers everywhere who labor because they are **Specific Historians**; they want to know how things really were and who was really there. A widely accepted fact is that "Washington crossed the Delaware." Specific Historians want to know who was rowing the boat.

    Isam and Willene Keith, Baxter, TN, who provide me a home base away from home.

    Christine Spivey Jones, Special Collections, Tennessee Technological University, Cookeville, TN.

    Teresa Boaz, Marion, IL. Librarian, friend and cousin who accompanied me on the first and subsequent field trips to Jackson County.

JACKSON COUNTY, TENNESSEE
BUILDING NEIGHBORHOODS

Table of Contents

Original Record Book	Entry Numbers	Page
Introduction		1
Reel 4 Bk8	Misc.	
Bk9		
Bk10		
Reel 17 Bk53	7524-8194	5
Bk54	2-237	7
Matthew Rhea's map		28
Bk55	23- 71	29
Bk56	None	29
Bk57	None	29
Bk58	69-354	30
Reel 5 Bk16	3-154	35
Reel 6 Bk23	328-1724	39
Bk24	1902-4147	42
Reel 7 Bk26	4180-5500	51
Bk25	5543-7235	59
Bk27	7254-9364	71
Reel 8 Bk28	9375-11365	93
Bk29	11413-14425	123
Reel 9 Bk30	14484-18307	147
Bk31	18385-22420	175
Conclusion		197
1836 Map of Jackson County		202
Field Notes		202
Index by Entry Numbers		215

Note: Changes of officials and jurisdictions resulted in some duplicate entry numbers. Prior to filming, original books were arbitrarily assigned identifying numbers which are not in date sequence. Consequently, in order to access an original record, both Book Number and Entry Number must be known. To use the index to "Building Neighborhoods," you must first find your ancestor's name and entry number. Then refer to this Table of Contents to determine **Original Record Book** and the page number herein on which abstractions from that Original Record Book begin. Examples: If Entry Number in the index is 10, the entry might be in Book 54 or Book 16. If Entry Number is 8000, it might be in Book 53 or Book 27. Good luck!.

JACKSON COUNTY, TENNESSEE
BUILDING NEIGHBORHOODS

Abbreviations and Terms

ase	assignee of
Cr	Creek
R	River
Br	Branch
E	East
W	West
N	North
S	South
ac	acre
acs	acres
Co	County
incl	include/including
excl	exclude/excluding
Loc	Locator
Fk	Fork
beg	Beginning
Dec	Deceased, except when in a date
?	I can not decipher or understand
sd	said
SR	Senior
JR	Junior
adj	adjacent (Terms in records are sometimes "jinin" or "up agin.")
Sur	Survey
rtd	returned
DS	Deputy Surveyor

Things to remember:

Surveyor's term - 1 pole = 16.5 feet or 5.5 yards.
640 acs = 1 square mile
Including and excluding = surrounding but not counted in acreage.
Spelling of proper names follows the source so is not consistent.
E. G. Huff may be Hough; Pharis may be Farriss; McCown may be McCowan or McKaughan.

BUILDING NEIGHBORHOODS
From
EARLY LAND RECORDS OF TENNESSEE

INTRODUCTION

Complete enjoyment of "Building Neighborhoods" requires prior study of a leaflet "Land Records in the Tennessee State Library and Archives" prepared by and available from the Library and Archives in Nashville. A second step should be study of *The Preemptors: Middle Tennessee's First Settlers* compiled by Irene M. Griffey of Clarksville, TN 37041.

The Preemptors catalogs persons already living on the land before the first day of June 1780 as determined in 1782 and 1783 when Commissioners Anthony Bledsoe, Isaac Shelby and Absalom Tatum surveyed the Military Reservation authorized by North Carolna in 1782 as recorded by David Shelby, whose original record book is preserved in the North Carolina State Archives.

One of those preemptors, Spilby or Spelsby Coleman, is recorded as living on the south side of the Cumberland near the mouth of Obey's River. He is probably the earliest recorded settler in what became Jackson County because his name also appears on the 1802 tax list.

"Building Neighborhoods" was conceived as an attempt to discover exactly who were the earliest settlers on Martin's Creek. The project grew in scope to include all of Old Jackson County as it was prior to the alphabetized census of 1820 which gives no sense of neighborhood. Obviously, there were individuals and family members who are not mentioned in land entries. Early surveys, courts, and churches provide more names. Significantly, the 1990 census of Jackson County lists several hundred **fewer** residents than did the census for 1830.

In its earliest occupation by non-Indians, Martin's Creek was the geographical center (north-to-south axis) of Old Jackson County. Before that, it was a mere wrinkle in the aspirations of North Carolina's Washington County. Washington County was divided in 1777 to create Sullivan County.

RG 50 SERIES 2 - LAND ENTRIES - BOOK 8 REEL 4
NORTH CAROLINA - SULLIVAN AND WASHINGTON COUNTIES
1778 - 1783

The bounds of Sullivan County were established by an Act passed in November 1777.

"Washington shall be divided into two distinct counties by a line beginning at the Steep Rock, thence running along the dividing ridge that divides the waters of the Great Kanaway and the Tennessee to the Head of Indian Creek, thence along the Ridge that divides the waters of Holston and Wattauga to the Mouth of Wattauga; thence a direct line to the highest part of the

Chimneytop Mountain at the Indian Boundary, and that all that part of the said County of Washington which lies Northwardly of the said dividing line shall be erected into a new and distinct County by the name of Sullivan County; and that all the other part of said County which lies Southwardly of said dividing line shall continue and remain as a distinct County by the name of Washington."

Notice no western boundaries were stated except for the vague "Indian Boundary," and no southern boundary was described for Washington.

"A Report of the quantity of acres of land entered
In the Entry taker's office kept in Sullivan County, North Carolina
By
Gilbert Christian, late Entry Taker in said County."

The list has dates, names and quantities, but no locations. After years of studying Martin's Creek, Jackson County, names that seem relevant are:

Col. William Russell	Joseph Wallace
Evan Shelby	William Anderson
Moses Shelby	William Young
Samuel Wilson	Elizabeth Young
Joseph Martin	John Anderson
Thomas Houghton	**Henry Turney**
Joshuah Houghton	David Gamble
Anthony Bledsoe	Robert Allison
John Looney	Thomas Taylor
Josiah Ramsay	John Hannah
John Hagard	Andrew Leeper
John Donaldson	Robert Gilliland
Timothy Ecuff	William Blevins
(Sometimes transcribed as Huff.)	
John Shelby	Robert Preston
Stockley Donaldson	Patrick Henry
Joseph Martin	Samuel Wilson
Thomas Sharp	**Garet Fitzgerril**
William Hughs	**Isin Faris**

Many more names are on the list, but the Sullivan County list consists of explorers, soldiers, and speculators rather than permanent settlers. And in 1778, there were no recorded settlers on Martin's Creek.

The next list is for Washington County, 1778. It contains John Sevier, Garret Fitzgerrald, **Stephen Huff**, John Denton, Joseph Martin, and many more, but 1778 is still too early for Martin's Creek. These early lists are of folks who pushed first through the mountains and later to the Cumberland. They were not settlers by nature but pushers and speculators.

Series 2, Book 9 - Has more lists for Sullivan and

Washington Counties for the 1780's. Two names that capture the imagination are **Henry Turney and Josiah Ramsey.** These two names surface on Martin's Creek, and they were on the list of captives released by the Shawnees and their Cherokee guests on the Scioto River in 1765 after Col. Bouquet's campaign and the resulting Peace of Paris. **Samuel Huff** was one of those captives, also, and he surfaced in Old Jackson County, Tennessee.

Series 2, Book 10 contains a list of North Carolina Invalids' Entries (Continental Line) 1787 - 1805. The fourth page into the Book, has Entry No. 115 - Joseph Williamson Heirs.

"William White, Secretary of State to William Christmas, Esq. Surveyor.

"Greeting:

"You are hereby required to lay off and survey for the **Heirs of Joseph Williamson**, a private in the line of this State, Six hundred forty acres of land within the limits of the land reserved by law for the officers and soldiers of the Continental line of this State: Observing the directions of the acts of assembly in such cases made and provided .. Two just and fair plans thereof with a certificate to each annexed. You are to transmit, with this warrant, to the Secretary's office within the time limited by law. Given under my hand at Raleigh, 16 May 1804. Signed Will. White."

Children of Joseph Williamson were among the earliest settlers on Martin's Creek as documented in records of Smith County, TN, and Montgomery County, VA.

Series 2, Books 11 and 12, still Reel 4 are for Davidson and Dickson Counties. Book 13 is for Jackson County 1832 and later and will be abstracted as chronology requires.

The purpose at hand is to discover the earliest folks in Jackson County and on Martin's Creek. Tax lists exist for 1802 and 1803 but they do not include Martin's Creek and points south because those areas were still in Smith County until 1806. A list of qualified voters in 1812 exists, but two companies are missing - the lists for Martin's Creek and points south. Then the early census schedules were alphabetized before they were preserved.

Tax lists for 1836 are the earliest reliable lists we have. Because the County was formed in 1801 with many folks already present, most of the people on that 1836 list were **not** the earliest settlers but second generation or later arrivals.

Study in Tennessee State Library and Archives Record Group 50, Early Land Records, holds many frustrations. First there is deciphering ancient handwriting by clerks and surveyors of varying degrees of talent, sobriety and conscientious care.

Many of the land descriptions are vague and incomplete. Creeks and other landmarks have disappeared or their names have changed. Record Books do not surface in a perceivable order. Changes in political jurisdiction or government agency required copying of records with resultant errors. When a new agency was formed, it quite naturally started a new series of numbers causing duplications in Entry Numbers. Consequently, in searching for a record, the Number of the **Book** must be known along with the Entry Number.

Sometimes the County Lines were vague and frequently changed. Creeks, cornfields and jack rabbits did not care anyway. Folks also moved across County lines, so some references herein are to counties other than Jackson because the folks involved are known to have moved back and forth.

These frustrations were over-shadowed by the humor, pathos and drama. As this study progressed, I fell in love with a clerk who tried (and failed!) to determine the possessive for a man named Waters.

And late one night, my laughter aroused my family. They peered over my shoulder at the film, but failed to see the humor. I was reading land conveyances.

"Look how the handwriting changes between 10:00 a.m. and 5:00 p.m.," I said.

Still no one caught the joke, so I said

"Look at the **date**."

It was December 24, Christmas Eve in 1819. One son observed, finally, that the worthy clerk must have been celebrating. The word for it then was "tippling," and our friend, the clerk, should have re-copied those last several registrations! He was certainly in the "spirits" before his workday ended because of all the "cheer" he shared with his callers.

For drama, there was the unexpected discovery of a young wife mortgaging the family farm to an attorney for his defense of her husband on a murder charge. Then her family and the young husband's parents, brothers, etc. mortgaged **their** farms. Followed through the records, that story was a tragedy that unfolded more compellingly than any piece of fiction.

If the approach to this study seems less scholarly than might be expected, consider the emotional impact of all these real folks whose feet and backs hurt, whose hands were calloused and cold, whose hopes, courage, and spirit sustain us even now.

Let's find ancestors, their landmarks and their neighbors. Listen to them laugh and cry. They are ours. Yours and mine.

BUILDING NEIGHBORHOODS
From
EARLY LAND RECORDS OF TENNESSEE
RG 50 SERIES 2 - LAND ENTRY BOOK 53 - REEL 17
MIDDLE TENNESSEE 1797 - 1799

Trust no index. Book 53. Begin. Jackson & Smith Counties did not yet exist, so we read for Sumner. This is early material, much of it illegible, dealing with early heroes chronicled by other historians. Book 53 contains references to land which would later fall into Smith or Jackson, present-day Clay and Macon Counties.

BK PG   NUMBER   DESCRIPTION

53 158?   7524   **Martin Armstrong** ase of George Freelocks heirs (Trulock's?) .. 640 acs on a small branch of the Middle fork of Big Barren River near the head of the branch where **William Barker and Elijah Allen** killed two Bufaloes in a beaver dam on the south side of the middle fork of said Barren River to run on both sides of the branch to incl a spring on the north side and the beaver dam for compliment. Wm. Barker, Loc. Warrant No. 2974. 9 June 1797

53 163   7591   **Delilah Roberts** ase Guilford Reed .. 640 acs .. Cedar Cr .. beg at James Davis NW corner ... at a sugar tree & lyn .. S 320 poles to 2 lyns then W for compliment. Delilah Roberts. Saml Barton, Loc. 17 June 1797.

Someone determine where that land was! No County, no major waterway, a name like James Davis, and 4 trees -- one sugar and three lynns. And who was Delilah Roberts, we wonder.

Press of land entries in 1797 was on waters of Barren River which is in Kentucky. Creeks, like jack rabbits, have no respect for political jurisdictions. They follow the path of least resistance. Few settlers are mentioned in Book 53. Robert Stothart was prominent with Locator Thomas Johnson and/or Thos John.

53 172   7694   **James Caman** ase heirs of John Empson .. 640 acs .. both sides of Muires fork of Caney fork of Cumberland R. Robert King, Loc. 7 July 1797.

That's the earliest entry discovered for Caney Fork. And could James Caman possibly be Cammorn or Cameron? He made several entries on Caney Fk mentioning Muire's or Mures Fk, an island, junction with the Calf Killer, and a 5,000 ac survey for Eliz. Williams.

53 174   7722   **James Winchester** .. 1,280 acs .. to begin at the 53 mile tree marked U S standing in the north line established as a boundary between the United States and the Cherokee Indians to run northeast with said line and north for complement. J. Winchester. 13 July 1797.

5

The date of that entry almost coincides with the dates of the survey of the Cherokee Boundary by General Winchester's survey party accompanied by Cherokee Chief Culsatehee and 20 Cherokee warriors.

53 175 7733 **Daniel Wilbourn** ase of Thomas Vaney .. 640 acs .. Sumner Co .. S side of Cumberland above the mouth of the Caney Fk on the **waters of Martin's Cr** .. on the first W fork of Martin's Cr .. head of a spring .. beach marked AP & DW .. E and N .. Daniel Wilbourn. 14 July 1797.

That's the earliest land entry found for Martin's Creek, and notice, it was still in Sumner County in 1797.

53 176 7743 **Robert Stothart** .. 640 acs .. S side of Cumberland .. on the Caney Fk joining Mr. or Wm. Hughlett's survey .. joining Gen'l Hogan's tract of 12,000 acs .. James Mulherrin, Loc. 20 July 1797. Survey rtd 14 June 1809 by Willis Jones.

Many entries appear for James Easton on Caney Fk in 1797, and for Redmond D. Barry. Barry was not, relatively speaking, a small operator. A later entry informs that his middle name was Dillon.

His is one of several names i.e. William Tyrell, William Terrell Lewis, Stokely Donelson, Robert Stothart, James Mulherrin, Howell Tatum, etc. associated with the early history of Martin's Creek and Jackson County. They were politicians and speculators who possibly never saw the land beyond the path they traveled and had little if any personal impact on the social history. They took their profits or losses and moved on.

53 204 8127 **William Christmas** .. ase Nehemiah Williams .. 228 acs .. on road leading from Cumberland mountain to **Fort Blount** .. beg ..in the Military line .. 13 Nov 1797.

53 206 8161 **Joseph Woodfork** .. 640 acs .. E fork of War Trace .. J. Murrey, Loc. 20 Nov 1797. (Apologies to descendants who do not like that spelling, but the entry is very legibly "Woodfork.")

53 209 8194 **Joseph Woodfork** .. 640 acs .. a fork of Dixon's Cr .. where **Frederick Debo**, Patrick Forbush and Peter Turney killed a buffaloe .. to incl .. improvement made by Peter Turney. Joseph Woodfork, Loc. 14 Dec 1797

53 210 "Martin Armstrong, Surveyor and Entry taker of lands granted to Officers and soldiers of the Continental Line .. certifies .. the foregoing entries .. are true and perfect copies .. 12 July 1799."

RG 50 SERIES 2: ENTRY BOOK 54, MIDDLE TENNESSEE 1802-1806.
INDEXED
(AT THE END-MILITARY WARRANTS)

Whatever that heading means, be aware. The index at the beginning is incomplete. Use of the term "Middle Tennessee" is confusing. These entries were in what we know as Middle Tennessee, but at the time, everything west of Knoxville was still West Tennessee. Later, the Mountain District was formed encompassing Jackson and White Counties. The abbreviations "Mtn" or "MTN" or "M TN" can mean "Middle Tennessee" or "Mountain" District.

The following abstracts are **all in Jackson Co unless otherwise noted.** Recall: 1801 - 1806 Jackson Co included what became Overton, part of Fentress, part of White, et al. It was a huge, vaguely defined area extending to the southern state line, wherever you perceived that line to be - depending on your ethnic and political orientation. Land Entries in Book 54 which can be identified as definitely falling outside of what became Jackson County in 1806 are generally omitted from this transcription. Recall also that the Smith County line followed the ridge between Martin's and Flynn's Creek, leaving Martin's Creek in Smith County until 1806.

BK	PG	NUMBER	DESCRIPTION
54	1	2	**James Lock** .. 200 acs .. Jennings Cr .. 9 Mar 1802.
54	2	3	**Garrett Fitzgerald** .. 170 acs .. Doe Cr .. Armstrong's and Gourd's improvement. 9 Mar 1802.
54	2	4	**Garrett Fitzgerald** .. 670 acs .. dividing ridge between Doe and Flynn's Cr " .. incl my improvement on the ridge and a pond." 9 Mar 1802.
54	3	5	**Garrett Fitzgerald** .. 270 acs .. E side of Flynn's Cr .. adj his own. 9 Mar 1802.
54	3	6	**John Russell** .. 300 acs .. adj William Russell. 9 Mar 1802.
54	4	8	**Rich Ratton** .. 200 acs .. S Br of Spring Cr .. to incl sd Ratton's improvement. 9 Mar 1802.
54	4	9	**Joseph Russell** .. 640 acs .. Jenning's Cr .. adj Buckner Russell's line .. to incl sd Russell's improvement. 9 Mar 1802
54	4	10	**Joseph Lock** .. 640 acs .. adj Haner's corner .. N side of Cumberland .. 200 yards above mouth of Roaring R .. to incl part of a large knob .. 10 Mar 1802.
54	5	11	**Joseph Lock** .. 200 acs .. S side of Cumberland .. adj Hickman .. 10 Mar 1802.

54	5	12	**Garrett Fitzgerald** .. 200 acs .. on Doe Cr beg above Armstrong's improvement .. 12 Mar 1802.
54	5	13	**Garret Fitzgerald** .. 50 acs .. Doe Cr .. to incl **James Isham's** spring and improvement. 12 Mar 1802.
54	5	14	**David Harbert** .. 400 acs .. ridge between Flynn's Cr and Roaring R .. adj Garret Fitzgerald .. 12 Mar 1802.
54	5	15	**John Houser** .. 640 acs .. ridge between Flynn's and Roaring R **where sd Houser now lives**. 12 Mar 1802.
54	6	16	**James Taylor** .. 640 acs adj his own .. in The Barrens adj William Pryor .. John Sullivan, Loc. 16 Mar 1802.
54	6	17	**Benjamin Ford** .. 150 acs .. waters of Cumberland beg on the Cave Spring Br adj Henry McKinny .. 16 Mar 1802.
54	6	18	**David and John Womack** .. 640 acs .. E fork of Russel Mill Cr .. westwardly to Prior's line .. incl sink hole, spring and improvement **where sd Womack lives** .. then to incl the content between James Taylor and Womack .. 19 Mar 1802.
54	6	19	**Garret Fitzgerald** .. 50 acs .. S side of Cumberland .. adj his on the R. 19 Mar 1802.
54	7	20	**Joseph Pryor** .. 460 acs .. E fork of S fork of Roaring R .. 20 Mar 1802.
54	7	21	**John Fitzgerald** .. 200 acs .. on Doe Cr adj Garret Fitzgerald name of **Gord's improvement** .. 20 Mar 1802.
54	7	22	**William Robertson** .. 100 acs on a small branch of Roaring R .. 25 Mar 1802.
54	7	23	**William Robertson** .. 100 acs .. on the creek **that he lives on** .. 20 Mar 1802.
54	8	24	**John McNairy** .. 640 acs .. S of Golston's tract .. adj Moses Fisk's location entered May 1801 .. adj .. improvement **McLane got of Goodpasture and now lives on** .. Moses Fisk, Loc. 25 Mar 1802.
54	8	25	**William Terrell Lewis** ase of Stockley Donnelson .. 640 acs .. headwaters of Sugar Cr .. beg at a chestnut and poplar marked by Capt. Williams in Apr 1800 as mile trees .. surveying for John Love .. Moses Fisk Loc. 25 Mar 1802.
54	9	26	**Edward Harris** ase of Henry Bonner, Executor and devisee of James and John Bonner, ase of heirs of Solomon Overton .. 1,000 acs .. Sugar Cr and Roaring R .. near

path leading from Hutcheson's towards Mr. Ewing's .. 640 acs **John Hutcheson Jr has settled** as tenant for trial by Moses Fisk, Benjamin Stowell etc sometime in December last .. Moses Fisk, Loc. 25 Mar 1802.

54	9	27	**William T. Lewis** .. 640 acs .. headwaters of Sampson's fork and some of the branches of Roaring R .. ridge near where the path leading from David Mitchell's to Hutcherson's and another leading from Black's to Hutcherson's .. Moses Fisk, Loc. 25 Mar 1802.
54	10	28	**William Hale** .. 170 acs .. on Doe Cr adj Armstrong's and Gord's improvement to incl sd improvement. .. 9 Apr 1802.
54	10	29	**Ephraim Payton** .. 480 acs on S side of Cumberland .. at the mouth of a creek known by the name of Sugar Run .. 16 Apr 1802.
54	10	30	**Ambrose Gore** .. 500 acs .. headwaters of Copeland's Cr a branch of Roaring R .. to incl his improvement .. 22 May 1802.
54	11	33	**Jacob Work** .. 150 acs .. Lamb's Cr a branch of Roaring R .. a path that leads from sd cr to Flat Cr .. to incl an improvement **where Joseph Copeland now lives.** 22 May 1802.
54	11	34	**Jacob Work** .. 300 acs .. E fork of Flat Cr the waters of Roaring R .. the Rocky Spring on the W side of sd Cr .. to incl Robert Seypert's improvement. 22 May 1802.
54	12	35	**Nathaniel Taylor** .. 350 acs .. waters of Roaring R .. near Walton's Branch .. James Taylor, Loc. 22 May 1802.
54	12	36	**James Taylor** enters for **Thos Michison** 213 1/3 acs (if sd Thos Mickson & sd James Taylor agrees & Mickinson buys sd warrant and if not the entry stands in the name of Nathaniel Taylor) on waters of Roaring R adj tract of Watson's .. James Taylor, Loc. 22 May 1802. (BHB Note: Three spellings of the same name are exactly as they appear in the entry.)
54	12	37	This entry is almost identical to No. 36. The name appears "Mickinson" twice and "Mickison" once. Entry No. 38 is more of the same.
54	12	39	**James Taylor for Nathaniel Taylor** .. 640 acs .. waters of Roaring R .. up the valley above where William Fitzgerald now lives .. to incl the improvements **where William Fitzgerald lives and others** .. James Taylor, Loc. 22 May 1802.

54 14 40   **Isaac Taylor for Nathaniel Taylor & Co.** .. 400 acs on waters of Roaring R .. N side of a small branch running thence southwest with the Indian Line .. not interfering with Indian Land. 28 June 1802.

54 14 41   **David & John Womack** .. 350 acs .. waters of Roaring R .. adj Jonston Womack .. to incl improvements where sd **Womack now lives.** 2 July 1802.

54 14 42   **Christopher Bullard** ase of Sampson Williams .. 640 acs N side of Cumberland R at the mouth of a small creek above **where he lives called Trace Cr** .. 5 July 1802.

The following entry seems worthy of a complete transcription.

54 15 43   "Moses Fisk ase of Sampson Williams of Stockley Donelson and Will Tyrrell of the heirs of John Keith enters 640 acs in Jackson Co on waters of Roaring R between the E fork and the ridge which divides its waters from those of Sampson's fork of Mill Cr incl the best part of a flat that lies westerly of the path leading from old Mr. Officer's to Captain Mitchell's Beginning about ninety poles northwest of an oak marked T O, which stands close by a pen made, perhaps, to catch turkeys; thence from sd beginning to extend E and S so as to cover the sd quantity of 640 acs of land fit for cultivation exclusive of prior claims. John Bowen Esquire was present with sd Fisk at sd pen and oak marked T O on the 6th instant, namely July 6 1802. Moses Fisk, Loc."

    That seems to indicate that John Keith was a private and was given a piece of paper good for 640 acres. He died, and his heirs sold (or otherwise assigned) it to William Tyrell. William Tyrell sold (?) it to Stockley Donelson, son of John Donelson and brother to Andrew Jackson's wife. Stockley Donelson sold (?) it to Sampson Williams. Sampson Williams sold (?) it to Moses Fisk. All before 6 July 1802.

    Historical perspective: Double Head was still alive and would be for another five years. Our so-called Bill of Rights, the First Ten Amendments to our Constitution, was not quite ten years old. In 1802, a Cherokee named Stone was accused of stealing a horse, captured within the Indian Boundary, and imprisoned in Nashville without trial for several months. John Richmond and Alexander Irwin killed one or two Cherokees about 3 miles from Benjamin Blackburn's at Double Springs which threw the neighborhood into an uproar.

54 15 44   **John and Robert Allen** .. 274 acs .. on Dry Cr which empties into the E fork of Roaring R .. Moses Fisk, Loc. 9 July 1802.

54 16 45   **Moses Fisk** .. 640 acs on the highlands S of Sampson's fork of Mill Cr .. 120 poles S of the 13-mile tree marked by Captain Williams in April 1800 to denote the

distance from the intersection of the State Line with the Cumberland R .. E and S so as to **incl the plantation on which George Hutcheson, his mother, etc now live** .. Moses Fisk, Loc. 26 July 1802.

54 16 46 **David Henley** ase of John Overton of Redmond D. Barry of the heirs of John Seagrave .. 640 acs .. W fork of Roaring R joining the tract **John Richmond lives upon** .. S. Williams, Loc. 26 July 1802.

54 17 47 **David Ramsey** ase of James G. Gaines .. 100 acs .. E side of D. Ramsey's other entry "to incl my spring and improvement with one hundred acs **where I know live.**" David Ramsey, Loc. 3 Aug 1802.

54 17 48 **David Ramsey** .. 100 acs .. beg on **William Russell's line** on the S fork of his mill creek .. to incl **John Russel's improvement where he lives** .. David Ramsey, Loc. 3 Aug 1802.

54 17 49 **Jessey Starkey** .. 100 acs .. W fork of Roaring R adj Russell. Jessey Starkey, Loc. 5 Aug 1802.

54 18 50 **Nathaniel Taylor** .. 640 acs .. S side of N fork of Roaring R .. James Taylor, Loc. 5 Aug 1802.

54 18 51 **Jacob Work** .. 250 acs .. Roaring R .. S side of a path that leads from William ___ to John ___. 5 Aug 1802. (BHB Note: The surname for William and John is apparently legible but undecipherable. It could be Bryan, Cryor, Boyor, etc. See print-out of original on Page 20.)

54 18 52 **Nathaniel Taylor** .. eastern branch of Roaring R .. adj Ambrous Gore's .. 5 Aug 1802.

54 19 53 **Nathaniel Taylor** .. 640 acs .. branch of Roaring R .. 5 Aug 1802.

54 19 54 **Jacob Work** .. 640 acs .. waters of Roaring R .. beg at a black oak and post oak on the Indian Line between the 54 and 55 mile trees on a ridge .. 5 Aug 1802.

54 20 55 **Nathaniel Taylor** .. 640 acs .. S fork of Roaring R .. 5 Aug 1802.

54 20 56 **Joseph Copland** ase of Stephen Copland .. 400 acs .. eastern branch of Roaring R .. Stephen Copland, Loc. 5 Aug 1802.

54 20 57 **William Tilghman** .. S side of Roaring R .. Alaxander Finn's improvement. William Tilghman, Loc. 5 Aug 1802.

54	21	58	**John Gray Blount** .. 640 acs .. waters of Roaring R .. near the Indian Boundary. Thomas Dillon, Loc. 5 Aug 1802.
54	21	59	**John G. & James Porterfield, heirs of Drury Porterfield** .. middle fk of Roaring R .. Thomas Dillon, Loc. 5 Aug 1802.
54	22	60	**Wm. Shepherd** .. 1,252 acs .. W fork of Sugar Cr .. Thomas Dillon, Loc. 5 Aug 1802.
54	22	61	**Edward Harris** .. 640 acs .. Doe Cr a branch of Roaring R .. 5 Aug 1802.
54	23	62	**John Morriss Heir of Ben** (See Bk 54 No. 86) .. 640 acs .. middle fork of Roaring R. 5 Aug 1802.
54	23	63	**The Heirs of Wm. Haynes** .. 640 acs .. Roaring R .. adj Russell's line. 5 Aug 1802.
54	24	64	**Heirs of Solomon Mollorn** .. 1,000 acs .. eastern branch of Roaring R ..5 Aug 1802.
54	24	65	**Mordica Mindinhall** 228 acs .. Roaring R. 5 Aug 1802.
54	25	66	**Wm. Person** .. 640 acs .. middle fork of Roaring R .. adj William Russell's .. Thomas Dillon, Loc. 5 Aug 1802. Notation in margin: "This was returned, lifted and assigned to Garrett Fitzgerald and from Fitzgerald to John Talley. Re-enters sd warrant on Page 46."
54	25	67	**Nathaniel Taylor** .. middle fork of Roaring R .. 5 Aug 1802.
54	26	68	**Joseph Pryor** .. 150 acs .. W fork of Russell's mill creek a branch of Roaring R .. path that leads from sd Pryor's to John Starky's .. to incl sd Pryor's improvement. Joseph Pryor, Loc. 5 Aug 1802.
54	26	69	**William Robertson** .. 300 acs .. Spring Cr a branch of Roaring R .. on the Indian Line .. to incl Cline's improvement. William Robertson, Loc. 9 Aug 1802.
54	27	70	**No name** .. 100 acs .. N side of Roaring R .. to incl Hesty's improvement "now in my possestion." Benjamin Blackburn, Loc. 11 Sep 1802. Note in margin says "Mrs. Embry in the name of Tyler. Made void by Benjamin Blackburn."
54	27	71	**Moses Fisk** .. 200 acs .. adj Robert Cartwright to incl improvement of John Black's. Moses Fisk, Loc. 11 Sep 1802.

54	28	72	**Moses Fisk** .. 200 acs .. on waters of Coperace Cr sometimes called Dry Cr of Roaring R .. 11 Sep 1802.
54	28	73	**Moses Fisk** .. 640 acs .. Roaring R .. near path that leads from Old Mr. Officer's to Captain Mitchell's. 11 Sep 1802.
54	29	74	**Moses Fisk** ase of James T. Gains .. 640 acs .. S of the Golston tract so-called which is part of a tract of 60,400 acs granted to Stokley Donelson in 1795 incl the mouth of Oby River .. adj a 640 ac tract surveyed for Samuel Sanford. Moses Fisk, Loc. 11 Sep 1802.
54	29	75	**Redmond Dillon Barry** .. 300 acs on Flynn's Cr .. 17 Sep 1802.
54	30	76	**Uriah Anderson** .. 100 acs .. waters of Roaring R to incl the improvement **whereon Joseph Weaver now lives** which improvement was first made by **Jacob Harty** below sd Blackburn's. 17 Sep 1802.
54	30	77	**James Taylor** 400 acs Roaring R .. incl improvement **where Richard Copeland now lives.** 17 Sep 1802.
54	31	78	**Henry Harris** .. 274 acs .. Roaring R .. edge of The Barrens .. S of a path that leads from William Russell's to Bartholomew Donehues .. incl 3 small improvements .. Berryman Stuart's, the widow Davises and Mr. Cowan's ... Thomas Dillon, Loc. 18 Sep 1802.
54	31	79	**Willoughby Williams** .. 274 acs .. dividing ridge between Roaring R and waters of Flynn's Cr .. near the head of Doe Cr a branch of Cumberland .. 18 Sep 1802.
54	32	80	**Lewis Whortner** .. 250 acs .. Roaring R .. incl improvement where **Cornelis Crowly now lives.** 18 Sep 1802.
54	32	81	**Elijah Robertson** .. 624 acs .. E side of Salt or Lick Cr of Roaring R .. 18 Sep 1802.
54	33	82	**John Porterfield** .. 228 acs .. N side of Cumberland on Jennings Cr .. incl improvement made by Joseph Russell on 10 acs to incl improvement that was sd Russell's 9 March 1802 .. 18 Sep 1802.
54	33	83	**John Gray Blount** .. W fork of Roaring R .. adj Taylor. 18 Sep 1802.
54	34	84	**William Parson** .. 320 acs .. main fork of Roaring R .. Thomas Dillon, Loc. 18 Sep 1802.
54	34	85	**Edward Harris** .. 320 acs .. S fork of Roaring R .. Thomas Dillon, Loc. 18 Sep 1802.

54	35	86	**John Harris Heirs of Ben** .. 320 acs .. eastern branch of Roaring R .. 18 Sep 1802.
54	35	87	**Heirs of William Haynes** .. 320 acs .. main fork of Roaring R .. S side. 18 Sep 1802.
54	36	88	**William Shepherd** .. 417 acs .. beg at two hickories on the N side of a creek .. Thomas Dillon, Loc. 18 Sept 1802.
54	36	89	**William Shepherd** .. 417 acs .. begins at two beaches and a sugar tree on the N side of a creek .. Thomas Dillon, Loc. 18 Sept 1802.
54	37	90	**James Porterfield,** heirs of Henry Porterfield .. 1,208 acs .. middle fork of Roaring R .. 19 Sep 1802.

Thomas Dillon's locations are so indefinite, the following amuses:

54	37		An incomplete entry is followed by a note: "This entry is not worded agreable to the location and it is moved to the following page 38." Then:
54	38	91	**James Porterfield** .. 1,280 acs .. **a branch** of Roaring R .. at a post oak and black oak on S side of **the branch** .. Thomas Dillon, Loc 18 Sep 1802.

What branch, we wonder!!

54	38	92	**John Stukley** .. 320 acs .. Roaring R .. top of a hill above the mouth of Blackburn's Branch .. Benjamin Blackburn, Loc. 23 Sep 1802.
54	39	93	**David Harbert** .. 400 acs .. on Dow (Doe?) Cr .. it being the first creek that empties into Cumberland below the mouth of Roaring R .. 8 Oct 1802.
54	39	94	**Christian Rhodes** .. 640 acs .. middle fork of Roaring R .. incl improvement of Martain Jobe and David Waldson. 8 Oct 1802.
54	40	95	**Robert King** .. 400 acs .. N side of Cumberland .. above mouth of Roaring R .. Haner's line .. 8 Oct 1802.
54	40	96	**Nathaniel Taylor** .. 100 acs .. southwest fork of Roaring R .. 8 Oct 1802.

Ceative phonetics are nice, but when someone breaks a name like Nathaniel Taylor onto four lines, the name is almost impossible to read i.e.

Nathani
al

Tay
Lor

54	41	97	**Nathaniel Taylor** .. 150 acs .. on Doe Creek .. Cord cabin and Noble's cabin .. 8 Oct 1802.
54	41	98	**Jacob Work** .. 100 acs .. branch of Roaring R incl plantation and improvement where **William Bradley and his brother now live** .. 8 Oct 1802.
54	42	99	**Jacob Work** .. 150 acs .. head of eastern branch of Roaring R beg nearly NE of **where James Warthen now lives** .. and incl sd plantation. 8 Oct 1802.
54	42	100	**Jacob Work** .. 600 acs .. N fork of Roaring R .. incl plantation where **Mr. Ledbetter the mill wright and Mr. Hins now lives** .. James Taylor, Loc. 8 Oct 1802.
54	43	101	**Abraham Bylor** .. 200 acs .. waters of Roaring R adj James Taylor .. where sd Taylor's line intersects the Indian Line .. 8 Oct 1802.
54	43	102	**Nathanial Taylor** .. 50 acs .. Blackburn's fork of Roaring R .. adj Watson's survey .. adj Jobe's survey .. incl Thomas Meginson's improvement .. 8 Oct 1802.
54	44	103	**Nathaniel Taylor** heir of Andrew Taylor, deceased .. 50 acs .. waters of Roaring R incl plantation **where Cornelious Crowley** now lives .. 8 Oct 1802.
54	44	104	**Nathaniel Taylor** and **Abraham Bylor** .. 640 acs .. waters of Mill Cr a br of Cumberland incl 3 beeches at the head of a spring marked MT .. 8 Oct 1802.
54	45	105	**Nathaniel Taylor** and Abraham Bylor .. 300 acs .. head waters of Roaring R .. head of Doe Cr .. fork of the creek **whereon Joseph Taylor now lives** .. Joseph Taylor, Loc. 9 Oct 1802.
54	45	106	**Nathaniel Taylor** .. 50 acs .. S side of Cumberland between lands of Garrett Fitzgerald and **Henerary McKinney** .. 9 Oct 1802.
54	46	107	**Joseph Lock** ... 640 acs .. adj **Thomases** corner - Hanna's upper corner - to incl **where Lock now lives**. 16 Oct 1802.
54	46	108	**John Tally** .. 640 acs .. Doe Cr near top of ridge between Doe Cr and Flynn's Cr .. to incl John Houser's improvement .. 18 Oct 1802.
54	47	109	**David Harbert** .. 175 acs .. Rushley fork of Flynn's Cr .. to incl John Hensen's improvement .. 18 Oct 1802.

54 47 110   **Ephraim Payton** .. 480 acs .. S side of Cumberland .. begin in the bend of the R **where Thomas Simpson now lives** .. 22 Oct 1802.

54 48 111   **Phillip Brittain** .. 428 acs .. N side of Cumberland adj Christopher Bullard's line on the bank of the R .. up the R .. Abner Henley, Loc. 25 Oct 1802.

54 48 112   **Robert Carmichal** .. 640 acs .. N side of Cumberland .. adj his own and Christopher Bullard .. Abner Henley, Loc. 25 Oct 1802.

54 49 113   **Levi Jarvis** .. 226 acs .. (Here is a rare Revolutionary soldier who claimed the land granted him. The complete entry is transcribed.)

"Levi Jarvis enters in Jackson County and State of Tennessee by virtue of a military warrant granted to Levi Jarvis a private in the Continental Line in the State of North Carolina two hundred and twenty eight acres of land number of the warrent No 26 lying on Doe Creek that emtys into Cumberland R below six hundred and forty acres of land entered by John Billingsley and Taylor beg at a cabbin partley rased against the mouth of a branch or near it and running up and down for compliment .. Entered this 30 day of October 1802. David Cox, Locater."

54 49 114   **William Megee** .. 640 acs .. adj William Warter's (BHB Note: Waters! This clerk consistently spells "waters" with two "r's.") He wants the possessive and writes "William **Wartersis** upper line on roaring river runing up sd roaring river to the best advantage for compliment." The locator seems to be Boz Burris. 4 Nov 1802. There is a blot between "Warters" and "is." Gives me a lump in my throat. I can see the poor devil sitting there thinking he has made an error - marking it out - and making what he hopes is a correction - wanting to do the job right. A note in the margin says "remove to the following page 50." I can hardly wait.

54 50   The sweet clerk tries again.

"Boz Burress for William Megee enters six hundred and forty acs of land in Jackson County on Roaring R on a melatery land warrant No five thousand one hundred and three Entred this twelveth day of novem 1802. Boz Burriss, Locter."

That's marked out, and the brave non-hero (probably near-sighted) tries again!

54 50 115   "**Boz Burriss for William Megee** enters six hundred and

16

> forty acres of land in Jackson County on roaring river on William Warters west line that runs down roaring river on a melatary land warrent N 5103 Entred this 12 day of november 1802. Boz Buriss Locater."

Passed inspection! No problem. Anyone who tries to spell "12th" is brave.

54 50 116 **"James Taylor and hennery reybourn** enters locates and clames one hundred and forty acres of land on the E fork of mill creek a branch of Cumberland R by virtue of a part of a millitary land warrent No 3765 baring date the sixth of september 1790 assigned to david grant for six hundred and forty and assigned from sd grant to Nathaniel Taylor and from nathaniel Taylor to James Taylor and Hennary rey bourn beginning at an oak on the S side of sd E fork marked thus TR running thence as the as the law will direct so as to include a buflow lick on sd fork and sd compliment. Hennery rey burn, Loc." 15 Nov 1802.

Do not trust what you see in print until you have looked at the original handwritten record ! ! ! I make mistakes. So do human and non-human printers. I wonder how many errors in our history exist because someone mis-read someone else's handwriting -- and the errors go on for ever. Remember there are books out there recording my father as a girl named Hannah. I do the best I can.

54 51 117 **Uriah Anderson** .. 290 acs .. warters of flin's creek .. and a branch by the name of wallises Br beg above the cabbin and improvement where **sd wallis did live** .. by virtue of a certificet obtained from a guard right warrant No 4420 assigned to sd anderson by Joseph Lock. 8 Nov 1802.

54 51 118 **Isaac Taylor** .. 640 acs .. on the main fork of roaring R and adj a tract **Elijah Ewings now lives one** .. S side of sd R .. to incl improvement where sd Ewing made corn last season .. Isaac Taylor, Loc. 6 Jan 1803.

54 52 119 **John McDonald** .. 110 acs .. N side of Wolf R adj John hines and frances Mayberry .. John McDonald, Loc. 15 Jan 1803.

54 52 120 **David Chester** .. 250 acs .. Trace Creek on the N side of Christopher Bullard survey .. and Abner Henley's .. and William Robertson .. Abner Henley, Loc. 2 Feb 1803.

54 53 121 **David Chester** .. 500 acs .. N side of Cumberland .. at the mouth of Cub Cr .. Abner Henley, Loc. 2 Feb 1803.

54 53 122 **David Chester** .. 250 acs .. Cub Cr .. incl improvements of James Simson and Skags at the big spring greenhow

??? improvements and .. sd Cub creek .. the first lines
belowe on the creek being a part of a thousand acs
warrent granted to sd David Chester for his sarvises as
a sargent .. 2 Feb 1803. Abner Henley, Loc.

54	54	123	**James T. Ganes** claimants of Gid Harris and William Nelston (Kelston?) .. 1,029 acs ... main N fork of Roaring R beg where the Obed **road** crosses sd R .. Locator is James L or T or S Gains. 16 or 17 Feb 1803.
54	54	124	**Nathaniel Menable** claimant of Joab Chamberlin .. 200 acs .. Coplin's fork of Roaring R adj Joseph Coapland's entry of "fore hundred acres" William Merchant, Loc. 17 Feb 1803.
54	55	125	**Nathaniel Taylor** claimant of Thomas Mitchel .. 100 acs .. on waters of Roaring R .. adj Joseph Copland .. ? Feb 1803.
54	55	126	**William Milcher** .. claimant of Timathey Nobaway ?? Holdaway ?? Holloway .. waters of Coapland's fork of Roaring R .. near the Obed **road** .. about 200 yards W of a large spring known as the double spring.. William Milcher, Loc. 17 Feb 1803.
54	56	127	**Nathaniel Taylor** .. 100 acs .. Spring Cr of Roaring R .. adj land granted to John Rice .. N of sd creek nearly W from **Elijah Chisholm now lives** .. 17 Feb 1803.
54	56	128	**William McCutcher** claimant of Joab Michell .. 100 acs Spring Cr .. 17 Feb 1803.
54	57	129	**John Stuart** .. 150 acs .. Roaring R .. path that leads from John Watson's to Isaac Bullard's .. to incl improvement made by George Talley .. 17 Feb 1803.
54	57	130	**Heirs of Christopher Lockey** .. 2,560 acs .. S side of Cumberland in the bend that **Thomas Simpson now lives in** .. 26 Feb 1803.
54	58	131	**Garrett Fitzgerald** .. 640 acs .. North side of Welcom Harris or Burress Cr .. waters of Brimstone Cr .. 1/2 mile below **Shary's where he now lives.** Jabez Fitzgerald, Loc. 28 Feb 1803.
54	58	132	**Benjamin Blackburn** .. 208 acs .. waters of Roaring R .. 3 Mar 1803.

There are two pages numbered 58.

54	58	133	**Edmond Timmons** .. 191 acs .. Dry fork of Flynn's Cr .. incl vacant land between Sampson Williams, Struthers, and John Anderson's. Edmond Timmons, Loc. 6 Mar 1803.

54	59	134	**Nathaniel Taylor and William McCutchen** .. 1,240 acs .. Coaplin's Fk of Roaring R .. adj Indian line and Joseph Coaplin's entry of 400 acs .. 7 Mar 1803.
54	59	135	**Nathaniel McNabb** .. 300 acs .. Spring Cr adj James Taylor's land that **he now lives on** .. 7 Mar 1803.
54	60	136	**Andrew Reed** .. 400 acs .. on Flynn's Cr of Cumberland .. N side of the wagon road and nearly opposite the mouth of a fork of sd creek by the name of the Rush fork .. 7 Mar 1803.
54	60	137	**John McDonold** .. 100 acs .. N side of Wolf R adj John Hinds and Francis Mayberry .. 8 Mar 1803.
54	61	138	**James Mayberry** 74 acs .. Wolf R between Lewis Harris and Fitsgerald's improvement .. incl improvement of sd Garret's. 16 Mar 1803.
54	61	139	**Benjamin Poor** .. 100 acs .. Wolf R .. incl the improvement. Benjamin Poor, Loc. 26 Mar 1803.
54	62	140	**John Swain and Armstead Stubblefield** .. 2,560 acs .. headwaters of Brimstone Cr .. to incl the salt lick and two banks of iron ore. 2 Apr 1803.
54	62	141	**William McNabb** .. 100 acs .. W fork of Russell's mill cr on which fork **William Prior lives** .. 21 Apr 1803.
54	63	142	**John Craford** .. 100 acs .. Roaring R .. mouth of Lick Cr .. to incl spring and improvement where **William Harple now lives** .. 22 Apr 1803.
54	63	143	**Benjamin Lockhart** .. 50 acs .. Eagle Cr a branch of Obed R .. **where Benjamin Totton now lives** .. 22 Apr 1803.
54	64	144	**John Williams** .. 150 acs .. waters of Wolf R .. Dry Cr .. incl place where sd **Williams now lives** .. Hennary Rowan, Loc. 23 Apr 1803.
54	64	145	**John Carter** .. 600 acs .. waters of Obed's R .. improvement made by Alexander Tait .. adj 3,000 ac tract granted to sd Carter and McNutty .. 23 Apr 1803.
54	65	146	**Hennary Rowan** .. 400 acs .. both sides of the waggon road leading from the Long bottom on Obed's R to the Hurricane Hill known by name of Parris Spring Place and **where William Mill now lives** .. 23 Apr 1803.

Jacob Work assignee of John Scott	Enters on a Land warrant of No. five hundred and eight assignee of John Scott two hundred and fifty acres of Land in Jackson county on the waters of greenen river begining at a black oak & several post oaks the black oak marked & tree standing on the south side of a path that leads from William bryor to John bryor & running then west and north for compliment James Taylor Houston	51 250	508 ... 1805
Nathaniel Taylor assignee of John Ware	Enter six hundred and forty acres of Land by virtue of a Land warrant No 201 assignee of John Ware gen on the head of an eastern branch of horning river joining an entry of Ambrous ... running thence ...	52 640	...

Entries for Jacob Work and Nathaniel Taylor. Book 54, Page 93

BK	PG	NUMBER	DESCRIPTION
54	65	147	**Conrod Peters** .. 320 acs .. both sides of the Spring Fork of Wolf R .. incl .. **where sd Peters now lives** .. 23 Apr 1803.
54	66	148	**Hennary Rowan** .. 320 acs .. on Caney Fork of Wolf R including where **Samuel Blair lives** .. 23 Apr 1803.
54	66	149	**Henary Rowan** .. 150 acs .. N side of Obed's R opposite and below the mouth of Eagle Cr near John Wilson's ?? line .. known as hors shew bottom .. 23 Apr 1803.
54	67	150	**John Jee** .. 50 acs .. both sides of Kany Fork of Wolf R including an improvement made by himself .. 23 Apr 1803.
54	67	151	**Moses Fisk** .. 640 acs .. between Roaring R and waters of Mill Cr .. adj tract granted to Samuel Sanford .. incl the plantation **where Andrew McLane lives** .. N to a tract of 60,400 acs granted to sd Donelson .. sd Sanford's tract granted to Bengomin Shepart. 30 Apr 1803
54	68	152	**Willia Cherry** ase Elizabeth McHoon heir of Ralph McHoon. 240 acs on first large br that crosses Walton's Road above sd William Cherry's house .. on sd road .. 2 or 3 miles from Cherry's improvement on Cub Run adj the Indian Boundary. 6 May 1803. Willie Cherry, Loc.
54	68	153	**Willie Cherry** .. 400 acs .. dividing ridge between Big Barren and headwaters of Jennings Cr .. adj survey granted to David Langston. 6 May 1803.
54	69	154	**Moses Fisk** ase Howell Tatum .. 100 acs S of Sampson's fk of Mill Cr W of **where John Black now lives** .. to incl improvements and spring where "**Widow Black and Samuel McCown lives occupied last year.**" 11 May 1803. John Hutcheson, Loc.
54	69	155	**Moses Fisk** .. 560 acs .. Roaring R SW of path leading from old Mr. Officer's to Captain Mitchell's .. said Mitchell's spring. Moses Fisk, Loc. 11 May 1803.
54	70	156	**Moses Fisk** .. 260 acs .. W of Samuel Sanford's **where Andrew McClaine lives** .. 11 May 1803.
54	70	157	**Moses Fisk** .. 100 acs .. Roaring R .. southwest of Captain Mitchell's and E of Coperas Cr .. **sd Mitchell's where he lives** .. 11 May 1803.
54	71	158	**Moses Fisk** .. 100 acs .. Roaring R .. path leading from Old Mr. Officer's to Captain Mitchell's .. 11 May 1803.

54	71	159	**Moses Fisk** .. 60 acs .. road leading by one of sd Fisk's fields to Elijah Ewing's .. both sides of sd road .. northwest of Captain Mitchell's .. 11 May 1803.
54	72	160	**Madison Fisk** ase of Moses Fisk .. 200 acs .. Roaring R near Mr. Officer and Captain Mitchell and other locations of Moses Fisk. 11 May 1803.
54	72	161	**George Geer** .. 250 acs .. Blackburn's Fk of Roaring R .. Thomas Williams corner on E side of sd Fk .. the plantation sd **Geer now lives on** .. George Geer, Loc. 17 May 1803.
54	73	162	**Tomas Williams** .. Blackburn's Fk of Roaring R .. E side .. including plantation **sd Williams now lives on** .. George Geer, Loc. 17 May 1803.
54	73	163	**William Lewis** ase Stockley Donelson .. 640 acs .. between Roaring R and Sampson's Fk of Mill Cr S of the place **which John Black got of George Hutcheson** .. adj Moses Fisk which incls improvement made by sd Hutcheson. 26 May 1803.
54	74	164	**Moses Fisk** .. 50 acs .. waters of Sampson's Fk on the N side .. adj his entry he got of George Hutcheson .. 26 May 1803.
54	74	165	**Moses Fisk** .. 100 acs .. southerly of the place **where Widow Black lives** .. near road passing John Black's towards Elijah Ewing and about half a mile W of the northwest corner of an entry this day made for William T. Lewis .. 26 May 1803.
54	75	166	**Moses Fisk** .. 230 acs .. on the road which goes along the ridge between waters of Roaring R and of sinking and Sampson's Fk of Mill Cr .. W of Samuel Sanford's tract which incls Andrew McLane's plantation .. 27 May 1803.
54	75	167	**James Elliott** .. 200 acs .. W side of Eagle Cr including where **Jacob Meeks now lives** being an improvement made by Carter Grigg .. 27 May 1803.
54	76	168	**Moses Fisk** .. 100 acs .. on Coperas Cr S of a location made for John and Robert Allen .. "S of a poplar and blackgum marked as sd Allen's southwest corner by sd Fisk present Moses Bingerman and Jackson's then to run E .. " 20 June 1803.
54	76	169	**Moses Fisk** .. between Roaring R and Sampson's Fk of Mill Cr .. 20 June 1803.
54	77	170	**Moses Fisk** .. 200 acs .. on Coperas Cr .. adj John & Robert Allen .. 20 June 1803.

54	77	171	**William Roberson** .. 640 acs .. N side of Cumberland on Bullard's Cr .. including John Lee's improvement and **Andrew Blackwood's improvement where he now lives** and Roberson's improvement. 21 June 1803. "This 29th day of July 1806, I do hereby transfer one hundred acres of the above warrant and entry to Andrew Blackwood, one hundred to Jehu Lee and two hundred forty to Jonas Bedford without recourse on me .. William Roberson."
54	78	172	**James Oar** .. 2,000 acs .. adj James Mayben's line of 5,000 acs .. adj Hennary Rowen's survey of 330 acs .. to incl Alexander Akemon's improvement. James Oar, Loc. 23 June 1803.
54	78	173	**John Chisum** .. 50 acs .. Roaring R .. including plantation whereon **sd Chisum now lives**. James Oar, Loc. 23 June 1803.
54	79	174	**John Chisum** .. 170 acs .. Spring Cr .. to incl sd Chisum's improvement where **he now lives**. James Ore, Loc. 23 June 1803.
54	79	175	**William McCutchen and Isaac Taylor** .. 50 acs .. S Fk of Roaring R .. adj James Blackburn's and Nathaniel Taylor .. E side of sd cr .. Warrant dated 27 Nov 1794. Isaac Taylor, Loc. 27 June 1803.
54	80	176	**William McCutchen** .. 200 acs .. Spring Cr a Fk of Roaring R .. on the Indian Line .. adj Nathaniel Taylor .. incls Cornelis Crowly's improvement 27 June 1803.
54	81	178	**John Fitzgerald** .. 640 acs .. N side of Cumberland .. Jennings Cr .. Ephraim Payton's and Pruets S boundary .. "I do hereby sartify that the above location was legally proven before me one of the justice of the peace for sd county" .. 28 June 1803. Henary McKinney."
54	81	179	**James Ore** .. 500 acs .. Eagle Cr .. to incl **where Jacob Coons now lives** .. 5 July 1803.
54	82	180	**James Ore** .. 122 acs .. adj William Sinclare .. 5 July 1803.
54	82	181	**James Ore** .. 295 acs .. Nathaniel Careger's Cr on the Indian boundary .. 5 July 1803.
54	83	182	**Robert Glenn** .. 50 acs .. adj Samuel Sandford's .. **that William Russell now lives on** .. 5 July 1803.
54	83	183	**James Officer** .. 400 acs .. Lick Cr of Roaring R .. incl .. where **Powell formerly lived**. 11 July 1803.

54	83	184	**"The members of the babtis church"** .. 50 acs .. beg on a black gum and white oak marked OC on the S side of Copland Cr .. Joseph Copland's line .. Stephen Copeland's line .. to include Cave Spring Meeting House. Stephen Copeland, Loc. 14 July 1803.
54	84	185	**Uriah Anderson** .. 640 acs .. on the main waggon road between old Mr. Henson's and Ervin's cabbin .. 26 July 1803.
54	84	186	**Garret Fitzgerald** .. 640 acs .. at the foot of the hurricain ridge on a small branch of Dowe Cr .. to incl Isom's spring and improvement. 26 July 1803.
54	85	187	**Moses Fisk** .. 640 acs .. to incl **where George Hucheson then lived and John Black now lives** .. adj W. T. Lewis .. 2 Aug 1803.
54	85	188	**Moses Fisk** .. 200 acs .. waters of Roaring R southwest of Old Mr. Officer's .. S of Madison Fisk .. 2 Aug 1803.
54	86	189	**Moses Fisk** .. adj his own **on which Samuel McCown lives** and E of William T. Lewis and S of the big tract but not to join either .. to incl a spring .. 3 Aug 1803.
54	86	190	**Nathaniel Taylor** .. 200 acs .. Copeland's Cr of Roaring R .. adj his own .. near Joseph Coapland's .. adj Baylor's .. including Walter Alley's improvement **where he now lives** .. 3 Aug 1803.
54	87	191	**William Robertson** .. N side of Cumberland .. on Bullard's Cr .. incl improvement which sd Robertson made. 11 Aug 1803.
54	87	192	**"The Hairs" of William Rhodes** .. 1000 acs .. N side of Cumberland .. few miles below the mouth of Oby .. mouth of Dry Cr .. 11 Aug 1803.
54	88	193	**Armstead Stubblefield and Hennary W. Lawson** .. on Roaring R .. adj Ewing .. .. 1803.
54	88	194	**Heirs of Christopher Lackey** .. 2,560 acs .. both sides of the Cumberland .. adj Bonnar's .. 1803.
54	89	195	**Elijah Chisum** .. 320 acs .. on Roaring R .. to take in Isaac Ogdon's claim and improvement and Thomas Boons claim and improvement by consent of each party. 15 Aug 1803.
54	89	196	**Elijah Chisum** .. 100 acs .. adj his former entry of 170 acs **he the sd Chisum now lives on** .. 15 Aug 1803.
54	90	197	**Elijah Chisum** .. 170 acs .. between Robert Prentis

			cabin and Isaac Ogdon's .. land known by name of Boon's purchase .. 15 Aug 1803.
54	90	198	**Elijah Chisum** .. 150 acs .. to incl a cabin that one Stout built on sd Chisum's improvement known by the name of sycamore spring .. 16 Aug 1803.
54	91	199	**Francis Maberry** .. 300 acs N side of Wolf R .. 16 Sep 1803.
54	91	200	**Simon Huddleston** .. W end of Huddleston's cove on James Maben's line .. 16 Sep 1803.
54	92	201	**Francis Mayberry** .. 100 acs .. John McDonald's SW corner .. top of a mountain .. 16 Oct 1803. Simond Huddleston, Loc.
54	92	202	**Simond Huddleston** .. 50 acs .. adj his own .. N side of Obed's R. 16 Sept 1803. Simond Huddleston, Loc.
54	93	203	**Francis Mayberry** .. 200 acs .. head of a rich hollow a small distance from said Huddleston's plantation .. James Maben's line .. line between "Craford's and myself" .. 3 Sep 1803. Simond Huddleston, Loc.
54	94	204	**Stephen Mayfield** .. waters of Roaring R .. to incl the big pond cove and sd Mayfield's spring .. and two warrents signed William Macklin .. 16 Sep 1803.
54	94	205	**Samuel Moore** .. 50 acs .. N side of W Fk of Russell's mill Cr .. conditional line made by Joseph Pryor and Enock Odle .. 25 Sep 1803.
54	95	206	**Isaac Taylor** .. 640 acs .. W Fk of Flat Cr on which **William Thompson lives** .. to incl the improvement of sd Thompson and where **William Ballon the trunkmaker lives** .. and Hennary Raybourn .. 27 Sep 1803.
54	96	208	**William Bradley** .. 100 acs .. black oak .. southwest course .. to incl sd Bradley's spring and improvement. 6 Oct 1803.
54	96	209	**Robert Price** .. a little beech marked R P .. W side of Uriah Anderson's .. N to Fitzgerald's .. Thompson's line .. Anderson's line .. 10 Oct 1803.
54	97	210	**Uriah Anderson** .. 640 acs .. Dry Fk of Flynn's Cr .. to incl Benjamin Foxes spring and improvement and also John Anderson's spring and improvement .. 17 Oct 1803.
54	97	211	**Edward Givins** .. 640 acs .. N side of Cumberland .. on the bank of the river above the mouth of Dry Cr .. to incl John Black's improvement and plantation. John Black, Loc. 1 Nov 1803. Re-entered 16 Sep 1807.

54	98	212	**Isaac Taylor** .. 502 1/2 acs .. N side of Spring Cr of Roaring R .. near a thousand acs granted to John Rice .. adj Christopher Rodes .. 4 Nov 1803.
54	98	213	**Garrett Fitzgerald** .. 640 acs .. N side of Cumberland .. left hand Fk of first creek that puts in Cumberland below Old Mr. Sanders .. southwest of Scantling's camp .. 4 Nov 1803.
54	99	214	**Garrett Fitzgerald** .. 50 acs .. Beginning on Hennary McKinny's line .. Transfered to Jonthan Nobles. 7 Nov 1803.
54	99	215	**Garret Fitzgerald** .. 274 acs .. at the Fk of the Hurricane ridge and running down both sides of the creek .. to incl Gaines' spring and improvement. 17 Nov 1803.
54	100	216	**David Spears** .. 799 acs .. N side of Cumberland .. waters of Barron .. 1/2 mile below John Fowler's .. to incl Fowler's improvement **where they now live** .. 8 Nov 1803.
54	100	217	**John Dale** .. 100 acs .. mouth of Spring Branch .. to the River .. 8 Nov 1803.
54	101	218	**Carter Dillon** .. 100 acs .. waters of Roaring R .. to incl improvement and house **where sd Dillon now lives**. 26 Dec 1803.
54	101	219	**Lawson Nourse** .. 100 acs .. southerly Fk of Sugar Cr to incl the falls usually called the mill seat or Mill shoals .. 26 Dec 1803.
54	102	220	**No enterer is named.** 73 acs .. waters of Roaring R .. to incl an improvement made by the Williams. Benjamin Blackburn, Loc. 26 Jan 1804.
54	102	221	**Isaac Fisk** .. 640 acs .. first large bottom above Little Island creek about 10 or 12 miles above Roaring R .. a small branch that runs into Cumberland **nigh** the lower end of sd bottom .. 9 May 1804
54	103	222	**Hugh Hueston** .. S side of the Cumberland .. first bottom above the mouth of Little Island Cr .. adj Isaac Fisk .. 9 May 1804.
54	103	223	**James Davis** .. 320 acs .. S side of Cumberland .. beg at a small br **nigh** the upper end of the first bottom above the mouth of Little or Settle Cr .. Isaac Fisk, Loc. No date.
54	104	224	**Isaac Fisk** .. 100 acs .. first bottom on S side of

Cumberland R below Hamelton ferry .. to incl cabin and improvements near Henderson's Ferry. 12 Nov 1804.

54 104 225 **Moses Fisk** .. 50 acs .. S side of Cumberland .. 12 Nov 1804.

54 105 226 **Ferdinand Hamilton** .. 100 acs Mill Cr .. beech marked EH .. incl improvements where **James Saxton now lives.** 9 Aug 1804.

54 105 227 **Moses Fisk** .. 640 acs .. on the highlands between Sampson's fk of Mill Cr .. 9 Aug 1807.

54 105 228 **Moses Fisk** .. 50 acs .. Mill Cr .. near Carter Dillon's .. 9 Aug 1804.

54 105 229 **Isaac Fisk** .. 80 acs .. Sugar Cr .. incl improvement **Mr. Abner now lives on.** No date.

54 107 230 **Howel Tatum** .. 86-3/4 acs .. N fk of Mill Cr .. beech and hickory marked **nigh** where sd creek forks.. 9 Aug 1804. Lawson Nourse, Loc.

54 107 231 **Isaac Fisk** .. 100 acs .. Sugar Cr .. 9 Aug 1804.

54 108 232 **Isaac Fisk** .. 50 acs .. adj Carter Dillon. 9 Aug 1804.

54 108 233 **Moses Fisk** .. 640 acs .. to incl the mouth of a large br which runs into the Cumberland betweeen tract granted to George Cummings and **Coleman's pre-emption** at the mouth of Oby. No date. (See Griffey, The Preemptors, for Spelsby Coleman.)

54 109 234 **Lawson Nourse** .. 100 acs .. Sampson's fk a br of Mill Cr .. to incl plantation **where Mr. Skeggs now lives.** Lawson Nourse, Loc. 9 Aug 1804.

54 109 235 **Moses Fisk** .. 640 acs .. N of Cumberland .. Dry Cr .. to incl Black's br. 16 July 1805.

54 110 236 **Andrew Peddy** (Petty?) .. 140 acs .. S of Cumberland above island Cr .. above heirs of William Rhodes .. opposite the mouth of Brimstone Cr .. 6 Sep 1805.

54 110 237 **Heirs of William Rhodes** .. 1,000 acs .. S side of Cumberland .. above Little Island Cr .. opposite mouth of Brimstone Cr .. 6 Sept 1805.

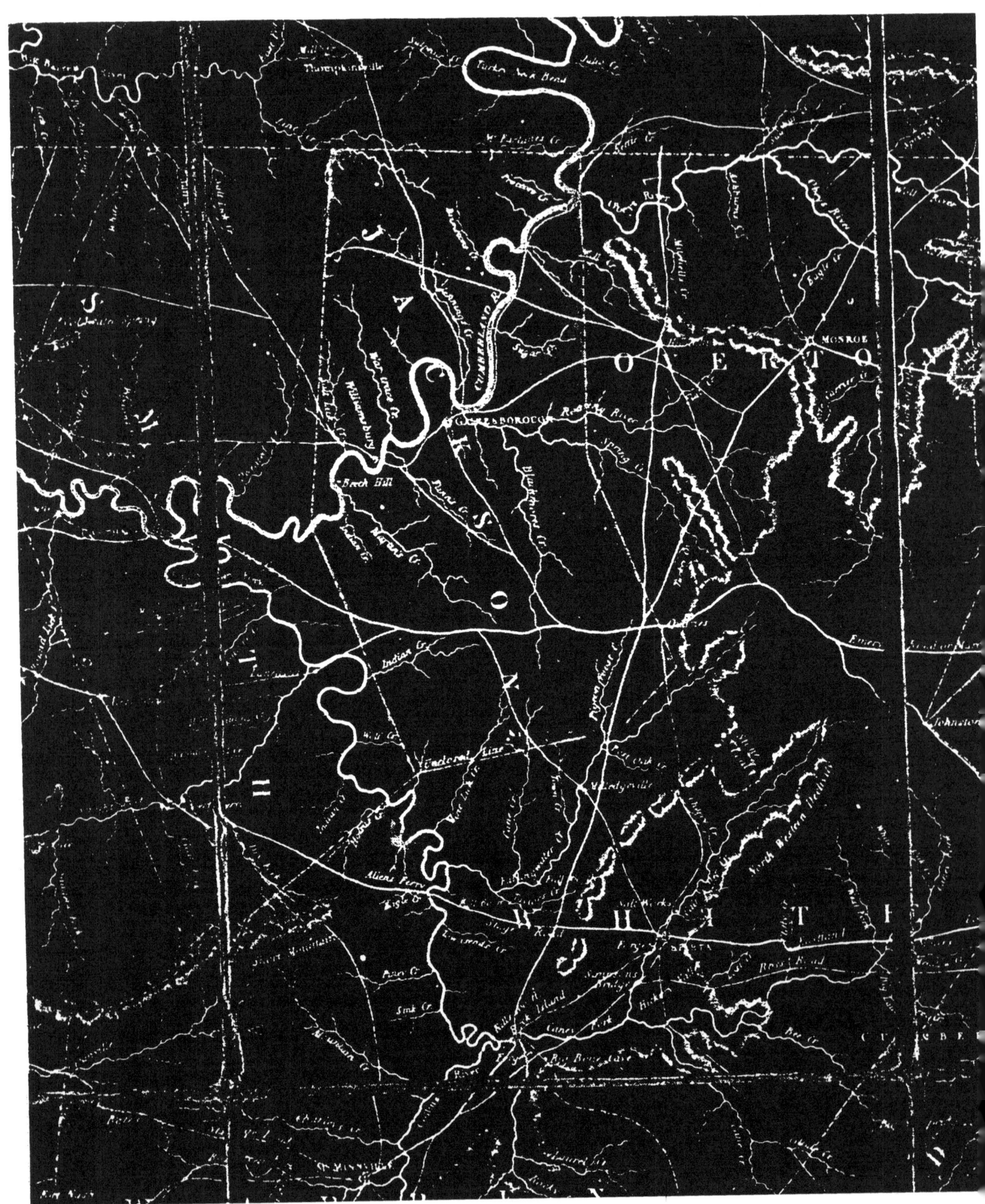

Matthew Rhea Map, ca1830. Courtesy of Tennessee State Library and Archives, Nashville, TN.

BUILDING NEIGHBORHOODS
From
EARLY LAND RECORDS OF TENNESSEE
RG 50 SERIES 2 - LAND ENTRY BOOKS 55, 56, 57 & 58 - REEL 17
WEST TENNESSEE

Books 55, 56, and 57 are of little help to Jackson County history. They deal with newer counties to the west and south, far away from Martin's Creek. Titles and dates of these Books remind us "West Tennessee" did not then exist as we know it. In essence, everything west of Knoxville was "West Tennessee" until 1807. As lands to the west were organized into counties, they became the new West Tennessee, and the term "Middle Tennessee" came into use.

The few pertinent entries in Book 55 follow. Page numbers are in question because they have been torn away, eaten away, folded down, or are illegible.

BK	PG	NUMBER	DESCRIPTION
55		23	**Thomas Shute** ase of Thomas Dillon attorney in fact for Joseph Scurlock ase of Robert Barge. Enters 640 acs .. Davidson Co .. Stuart's Cr .. Cox NW corner, Alexander's S boundary line. Thomas Shute Loc. 26 June 1802. **John C. McLemore** received Warrent No. 3993 for above 640 acs on 10 Apr 1807.

Entry No. 23 was abstracted to keep the cast of characters in focus. Thomas Shute and John C. McLemore were prominent all over Tennessee.

BK	PG	NUMBER	DESCRIPTION
55		32	**Thomas Shute ase of Philip Shute** .. 100 acs .. Davidson Co .. waters of Hurricane .. adj Stockly Donnelson .. and Ebenezar Brooks. 12 Nov 1802.
55		67	**Isaac Shute ase of Thomas Shute** .. 150 acs .. Davidson Co .. waters of Hurricane Cr .. incl the Sink Hole Spring. Isaac Shute, Loc. 27 May 1803.
55		71	**Howell Tatum** ase of James L. White ase of Stockley Donelson as attorney for **Robert Huff** enters 640 acs .. east fork of Stone's R .. adj heirs of Henry Wiggin .. Howell Tatum Locator. 13 June 1803.

Entry No. 71 is important to me, I record the Warrant Number 4090. It was rcvd by Howell Tatum on 22 Dec 1806. **That should be fuel for further research.** The record does not make clear who was attorney for Robert Huff. East Fork of Stone's River is in Rutherford Co created 1803 out of Davidson. Native Tennesseans pronounce that county "Rullerford."

At Entry No. 114, page format changes, almost as if these were loose pages from a different book. Entry numbers are inexplicably lower than the preceding ones.

55   82   **John Dean** .. 200 acs .. White Co .. waters of **Elk R** .. beginning at a red oak running west and south in a square to ???? end of page.

   The entry preceding John Dean's is dated 26 Aug 1807, and the following one, No. 83, is dated 15 Aug 1807, so we can safely date John Dean's entry in August 1807. **White Co** was created in 1806, before the treaty which legalized it was ratified. Cherokee Chief Double Head was assassinated on 16 August 1807, one day after Entry No. 83 was made.

55   83   **Samuel Bigham** ase of Joseph Martin .. warrant for 5,000 acs .. Enters 200 acs .. **White Co** .. waters of Boiling fork of Elk R to include his improvement .. Samuel Bigham, Loc. 15 Aug 1807.

   Boiling Fork of Elk River is in central Franklin Co (Ref. Fullerton and USGS maps) and partially drowned by Tims Ford Lake. It is incredible but seemingly true that one day before Double Head died, White County was assumed to extend to what is now the Tennessee State Line. It did not stay that way for long. The real estate was quickly carved into counties.

   Book 56 has familiar names but they are the speculators. A prominent surveyor was John Coffee. This book might better have been entitled **"Stampede to the Elk River."**

   Book 57 is entitled "Entry Takers' Reports, Middle Tennessee, No Dates." No general boundary or political jurisdiction is identified in the title. It consists of a long alphabetical list of names showing acreages, warrant numbers and waterways, and sometimes County names. To test its applicability to Jackson County, we looked for Thomas Shute. Typically, the "S" section is missing. We then read the "M" section, looking for McLemore, Martin, Moore, etc., and especially at the waterways and locations.

   Counties are Davidson, Tennessee, Knox, Sumner, Hawkins, and Green. There are interesting descriptions but nothing of real value to this study. Favorites are:

   "east side of Mill Creek." That's all it says.

   "Adj James Todd." That's all it says.

   "Beginning on the East side of a large pond." (That was for Thomas and Samuel Martin, and is the **entire** description.)

   Book 58 has entries made in Williamson, Robertson, Rutherford, Davidson, Stewart, Montgomery, Dickson, Wilson, Smith, Sumner, and Jackson Counties. This is basically what became the 1st Surveyor's District. We extract and abstract:

BK PG   NUMBER DESCRIPTION

58 21   69   **Isaac Smith** .. 640 acs .. Smith Co .. S side of

Cumberland .. Begin at a beech on the bank of the River 75 poles south of the mouth of **Martin's Cr** .. thence down the R and east .. lying in **5th section & 3rd range.** Wm. Stephenson, Loc. 14 Aug 1807. Notation says this is a re-entry, the same land on same warrant entered in Smith Co on 2 Dec 1802. "Survey & Rtd 10 Oct 1808 by James Raulston, D. S."

Reference to Book 16, Page 11, Entry No. 41, shows the same entry without the "5th section and 3rd range." Now we know part of Martin's Cr was **5th section and 3rd range.**

With ranges and sections in mind, consider the following, not abstracted but quoted in toto:

58 34 117 "**Isham Russell** ase of Thomas Dillon .. State of Tennessee White County first District first range and seventh section running from two post oaks one hundred and twenty two poles south of the one mile tree on the eastern boundary line of the afforesaid seventh section west one hundred and sixty poles to a hickory and post oak in the Barrens for his beginning thence north fifty five degrees west on a conditional line made between Mathew Wilkinson and the afforesaid Isham Russell one hundred and twenty seven poles to a black oak cherry and black gum corner thence south thirty five degrees west one hundred and twenty seven poles to a white oak thence south fifty five east one hundred and seventy seven poles to a post oak and red oak corner thence to the beginning containing by estimation 100 acres an occupant right to include his improvement in the centre. 25 Aug 1807. Removed this entry this 10 Sep 1810. Isham Russell."

Abstracted, that entry would read "Isham Russell .. White Co .. the Barrens .. line between Mathew Wilkinson and Russell .. to include his improvement. 25 Aug 1807."

58 43 145 **Thomas Dounell** ase of James Winchester .. Sumner Co .. 3rd sec 9th range .. Begin at **James Faris** corner .. being the surplus land within the bounds of Grant No. 53 to Edward Cox. Thomas Dounell, Loc. 27 Aug 1807.

James Faris in Sumner Co? Prudence requires further research on Edward Cox's Grant No. 53.

58 60 206 **Abner Henley** ase of David Chister .. 150 acs .. Jackson Co .. ase of John Anderson by purchase of his improvement .. head waters of Flynn's Cr .. on the Ft. Blount Rd .. Bowman's .. 1st range .. Talley's road .. crossing said section line (Jackrabbits didn't care, either) to beginning. Abner Henley, Loc. 29 Aug 1807. Survey returned 30 July 1808 by Genl. L. Nolen, D. S.

31

58	61	209	**William Stafford** ase of Abner Henley ase of David Chister. 30 acs .. N side of Roaring R .. incl improvement of William Gray .. 3rd section 1st range. 29 Aug 1807.
58	62	210	**William Stafford** .. 100 acs .. S side of Roaring R .. improvement of William Stafford .. 29 Aug 1807.
58	62	213	**Abner Henley** .. 43 acs .. near Ephraim Payton's SW corner .. Smith's Fork .. James Simpson .. one Ratliff .. Yelveton Nevels .. range 3 and section 3. 29 Aug 1807.
58	62	214	**Edmond Jennings** .. 200 acs .. Smith Co .. Payton's Cr .. William Fout's NE corner .. to incl his improvement .. 5th range 4th section. 29 Aug 1807.
58	63	215	**John Anderson** .. 100 acs .. Flynn's Cr .. near Hugh Forgey's E corner .. where Benjamin _?_ lives .. 29 Aug 1807. (On original record, Benjamin has no surname.)

In the margins of Entry No. 215: "Survey Retd 10 Feb 1817 in name of W. Billingsley." and --

"I, James Raulston, Sheriff of Jackson County do hereby transfer this entry No. 215 unto Walter Billingsley the same having been sold by James Cook, former sheriff of Jackson County to said Billingsley by Virtue of an execution Walter Billingsley vs John Anderson. 23 May 1816. J. Raulston Shff Jackson Co."

Who is James Raulston, Sheriff of Jackson County in 1816? Is he the early settler, surveyor, financier, Colonel, friend of Andrew Jackson, the one who moved to Jackson Co, AL, but who supposedly owned and operated a stand on Walton Road although the DAR erected a monument to Moses Raulston?

58	63	216	**Abner Henley** .. 6-1/4 acs .. Smith Fk of Jennings Cr .. where **Yelveton Nevils now lives** .. 29 Aug 1807.
58	64	219	**John Armstrong** .. 200 acs .. White Co .. incl improvement of Ferris .. both sides of Caney Fk .. John Bowen, Loc. 29 Aug 1807. John Bowen removed entry 26 Oct 1808. Sur rtd 3 Apr 1809 by John Bowen DS.
58	66	228	**George Raburn** .. 200 acs .. White Co .. br of Caney Fork .. James Raulston, Loc. 31 Aug 1807.
58	66	229	**Richard Porterfield** .. 50 acs .. White Co .. S side of Little Caney Fk .. James Raulston, Loc. 3 Aug 1807.
58	67	231	**Samuel Roulston** ase of James Roulston .. 49 acs .. 6th section .. 3rd range .. 3-mile tree .. to incl his occupant claim .. James Roulston, Loc. 31 Aug 1807.

58	68	232	**Joseph Brown** ase of James Roulston .. 25 acs .. 5th and 6th sections .. 3rd range .. two mile tree .. to incl his occupant claim .. James Roulston, Loc. 31 Aug 1807. Sur Rtd 23 Feb 1809 by Jas. Roulston, D. S. (Martin's Cr.)
58	68	233	**Thomas Dillon** .. 200 acs .. Jackson Co .. 6th section .. 3rd range .. 31 Aug 1807.
58	68	234	**James Vance** .. ase of James Roulston.. 105 5/8 acs .. 6th section .. 3rd range .. N of said **Vance's dwelling house** .. James Roulston, Loc. 31 Aug 1807.
58	68	235	**William Jarred** ase of James Roulston .. 45 acs .. Jackson Co .. 6th section .. 3rd range .. 31 Aug 1807.
58	68	236	**Orsburn Dillard** .. 100 acs .. Smith Co .. Beg on the north boundary of a 3,500 ac survey of the **heirs of Richard Pryor** 560 poles west of the NE corner on a beech marked "R" .. north 160 poles .. west 100 poles .. south 160 poles to Pryor's line .. east with said line 100 poles to the beg to incl his occupant claim **on which he now lives** .. 31 Aug 1807. James Roulston, Loc.

"Heirs of Richard Pryor" means it was a survey of the Howell Tatum tract, his Grant No. 824!

58	69	237	**William Stewart** .. ase of James Roulston .. 50 acs .. White Co .. James Roulston, Loc. 31 Aug 1807.
58	69	238	**James Roulston** .. 39 3/8 acs .. 6th section .. 3rd range .. Begin on the south fork of Indian Cr of the Caney Fork .. on a beech marked "A. S. I. V." Martin Johnson's beginning corner .. to incl said Roulston's improvement .. 31 Aug 1807. James Vance, Loc.
58	76	262	**Christopher Bullard** 640 acs .. N side of Cumberland .. adj John Richman .. 3rd section .. 3rd range .. 31 Aug 1807.
58	76	263	**James D. Henley** ase of Abner Henley .. 100 acs .. adj his own .. to incl his improvement. 31 Aug 1807. James D. Henley, Loc. Made void by James D. Henley 3 Feb 1813.
58	78	265	**James Roulston** .. 50 acs .. 6th section .. 3rd range .. 4-mile tree .. Richard Porterfield, Loc. 31 Aug 1807.
58	85	296	**Edward Givin** .. 640 acs .. North side of Cumberland .. mouth of Dry Cr .. to incl **John Black's improvement and plantation** .. 11 Sep 1807. John Black, Loc. Sur rtd 13 May 1808 by Genl. L. Nolen, DS. Entered 1 Nov 1803

.. re-entered .. in the 2nd section and 1st range.

| 58 | 91 | 314 | **Willie Cherry** ase of Elizabeth Mahoon heir of Ralph Mahoon .. 220 acs .. Jackson Co .. first large br that crosses Walton's Road above said Willie Cherry's house .. on sd road supposed to be 2 or 3 miles from sd Cherry's improvement at Cub Run to adj **the Indian boundary** on the N near where it crosses sd branch and on the west side of sd branch to run down and up the branch on both sides for complement. **6 May 1803.** Willie Cherry, Loc. Re-enters same 220 acs .. 13 Nov 1807 in **5th section and 3rd range.** (Martin's Cr.) |

| 58 | 92 | 316 | **William Patterson** ase of Job Smith .. ase of heirs of John Davis. 640 acs .. Smith Co .. S side of Cumberland in the first bend above the mouth of Caney Fk .. adj tract belonging to heirs of Lewis Gutridge .. 24 Oct 1802. A. Stubblefield, Loc. **Benjamin Clark** re-enters said land by virtue of same Warrant No. 4339 as ase of heirs of John Davis .. 4th section .. 4th range .. 14 Nov 1807. |

| 58 | 93 | 318 | **Thomas Stubblefield** ase of Armstreat Stubblefield ase of Cullen Smith Heir at law of Stephen Smith .. 20 acs beg at **Spel Coleman's** west corner in McCall's line .. to incl land between sd McCall's & his own. 11 Oct 1797. Re-entered 17 Nov 1807. |

| 58 | 109 | 354 | **John Fitzgerald** .. 640 acs .. N side of Cumberland .. Jennings Cr .. adj Ephraim Payton and Prewet's .. on a military land warrant No. 4711 issued in favor of the heirs of William Corbin ase of Charles J. Love ase of James Easten attorney in fact for said Heirs .. 13 Sep 1808. Survey returned 17 July 1809 by Genl. L. Nolen, D. S. "I do hereby certify that the above location was legally proven before me, one of the Justices of the Peace for said County given under my hand this 28 June 1803. **Henry McKinny, J.P.**" (See Entry 178 in Book 54.) John Fitzgerald transferred his entry No. 354 to John Wilson and Abner Lee on 29 Sep 1803 attested by David Vance. |

BUILDING NEIGHBORHOODS
From
EARLY LAND RECORDS OF TENNESSEE

RG 50 SERIES 2 - LAND ENTRY BOOK 16 - REEL 5
1ST SURVEYOR'S DISTRICT - SMITH COUNTY

Reel 5 contains Book 15, Franklin and Marion Counties Occupant Entries 1820 - . Then comes Book 17 which is Sullivan County 1780 - 1802 and Adair and Hardin Warrants, Indexed. Next on the Reel is **Book 16**, Smith County Entry Book for 1802 - 1803. During those years, Smith County encompassed much of what is now Jackson, White and Putnam Counties. We look for place and people names associated with Old Jackson County.

BK	PG	NUMBER	DESCRIPTION
16	1	3	NC Warrant 3240. John Sloan ase Zebulon Massey. 25 June 1802. 640 acs in Smith County beg .. 60 poles southwest .. the Indian Boundary line .. the Walton Road and running northeast with said Indian boundary line .. or compliment so as to incl a small improvement. A Stubblefield.
16	5	19	NC Warrant 9. Reece Porter, ase Philip Merrinor. First entered 3 Aug 1802. Reentered in the name of Reece Porter the 28th Nov 1809. 640 acs in Smith County on **Rock Spring Cr** of Caney Fk to join Patten Saul where his lower line crosses said Cr .. down the Cr for complement so as to incl a small improvement made by Kennady and Coyle. A. Stubblefield, Loc.
16	6	22	NC Warrant 48. Michael Santee .. 640 acs in Smith Co on the Ridge between the waters of Caney Fk and Indian Cr of Cumberland on both sides of Walton Road to begin 60 poles west of Lewis Pyburn's improvement and run north and east ... to incl the said improvement. A. Stubblefield, Loc. 11 Aug 1802. Removed by Stubblefield 24 Oct 1802.

This Book has some totally illegible pages.

16	8	31	NC Warrant 48. Michael Santee .. 640 acs in Smith County on head waters of South Fk of Indian Cr of Caney Fk to begin 60 poles west of a maple tree marked A S to run south and east .. to incl said maple. A. Stubblefield, Loc., 24 Oct 1802.
16	10	39	NC Warrant 48. Michael Santee .. 640 acs in Smith County on Indian Cr of Caney Fk to begin 50 poles above Taylor's Spring in the Little Bear Valley and run down said valley .. to incl Grimeses improvement. **James Vance, Loc.** 1 Dec 1802. Removed 26 Oct 1803. Peter Turney.

35

16	11	41	NC Warrant 5062. Isaac Smith, ase Thos. Jethro, .. 640 acs in Smith County on south side of Cumberland R beg. at a beech tree on the bank of the river 75 poles below the mouth of **Martin's Cr** running thence down the river ... William Stevenson, Loc. 2 Dec 1802.
16	11	42	NC Warrant 269. Joseph Martin .. 132 acs in Smith Co beg. on Richard Bankses south boundary .. northeast corner of tract located by William Pillow and sold to William Thompson being tract Daniel Burford now lives on ... Willis Jones, Loc. 3 Dec 1802.
16	11	44	NC Warrant 269. Joseph Martin .. 133 acs in Smith Co on Fall Cr beg on Wilson Cage's upper boundary ... Joseph Bishop, Loc. 8 Dec 1802.
16	13	50	Wilson Cage .. 100 acs in Smith Co on south side of Cumberland on branch of Indian Cr that **Mr. Young** lives on .. Wilson Cage, Loc. 2 Dec 1802.
16	13	52	NC Warrant 5192. Alnr. Carmichael ase Jonas Colgrove .. 640 acs in Smith Co on branch of Spring Cr to incl place where Richard Porterfield now lives to incl also the place where Bilderback lives to begin 1/4 mile southwest from said Porterfield's .. to incl both said improvements. Richard Porterfield, Loc. 20 Dec 1802. Removed by Peter Turney 24 Mar 1803.
16	17	65	Charles Marshall .. 320 acs .. on the ridge between waters of Caney Fk and Indian Cr of Cumberland .. both sides of Walton's Road .. near Lewis Pyburn .. 24 Mar 1803.
16	18	69	William Holliday ase of Sampson Williams .. 116 acs .. **where he now lives** on a branch of Salt Lick Cr .. 7 Apr 1800.
16	20	77	NC Warrant 3889. **Henry Turney** ase Reuben Goad .. 207 acs in Smith Co on Clear Fk, branch of Smith's fork to beg 10 poles above the Cave Spring .. by virtue of a certificate from the county surveyor bearing date 5 May 1803. Henry Turney, Loc. 5 May 1803.
16	20	79	TN Warrant 248. Richard Porterfield, ase Samuel Jackson .. 50 acs in Smith Co to incl a rocky sinking spring about 1-1/2 mile above **William Young's** on Indian Cr to beg on a beech tree marked R P on west side of a hill near the trace leading from said Young's to Walton's Road and .. west and south .. incl the spring. Richard Porterfield, Loc. 23 May 1803. Removed by Richard Porterfield 28 May 1803.
16	21	82	TN Warrant 248. Richard Porterfield, ase Samuel

Jackson, .. 50 acs in Smith Co on **Rock Spring Cr to incl the place he now lives upon** to begin between the said Cr and Walton's Road on a sugar tree and ... east and south .. to incl his own improvement. Richard Porterfield. 28 May 1803.

16 22 87   TN Warrant 124. Magness McDonald ase Howel Tatum, .. 100 acs in Smith Co on South Side of Cumberland R to beg on bank of said R at said McDonald's west corner to run east with said line thence north for compliment so as to incl the vacant land. Magness McDonald, Loc. 20 June 1803. Removed by order of Magness McDonald 1 Oct 1803.

Note: Magness McDonald lived in Wilson County. He registered a stock mark in Smith County, and his land entry reminds us that for a short period of time, the eastern boundary of southern Wilson County was the Caney Fk R. One of his sons moved on into Jackson County.

16 22 88   John Lancaster ase Benjamin McCullock ase heirs of John Jones .. 640 acs in Smith Co between Smith's Fk and Caney Fk at the place called the Cove .. beg at a beech .. 20 poles above the Sinkhole where the branch sinks ... east and west .. John Lancaster, Loc. 21 June 1803. Made void 25 Mar 18??.

16 29 115   NC Warrant 1053. **James Roulston**, ase Joseph Woolfolk .. 32 acs in Smith Co on waters of Indian Cr that empties in Cumberland 1/2 mile above James Narrock's to beg on a hernut(?) tree about 20 poles from Walton's Road ... west and south ... **James Roulston, Loc.** 15 Aug 1803.

16 30 120   TN Warrant 124. Magness McDonald, ase Howel Tatum .. 100 acs in Smith Co on south side of Cumberland beg. at southwest corner of .. Lewis Gutredge's .. 320 acs .. John Warren's corner on the river and said McDonald's .. north with Gutredge's line and west. Magness McDonald, Loc. 13 Sept 1803.

16 33 131   NC Warrant 48. Michael Santee .. 640 acs in Smith Co on Indian Cr of Caney Fk .. little Bear Valley .. **James Vance, Loc.** 25 Oct 1803.

16 34 133   NC Warrant 3761. Henry Bohannan, ase Nathaniel Taylor ase David Grant .. 50 acs in Smith Co on dividing ridge of the Caney Fk and Indian Cr on Walton's Road beg nearly west from where **said Bohannan now lives** .. to incl Spring and Improvement where he now lives. By virtue of a certificate from James Taylor bearing date the 3rd September 1803. Henry Bohannan, Loc. 26 Oct 1803.

16 35 139   Michael Santee .. 200 acs .. the head Spring of the

south fork of Indian Cr of the Caney Fk .. **James Vance.** 28 Oct 1803.

16 36 143   Howel Tatum .. 100 acs .. south side of Cumberland on waters of Indian Cr .. adj 100-ac tract surveyed for E. Jennings that the Widow Kerkindall now lives on .. Willis Jones, Loc. 30 Oct 1803.

16 36 144   TN Warrant 359. Wilson Cage .. 51 acs on certificate .. given by Willis Jones, Surveyor of Smith County, in Smith Co on south side of Cumberland R on waters of Indian Cr beg where Redmond D. Barry's upper boundary of his 640 ac tract **that William Sadler lives on** crosses sd Cr running up sd Cr on both sides .. to incl a spring and small branch. 30 Oct 1803. Willis Jones, Loc.

16 39 154   Solomon Blair .. 88 acs .. Payton's Cr .. so as to incl **James Morgan's and Vachel Clark's improvement.** Solomon Blair. 10 Nov 1803.

Book 16 seems to have had approximately 100 or more pages removed at the end with assistance from a pocket knife or razor blade - definitely cut out with a sharp-bladed tool.

****

Book 16 is followed by part of Book 17 **again** (Sullivan Co). Book 18 contains White County Occupant Entries No. 1 to 1816, 1824-1826. It is largely indexed, but no one should hope to use these records by indexes alone.

We read Book 18 quickly, looking for our neighborhoods. Knowing that our families were there, and remembering that casual references are sometimes more informative than formal statements, we abstracted what seemed pertinent, but those abstracts will appear in another volume as history of later decades develops.

BUILDING NEIGHBORHOODS
From
EARLY LAND RECORDS OF TENNESSEE

RG 50 SERIES 2 - BOOKS 23 & 24 - REEL 6
1ST SURVEYOR'S DISTRICT LAND ENTRIES - JACKSON COUNTY FOLKS

BK	PG	NUMBER	DESCRIPTION
23	47	328	**James Vinson** in **Sumner Co** .. land granted to James Clendennen **on which James Vinson now lives** .. Ephraim Farr's south boundary adj James Saunders line. 24 May 1807. Sur rtd 11 Sep 1807.

Note: Entry No. 328 reminds us of problems with wandering ancestors with same or with similar names. James Vinson will be mentioned several times in **Jackson** County, but we do not know if he lived in Sumner County in 1807 or if he helped survey the Indian Boundary in 1797.

23	52	364	**Mathew Gutrage** .. on Proctor's Cr adj Stephen Cantrell. 27 Aug 1807. Note: Gutrage, Gray et al had several entries in this area.
23	70	498	**Richard Porterfield** .. 50 acs ".. four-mile tree .." 31 Aug 1807. Sur rtd 23 Feb 1809 by Jas. Roulston, DS.
23	72	511	**William Jared** ase of James Roulston ase of Moses Newson .. 100 acs adj Jared's 45-ac tract. 31 Aug 1807. Jas. Roulston, Loc. Sur rtd 3 Aug 1808 by James Roulston, DS.
23	75	536	**James Roulston** ase of Jno Waddle and Jno McMillin .. near Walton Road. 31 Aug 1807. Henry Buchannon, Loc.
23	82	585	**Alexander Irwin** ase of Thomas Dillon .. 100 acs adj John Rhea .. the 4-mile tree and William Terrell's 2,000 acs. 18 Sep 1807. **White Co.**
23	82	588	**Alexander Irwin** ase of Thos. Dillon .. 50 acs adj Entry No. 585. **White Co.** Removed 13 May 1808 by Isaac Taylor Jr, atty in fact for Alex Irwin.
23	83	594	**William Irwin** ase of Thomas Dillon .. 50 acs in the Barrens. 1 Sept 1807. **White Co.** Isaac Taylor, Loc. John Bowen DS.
23	135	948	**James Simpson** .. 70 acs on Cub Cr. 5 Oct 1807. Sur rtd 24 Dec 1807 by Gen. L. Nolen, DS.
23	135	949	**James Simpson** .. 52-1/2 acs on Jennings Cr near Thomas Patton's NW corner. 5 Oct 1807. Sur rtd 24 Dec 1807. Gen. L. Nolen, DS.
23	136	950	**David Porter** ase of Abner Henley ase of David Chester

			.. 30 acs on Cub Cr of Cumberland adj James Simpson. 5 Oct 1807. Sur rtd 24 Dec 1807 by Gen. L. Nolen, DS.
23	176	1141	**Heirs of David Joyner** enter 200 acs (their warrant was for 3,340 acres) on Hurricane Cr of Cumberland adj McCann's 60 acs. 18 Nov 1807. A. Stubblefield, Loc.
23	197	1247	**Jeremiah Bush** ase of Benjamin Clark ase of Howell Tatum. Enters 13 acs on Lick Log Br of Dillard's Cr. Beg on an elm 19 poles N of Wilburn's line ... 24 Dec 1807.
23	199	1261	**Stephen Cantrell** .. 30 acs on Proctor's Cr Beg at NW corner of an entry of said Cantrell's for 100 acs at a beech and elm running S with the W boundary of said claim ... 5 Jan 1808.
23	209	1321	**George White** ase of John Rork of Isaac M. Bledsoe. Enters 20 acs .. Walton's Road incl improvement **whereon said White now lives.** 8 Feb 1808. James Roulston, Loc.
23	232	1451	**Edmund Jennings** ase of Peter Poiner .. 100 acs on Dry Fork of Flynn's Cr near Hartley's. 22 Mar 1808. Edmund Jennings, Loc.
23	234	1462	**Edmund Jennings** .. 100 acs N of Cumberland below **Simpson's old floating mill** along the R. 23 Mar 1808. Made void 1 Aug 1812.
23	234	1463	**Edmund Jennings** ase of John Richmond .. 21 acs on Indian Cr near where **Saml Stalcup lives** .. to incl said improvement. 23 Mar 1808. Removed 10 Feb 1809.
23	235	1469	**John Smith** originally of Patrick Moore. 23 Mar 1808. Enters 228 acs in Jackson Co on Knob Cr N waters of Cumberland beg. at **Thomas Lee's improvement.** Removed 16th Jun 1808. Test. John C. McLemore. (Brimstone Cr)
23	249	1543	**Joshua Hadley** .. 126 acs on N bank of Cumberland Beg at mouth of Jenning's Cr. 6 Apr 1808. Henry Lyon Loc. Removed 10 May 1809.
23	247	1546	**Gen. L. Nolen** ase of Wm. Christmas .. 83 acs on Jonas Griffith's S boundary of his occupant claim .. on W side of Jennings Cr. 8 Apr 1808. Removed 13 Feb 1810.
23	249	1547	**Brice Collins** .. 823 acs on both sides of Jenning's Cr meandering with bends of Cumberland to corner of tract **whereon John Burress now lives** formerly granted to Rich Fenner thence N to NW corner E of **Michael Harmon's stillhouse** thence N and W. Gen. Nolen Loc. Sur rtd Feb 1815 for 134 acs. **John Murrey,** DS.

23	255	1580	**James Taggart** ase of Thomas Dillon .. 65 acs in Jackson Co on the middle fork of Proctor's Cr northwest of Stephen Cantrell's. 13 May 1809. James Taggert, Loc. Sur rtd 1 Dec 1814.
23	257	1590	**Francis Kendall** ase of Thomas Gist ase of James Campbell .. on waters of Barren R adj land belonging to one Ervin **whereon John Frame now lives.** 16 Apr 1808. Garrett Moore, Loc. Sur rtd 27 June 1808.
23	257	1591	**Hezekiah Oakes** ase of Thomas Gist ase of James Campbell .. 100 acs adj **John Denton whereon he now lives.** 16 Apr 1808. Garrett Moore, Loc. Sur retd 25 June.
23	258	1597	**Richard Porterfield** ase of Samuel Price .. 20 acs on Falling Water of Caney Fk. **White Co.** 20 Apr 1808. Voided 15 June 1814 per order of Richard Porterfield.
23	259	1598	**Prettyman Jones** ase of William Christmas ase of John Whitecox heirs. .. on Indian Cr of Caney Fork. Improvement made by **Zachariah Jones where Samuel Brady now lives.** 20 Apr 1808. James Vance, Loc. Sur Rtd 3 Aug 1808. James Roulston, DS.
23	259	1599	**Prettyman Jones** ase ditto. .. in the Little Bear Valley, a draft of Indian Cr of Caney Fork .. **to incl where he now lives.** 20 Apr 1808. James Vance Loc. Sur rtd 22 Feb 1809. James Roulston, DS.
23	259	1600	**John Clemmons** ase ditto. ..on waters of Indian Cr of Caney Fork .. **where Henry Honnors now lives.** 20 Apr 1808. James Vance Loc. Sur rtd 3 Aug 1808. James Raulston DS.
23	260	1609	**Thomas Dillon** .. 200 acs on Roaring R adj John Haywood's tract. 25 Dec 1808. Removed by Dillon 13 May 1808.
23	148	1643	**David Cox** ase of Levi Jarvis .. 528 acs on Doe Cr. 5 Nov 1808. Sur rtd 5 Sept 1811 by John Murrey, DS.
23	274	1687	**George Smith** ase Jno Donelson ase Sterling Brewer ase of Silas Marshall. Enters 560 acs near three forks of Jinking's Cr .. adj John Payton's .. **to incl the plantation of James Crabtree.** 10 May 1808. Removed by Smith 31 Dec 1808.
23	280	1716	**Edmund Jennings** .. 66 acs on William Grenade's boundary incl **where Leonard Jones formerly lived.** 13 May 1808. Sur rtd 15 June 1809. Willis Jones, DS.
23	281	1723	**Isaac Taylor Jr** .. 200 acs on Roaring R adj John Haywood's tract .. beg 80 poles N of where said W boundary crosses the Wagon Road leading from Southwest

Point to Nashville .. 13 May 1808. Removed 24 Oct 1811.

23 282 1724 **Alexander Irwin** ..in the Barrons west of Wagon Road north of a sink hole spring. 13 May 1808. Isaac Taylor, Jr., Loc.

24 12 1902 **John Smith** ase of John Griffith ase of Archibald Lytle .. 101 acs .. on Knob Cr N waters of Cumberland R. Beg 46 poles east of **Thomas Lee's improvement** .. . David D. Mitchell's north boundary .. 15 June 1808. John Smith, Loc. Sur rtd by Gen. L. Nolen.

24 22 1955 **Benjamin Blackburn** .. on Blackburns Fork adj John Richardson's line. 27 June 1808. Sur rtd 18 July 1808. James Raulston DS.

24 23 1959 **Abner Henley** .. 43 acs on Jennings Cr. 27 June 1808. Sur rtd 1 July 1808 by Gen. L. Nolen, DS.

24 23 1960 **Abner Henley** .. 61-1/2 acs on Jennings Cr. 27 June 1808. Sur rtd 30 June 1808. Gen. L. Nolen, DS.

24 23 1962 **Thomas Hopkins** .. 113 acs on Pigeon Roost Cr of Caney Fk of Cumberland R at 3-mile tree. 28 June 1808. Made void 20 July 1820.

24 27 1981 **Uriah Anderson** ase of Roddom Home .. 75 acs .. on Dry Fk of Flynn's Cr .. with meanders of Knobs and Bluffs on both sides of the branch including an improvement belonging to said Anderson **whereon James Raglan now lives.** 30 June 1808. Sur rtd 9 Sept 1815.

24 27 1982 **Uriah Anderson** .. 74 acs on Dry Fork of Flynn's Cr .. beg opposite the fork of said Dry Fork .. on the east side of the Cr .. including two plantations joining to each other **whereon Thomas Brown and Elijah Simmons now live.** 30 June 1808. Sur rtd 22 May 1816.

24 28 1984 **Abner Henley** .. 420 acs beg near mouth of Henley's spring branch. SE corner of 640 ac tract of Christopher Bullard's on N side of Cumberland. 1 July 1808. Sur rtd 20 Nov 1808. S. Williams, DS.

24 35 2025 **William Gray** ase of William Stafford ase of Abner Henry ase of David Chester .. 10 acs on Roaring R .. adj John McGee's. 15 July 1808. Sur rtd 14 May 1814 by Jno Murrey, DS.

24 44 2070 **Sampson Williams** .. 118-1/4 acs .. E side of Caney Fork nearly opposite the upper corner of .. 2,550 acs granted to John Lancaster. 23 July 1808. Sur rtd 30 Sept 1822.

24	53	2118	**Richard Mansell** ase James Raulston ase Ichabod Radley .. on Martin's Cr .. Beason's Cr .. incl **whereon Richard Mansell now lives.** 3 Aug 1808. James Roulston, Loc. No sur.
24	54	2119	**James Roulston** ase **David Harburt** ase Ichabod Radley .. on ridge dividing Cumberland and Caney Fork near intersection of Lancaster's Road and Walton Road .. **whereon John Boyd now lives.** 3 Aug 1808. J. Roulston, Loc.
24	54	2122	**James Roulston** ase Ditto. On Indian Cr of Cumberland near Isaac Walton. 4 Aug 1808. Entry for 50 acres assigned to **Shadrick Bridges** 15 Oct 1811.
24	55	2123 & 2124	**Joseph Pryor** on 4 Aug 1808. Two entries in Jackson Co on Pryor's Fork of Roaring R. Total 460 acres on "Evans Warrant" dated 10 Jan 1794. James Roulston, Loc. Both entries made void per order 10 Sep 1810 by James Carter.
24	55	2125	**George Raybourn** .. 200 acs on Indian Cr of Cumberland adj Edmund Jenning's occupant survey .. N to Isaac Walton's line .. W to William's line .. 4 Aug 1808. J. Roulston, Loc. Sur rtd 23 Feb 1823.
24	65	2174	**Uriah Anderson** .. 100 acs .. on Doe Cr .. Beg on James G. Beecham's E boundary at David Coxes corner .. 15 Aug 1808. Sur rtd 20 Sep 1811 by John Murrey, DS.
24	66	2177	**Gen. L. Nolen** .. 50 acs .. N of Cumberland and on top of .. ridge between Knob Cr and .. **Black's Br.** Beg on a beech .. .. including a flatt on said ridge known by the name of Grape Vine Flatt. 15 Aug 1808. Gen. L. Nolen, Loc.
24	28	2183	**Philip Britton** .. 428 acs on N side of Cumberland near mouth of **Abner Henley's** spring branch. 30 June 1808. Removed 1 July 1808.
24	81	2267	**Robert Anderson** .. 50 acs on Spring Cr adj John Merriweather. 27 Aug 1808. Removed 24 July 1810. Jno Sterling, Loc.
24	117	2470	**William Tinsley** ase of Gen. L. Nolen ase of Uriah Anderson originally of Roddam Home .. 15 acs on S side of Cumberland R beg on the bank .. 16 Sept 1808.
24	117	2472	**Benjamin Blackburn** .. 100 acs on S Fk of Roaring R beg on a white oak "..not exceeding 400 yards NE from the Great Falls in said river .." 27 Sept 1808. Removed 12 June 1810 by Benjamin Blackburn.
24	118	2475	**Elisha Dillard** ase Robert and Thomas Anderson. **Smith**

Co. On Indian Cr of Cumberland **adj Daniel Wilburn's corner.** 27 Sept 1808. Made void 1 Jan 1814 Elisha Dillard. J. Roulston, Loc.

24	119	2479	**Gen. L. Nolen** .. 93 acs .. N of Cumberland on headwaters of Jenning's Cr .. adj Fifer's line. 29 Sept 1808.
24	119	2480 & 2481	**James McKnight** ase of William Stafford ase of Abner Henley ase of David Chester. Enters 10 acs .. on Sexton's Cr .. to incl **the lower improvement of Thomas Edwards.** 29 Sept 1808. Sur rtd 3 Feb 1815.
24	134	2570	**Aaron Lambert SR** .. 70 acs on S side of Cumberland between 4 and 5 miles above mouth of Roaring R. 18 Oct 1808.
24	448	2643	**David Cox** .. 28 acs .. beg on a Beech marked "D. C." on Doe Cr .. 5 Nov 1808.
24	153	2664	**James Bedford** .. 30 acs .. about 4 miles from mouth of Roaring R beg on a sycamore at the head of **his spring** .. to **incl said Bedford's improvement whereon he now lives** and the improvement of Thomas Gore. 10 Nov 1808. Sur rtd 5 Sept 1811. John Murrey, DS.
24	153	2665	**James Bedford** .. 7 acs on Roaring R ... to incl part of the improvement **where John McDaniel now lives.** 10 Nov 1808. Sur rtd 25 July 1814 by John Murrey, DS.
24	158	2699	**Wilson Cage** .. 51 acs .. on S side of Cumberland on waters of Indian Cr. Adj Redmund D. Barry's 640 acs .. that **William Sadler now lives on** .. 16 Nov 1808. Sur rtd 4 Oct 1809 by Willis Jones, DS.
24	158	2700	**Wilson Cage** .. 50 acs on S side of Cumberland R on Hurricane Cr .. near where **William Sullivan formerly lived** .. 16 Nov 1808. Sur rtd 8 May 1813 by James Roulston, DS.
24	169	2756	**William Marchbanks** ase Sampson Williams ase heirs of Thos. Hofarton?? Warrant No. 3978. 150 acs on the Spring Fork of Martin's Cr ..**incl place where Richard Anderson now lives.** Adj D Barry. 25 Nov 1808. S. Williams, DS.
24	169	2757	**Sarah Haliday** ase Sampson Williams ase heirs of Thomas Hofarton??? .. on Salt Lick Cr **incl place where she now lives** and joining tract in names of Francis Graves. Beg near lower corner of **her fence** on Graves' line. 25 Nov 1808. S. Williams DS.
24	169	2758 & 2759	**Sampson Williams and Charles Mundine** were also ase of the heirs of Hofarton??. One at the head of Flynn's

Cr where **Benjamin Fox now lives** and the other on Salt Lick and Defeated Crs adj Frances Graves, Nathaniel Williams and John Craddock adjoining Williams on the west. Both dated 25 Nov 1808.

24	172	2774	**John McDaniel** .. 10 acs on Blackburn's Fk .. to incl improvement **whereon William Rutledge now lives.** 4 Nov 1808. William Gray Loc. Made void 16 Apr 1824.
24	172	2775	**John McDaniel** .. 37-1/2 acs on west fork of Roaring R .. to incl improvement whereon **Abner Lee now lives.** 1 Nov 1808. William Gray, Loc. Sur rtd 20 Sept 1811 by John Murrey, D.S.
24	172	2776	**John McDaniel** .. 30 acs .. Roaring R .. south of Jacob Miller's Spring .. to incl **Jacob Miller's and Hatley Gore's improvement.** 4 Dec 1808. Sur rtd 29 Oct 1813.
24	172	2777	**John McDaniel** .. on Morrison's Cr of Roaring R .. beg where Elijah Ewing's S boundary crosses Morrison's Cr .. 1 Dec 1808.
24	172	2778	**John McDaniel** .. on Morrison's Cr .. **where William Morrison and David Lowry formerly lived.** 1 Dec 1808.
24	173	2779	**William Stafford** .. 15 acs on Roaring R .. beg 2 poles S of John Siscoe's spring .. to **incl John Siscoe's improvement.** 1 Dec 1808. Sur rtd 20 Sept 1811 by John Murray, DS.
24	174	2789	**Thomas Bounds and Thomas Lovelady** ase of Wm. Lyttle, Jr. and originally of Richard Phillips. Military Warrant No. 1026 for 640 acres: Enters 560 acres lying in White County on Falling Waters. Beg at a black oak and chestnut .. the black oak marked RR on the Military Reservation Line .. where the line dividing Jackson and White Counties crosses said Military Line: Running one ?? west with said Jackson Line thence South and East for complement to incl **Aaron Perrin, Reuben Ragland, James Bounds, Smith Hutchins, John Hutchins, James Dyer and part of Margaret Barton's and the whole of Thomas Lovelady's Improvements.** 3 Dec 1808. Thomas Bounds and Thomas Lovelady, Locators. Survey returned 10 April 1809 by James Roulston, DS.
24	174	2790	Same enterers - Same Military Warrant No. 1026. 88 acs in Jackson County on Pigeon Roost Cr .. waters of the Falling Water to incl the improvement **whereon John Young now lives.** 3 Dec 1808. James Roulston DS.
24	175	2791	Same enterers - Military warrant 4355 for 228 acres. They enter 70 acs in Jackson Co on Pigeon Roost Branch of Falling Water to incl place **where James Young now lives.** James Roulston, DS.

24	182	2835	**James Roulston** ase of Ichabod Radley. An Evans Warrant for 50 acs on Falling Water of Caney Fork adj entry of Elisha Davis. 10 Dec 1808. Sur Rtd 11 Oct 1814. James Davis, DS.
24	183	2838	**Edward Given** ase of Heirs of William Winwright .. 320 acs on Line Fk of Barren R. Beg on Johnson's Spring Br .. 10 Dec 1808. Sur rtd 20 Sept 1811 by John Murray, DS. Made void 2 Oct 1821.
24	198	2926	**Moses Fisk** ase of Stokley Donelson ase of James Chisum .. 10 acs on E bank of Cumberland just above mouth of Roaring R .. William Waller's lower corner. 14 Jan 1809. No survey shown.
24	218	3045	**Sampson Williams** .. 30 acs .. between lines of Selby Harney and Francis Graves and joining Thomas Woodward's north boundary. 18 Feb 1809.
24	218	3046	**Sampson Williams** .. 100 acs .. Flynn's Cr on both sides with meanders of the hills .. **to incl the place where Joseph Chaffin now lives.** 18 Feb 1809.
24	218	3047	**Sampson Williams** .. 200 acs on W fork of Roaring R including **where John Burleson and John Rutledge now live.** 18 Feb 1809.
24	222	3065	**Robert Anderson** .. 281 acs in Smith County on Williamson's Branch .. Howell Tatum's Survey of 3,565 acs about one hundred and fifty poles west of where said line crosses said Cr. 22 Feb 1809.
24	222	3073	**James Roulston** ase Levi Graham and originally George Brown Jr. .. .. 50 acs on Spring Branch of Caney Fork including **David Parker's improvement where he lives.** 22 Feb 1809. Voided 20 Aug 1814. James Roulston.
24	327	3100	**John Ward** .. 400 acs .. S side of Cumberland on Indian Cr .. adj tract in name of Isaac Smith .. to Poston's line .. 2 Mar 1809. Sur rtd 1 Aug 1810 by John Ward.
24	230	3114	**Stephen Cantrell Jr and Gen. L. Nolen** ase of Wm. Lytle Jr originally of **David Gholston** enter 294 acs on N side of Cumberland .. beg on a white oak .. supposed to be **Howell Parker's** NE corner .. the white oak standing between **James Richmond's** and a place claimed by **James Bedford** .. running S to Cumberland .. then down meanders of said river .. including **James Richmond, John Richmond, Andrew Blackwood and Clayton Roger's improvements.** 6 Mar 1809. Sur rtd 7 July 1809 by Sampson Williams, DS.
24	230	3115	**Stephen Cantrell Jr** et al ... 210 acs adj their own

including **John Sweazy's and James Bedford's improvements.** 5 Mar 1809. Sur rtd 7 July 1809 by Sampson Williams, DS.

24 230 3116 **Gen. Nolen** ase of Uriah Anderson originally of Rodham Home .. 143 acs on S side of Cumberland .. Beg where Howell Barker's N boundary crosses said river running E .. up the meanders of the R .. E with Parker's line .. including a place where **Dervin Jarmed** (might be James or Jarvis. Omits the word "lived.") .. last year .. opposite the mouth of Indian Cr. 6 Mar 1809. Removed 21 Dec 1810.

24 231 3118 **Isaac Moore** .. 640 acs on N side of Cumberland. Beg at **Samuel Parkin's** NW corner on Wartrace .. 7 Mar 1809. Edwin S. Moore, Loc. Made void 29 Jan 1812. Alfred Moore, a desc of Isaac Moore.

24 232 3125 **Jeremiah Denton** ase of Alexander Cook .. 50 acs .. 70 poles from **the dwelling house of said Denton** .. 9 Mar 1809.

24 250 3228 **Henry M. Rutledge** .. 400 acs .. Smith Co on the S side of John's Cr of Long Cr of Big Barren beg at Sam'l Dounel's SW corner .. of 274 acs on N boundary of 640 acs granted to Sampson Williams .. W and N so as to join **Thomas Wilkerson** on the W and Edward Given on the N. J. C. McLemore and E. Given, Locs. 31 Mar 1809.

24 252 3240 **Note:** Pages are mixed here, and some entries have duplicate numbers. First half of Double Page 252 has 3 entries for Henry M. Rutledge in **Sumner Co** numbered 3240, 3238, and 3239. The second half of that double page has the following entry also numbered 3240.

Henry M. Rutledge by virtue of a certificate warrant No. 213 for 5,000 acres: Enters 640 acs in Jackson Co, on the head of **Knob Cr** of Cumberland R adj Edward Givens .. being the tract **Leonard Huff lives on.** 31 Mar 1809. J. C. McLemore and E. Givens, Locs. Sur Rtd 24 Oct 1810 by Edwd. Givens DS.

24 255 3256 **Thomas Stubblefield** .. 60 acs on Mine Lick Cr of Caney Fork. Near **Samuel Maxfield's where he now lives.** 3 Apr 1809. A. Stubblefield, Loc.

24 255 3257 **Thomas Stubblefield** .. 40 acs .. on Caney Fork on south side of Walton's Road near **a field cleared by Samuel Walker.** 3 Apr 1809. A. Stubblefield, Loc.

24 255 3258 **Thomas Stubblefield** .. 25 acs on both sides of Walton's Road and on **the waters of Martin's Cr** of Cumberland R. Beg 20 poles N from said road where the west boundary line of a tract of Lytle's crosses the branch of said

creek. S and W .. to **incl where Reason formerly lived.** 3 Apr 1809. Sur rtd 30 July 1823.

24 256 3262 **Sampson Curling** .. 40 acs .. on both sides of Walton's Road .. near **where William Redkins now lives.** 8 Apr 1809. A. Stubblefield, Loc. Survey rtd Nov 10 1819.

24 264 3312 **Absolom Norris** ase of David Norris and originally of James Bryson Heir of David Shores. Enters 8 acs in Jackson and White Counties beg. on Thomas Bound's and Thomas Lovelady's northwest corner .. **incl the improvement where said Norris now lives.** 10 Apr 1809. Sur rtd 28 Apr 1814.

24 265 3313 **David Norris** .. 200 acs on headwaters of Town Cr .. Beg at 2 hickories in the Barrens .. **including his improvement.** 10 Apr 1809. David Norris, Loc.

24 266 3321 **James Carter** ase of James Maxwell .. 214 acs .. occupant claim on Cane Cr .. adj William King's 640-ac tract. 15 Apr 1809.

24 267 3325 **Gabriel Dillard** .. 100 acs .. waters of Caney Fk about 30 poles SE of head spring of Hutchin's Cr .. N and E .. to incl .. **whereon Joseph Hardin now lives.** 15 Apr 1809. Made void 29 Dec 1819.

24 283 3416 **Redmond D. Barry** .. 100 acs on N bank of Cumberland .. above **Fisher's Landing** .. so as to incl **Fisher's improvement.** 11 May 1809. Sur rtd 17 June 1809 by Gen. L. Nolen, DS.

24 299 3506 **George Raybourn** .. 74 acs in Jackson Co on Indian Cr of Caney Fk. Beg on S bank of said Cr where Phillip Phillips and Michael Campbell's E boundary .. crosses the said Cr thence N and E .. 25 May 1809. James Roulston, Loc.

24 300 3513 **Wm. T. Lewis and Wm. Tyrell** ase of Henry M. Rutledge. Warrant No. 215 enter 1,000 acres on south side of Cumberland R joining Thomas Clark's west boundary. "The above entry was originally made May 26, 1796, on Warrant No. 2116, Location No. 5863, and re-entered this the 27th day of May 1809 agreeable to an Act of Assembly in that case made and provided." Hayden Wills, Loc.

24 301 3521 **Wm. Woodfork** .. 73 acs .. on Salt Cr, N side of Cumberland. Beg on Benjamin Richardson's line where Selby Harney's line .. crosses said Richardson's line .. W .. with Gracie's line .. 30 May 1809.

24 321 3627 **Bartlett Gentry** .. 100 acs .. on Cane Cr. E boundary of said **Gentry's 200 ac occupancy survey** .. 14 July

1809. Removed 5 Feb 1811. James Townsend, Loc.

24 322 3629 **James Whitson** .. 200 acs .. his occupant claim .. on James Carter's N boundary .. including improvement **whereon said Whitson now lives.** James Townsend, Loc. (Date illegible. It is between 14 July and 15 July 1809.)

24 324 3643 **Jeremiah Denton** ase of Alexander Cook formerly ase of Thomas Dillon. Enters 80 acs in **White Co** beg at a Post Oak standing on the south side of the **Gum Spring Mountain** between the Gum Springs and Thomas McDonald's .. 18 July 1809. Removed 4 Aug 1811. Alexander Cook.

24 330 3678 **Tandy K. Witcher** .. 100 acs .. on Jenning's Cr .. including **improvement of Henry and Randall Webster.** 25 July 1809. Sur rtd 28 Oct 1817 by **Stephen DeBow.**

24 331 3679 **Tandy K. Witcher** .. 50 acs .. Jennings Cr to incl part of **Randall Webster's** improvement. 25 July 1809 Survey 25 Oct 1809 by Stephen DeBow.

24 331 3680 & 3681 **Tandy Witcher** .. 100 and 240 acs all on Jenning's Cr .. to incl **Joseph and Buckner Russell's improvements** and building on John Thackston's N boundary to **incl William and James Crabtree's improvement whereon they now live.** July 1809.

24 364 3902 **Anne Dyer** ase of Isaac Taylor Jr .. 50 acs on Roaring R adj **Edmund Finn's place** .. to incl **improvement of Anne Dyer.** 15 Sept 1809. Sur rtd 18 May 1813 by James Townsend, DS.

24 364 3905 **Edmund Finn** .. 100 acs .. on Roaring R .. including said **Finn's improvement.** Isaac Taylor Jr, Loc. 15 Sept 1809. James Roulston, DS.

24 366 3917 **Benjamin Clarke** ase of Howell Tatum .. 40 acs on S side of the Cumberland .. adj "WmS" SW corner .. 20 Sept 1809.

24 366 3918 **William Poston** .. 66 acs .. S side of Cumberland on N side of Indian Cr .. supposed to be 3/4 or a mile from the R. 20 Sept 1809. Made void 31 Dec 1811 by Poston.

24 367 3929 **Henry M. Rutledge** .. 600 acs .. in part in lieu of Location No. 3243 .. this day removed .. leaving a balance of sd warrant yet to satisfy of 40 acs lying in Sumner and Robertson Counties on the waters of Somers Br of Red R .. (Is entry No. 3929 in Jackson or Sumner Co??) Locators were John C. McLemore and Edmund Givin. 25 Sept 1809. Made void but date not entered.

24 392 4083 **Smith Hutchins** .. 200 acs covering an occupant claim in

name of **Bartlett Gentry** .. transfered by said Gentry to said Hutchins .. on Cane Cr .. adj James Wilson .. including **said Gentry's improvements.** 9 Nov 1809. James Townsend, Loc.

24 404 4147 **Isaac Taylor Sr** .. 15 acs .. Roaring R .. 20 Nov 1809. Sur rtd 14 Feb 1814 by James Blakemore.

BUILDING NEIGHBORHOODS
From
EARLY LAND RECORDS OF TENNESSEE

RG 50 SERIES 2 - BOOK 26 - REEL 7
1ST SURVEYOR'S DISTRICT LAND ENTRIES - JACKSON CO FOLKS

BK	PG	NUMBER	DESCRIPTION
26	3	4180	**Reece Porter** ase of Daniel Wheaton .. Smith Co. .. on Rock Springs Cr of Caney Fk to join Potter Saul where his lower line crosses sd Cr .. a small improvement made by Keneday & Cagle .. first entered in Smith Co on 3 Aug 1802 -- hereby re-entered. A. Stubblefield. 28 Nov 1809. Made void 10 Dec 1815. J. Roulston.
26	4	4187	**William Stephenson** ase of John Ward ase Henry Lenoir Heir at law of Thomas Lenoir. 50 acs .. on Dillard's Mill Cr .. Beg Benjamin Clark's W boundary .. Wilburn's line .. 1 Dec 1809.
26	4	4193	**William McGee** .. 320 acs on Roaring R .. adj William Martin. 2 Dec 1809.
26	5	4197	**Armstreat Stubblefield** .. 640 acs .. on Roaring R adj Ewing tract .. originally entered in Jackson Co on 27 Aug 1803 .. is now invalid. 3 Dec 1809.
26	5	4198	**Redmond D. Barry** .. 100 acs on Roaring R incl improvement **where Joseph Weaver now lives first made by Jacob Hartey** below Benjamin Blackburn's .. originally entered 17 Sept 1802 in name of Uriah Anderson. 3 Dec 1809.
26	11	4239	**James Moore** 40 acs .. White Co .. Beg west of the road leading from Harty's Tavern to the Rock Island .. N boundary of William Balch's occupant Survey .. where sd line crosses the wagon road from Joseph Banks to the Gum Springs. 19 Dec 1809.
26	13	4247	**Daniel Alexander** .. 18 acs .. W fork of Roaring R incl a Spring known as **Isaac Bullard's improvement** .. 22 Dec 1809.
26	13	4248	**Daniel Alexander** .. 11 acs on the W fork of Roaring R incl an **improvement made by Henry Lowery now called Winfrey Place** .. down both sides of sd river. Edward Robertson, Loc. 22 Dec 1809.
26	13	4250	**Daniel Harpole** .. 300 acs .. N side of Cumberland on Salt Lick Cr .. Selby Harney's W boundary .. Eaton's preemption .. **whereon Pleasant Kirby and others now live** .. William Woodfolk, Loc. 23 Dec 1809.

26	14	4252	**William Woodfolk** .. 240 acs .. N of Cumberland on Salt Lick Cr .. adj Harney and Eaton's preemption. 23 Dec 1809.
26	14	4253	**David Rutledge** ase of Thomas Dillon. 25 acs .. White Co .. N side of Caney Fk .. sd Rutledge's occupant Survey .. Mill Cr .. 25 Dec 1809.
26	16	4260	**Benjamin Richardson** 140 acs .. main fork of Salt Lick Cr .. near **sd Richardson's house** .. Grave's corner .. where Richardson lives. 27 Dec 1809.
26	16	4262	**Edmund Jennings** 100 acs .. headwaters of Salt Lick and Defeated Crs .. E boundary of Richard Andrew's tract. 15 Jan 1810.
26	18	4276	**William Young** ase of William T. Lewis .. one of the south branches of Indian Cr .. adj Augustus Davis tract **which includes Young's improvement.** 1 Jan 1810.
26	24	4315	**John Rayburn** .. 274 acs .. adj John Richmond .. 8 Jan 1810.
26	25	4324	**John Morgan** .. 150 acs .. on Cane Cr .. beg at mouth of first drean (?) emptying into Cane Cr on the north side .. below sd Morgan's spring .. incl Morgan's improvement. 10 Jan 1810.
26	26	4326	**Edmund Jennings** ase Solomon Blair .. 36 acs .. Indian Cr of Cumberland. SW corner of his occupant survey. 11 Jan 1810.
26	31	4354	**Daniel Witcher** .. 200 acs .. Smith Co .. Salt Lick Fk of Big Barron .. east from house **where Tandy K. Witcher now lives.** Tandy K. Witcher, Loc. 19 Jan 1810.
26	31	4355	**Daniel Witcher** .. 74 acs .. headwaters of Peyton's Cr .. east and south from the house and improvement **made by Thomas Terry..** west boundary line of **William Jenkins whereon he now lives** .. Tandy K. Witcher, Loc. 19 Jan 1810.
26	45	4449	**David Johnson** ase of Abner Henley ase of Philip Brittain. 15 acs .. on Roaring R .. **to include sd Johnson's improvement and Spring.** 19 Feb 1810.
26	45	4450	**John Chapman** .. Roaring R .. **incl sd Chapman's improvement where he now lives.** 19 Feb 1810.
26	45	4451 & 4452	**James Simpson** .. Roaring R **where Abner Lee now lives,** and **to include John Rutledge's improvement which he purchased of John Shanklin.** 19 Feb 1810. Also Entry No. 4453 **to include small improvement made by Benjamin Johnson.**

26	56	4519	**William Woodfolk** ase of John Bowen ase James Maxwell. 37 acs .. Salt Lick of Cumberland R .. north of Francis Graves. 12 March 1810.
26	56	4526	**Edmund Jennings** .. 47 acs on Salt Lick Cr adj Francis Graves. 13 Mar 1810.
26	58	4541	**William Coldwell** ase of Benjamin Blackburn. 20 acs on the head of Martin's Cr .. beg on Richard Mansell's W line .. south .. to include **sd Coldwell's house.** 19 Mar 1810. Sur rtd 12 June 1813 by Jas. Roulston, DS.
26	62	4570 & 4571	**William McGee** ase of David Cobb .. on Roaring R. 31 Mar 1810.
26			Many entries in this book for Thomas and Asa Shute show how very active they were in Middle TN particularly in the Big Bend area and "Old Boot" between the Cumberland and the Tennessee Rs.
26	87	4759	**Benjamin Blackburn** ase of Moses Steakley .. 40 acs in Buffalo Valley .. adj tract **whereon James Vance now lives.** 12 June 1810. Sur rtd 16 Oct 1810 by J. Roulston, DS.
26	88	4764	**John Plumley** ase of L. P. Simms .. 60 acs on head of Knob Cr .. about 40 yards below the head of a Spring at or near **John Lee's improvements .. Samuel Hays, Loc.** 13 June 1810. Made void 2 May 1815 by John Plumlee.
26	88	4765	**John Plumley** ase of L. P. Simms ase of William Evans. 2 acs .. on Brimstone Cr .. **to include sd Plumley's Mill.** Samuel Hays, Loc. 13 June 1810. Sur rtd 15 Oct 1816.
26	88	4766	**John Plumley** .. 28 acs on main Brimstone Cr .. to include where **Allen Bisby laid the foundation of a house.** Samuel Hays, Loc. 13 June 1810. Sur rtd 1 Dec 1814.
26	89	4767	**John Plumley** .. 60 acs .. between the heads of Knob Cr and Brimstone Cr .. a sinking spring .. about 100 poles nearly north from **Samuel Hays' house** .. Samuel Hays, Loc. Made void 21 Oct 1814 by order of John Plumley.
26	91	4789	**John Butler** .. 70 ac on Mill Cr .. 19 June 1810. Sur rtd 19 Apr 1811 by John Murray, DS.
26	91	4790	**James Cook** .. 200 acs on both sides of Roaring R .. 20 June 1810.
26	91	4791	**James Taggart** ase of Joel Lewis. Enters 12 acs on waters of Proctor's Cr .. 20 June 1810.

26	92	4792	**James Taggart** .. 18 acs .. on waters of Proctor's Cr .. 24 June 1810.
26	92	4793	**Archibald McLarren** .. 19 acs on waters of Proctor's Cr .. 1 pole east of **sd McLarren's cabin.** 24 June 1810. Sur rtd 20 Sept 1811 by John Murrey, DS.
26	92	4794	**Archibald McLarren** .. 19 acs .. Proctor's Cr .. 20 June 1810. (BHB note: This name might be "McLasson.")
26	93	4797	**Benjamin Blackburn** .. on Indian Cr of Caney Fk .. James Vance's east boundary where Vance's line crosses Indian Cr .. 22 June 1810.
26	94	4811	**Edmund Jennings** .. 36 acs .. waters of Flynn's Cr .. Beg. at **Robert Stothart's** NW corner running west with Uriah Anderson's S boundary. 29 June 1810. Made void 1 Aug 1812.
26	96	4824	**Sampson Williams** ase of Thomas W. Cosby. 200 acs on Martin's Cr .. Beg at NE corner of 640 acs granted Stokely Donalson .. 2 July 1810.
26	96	4827	**Benjamin Blackburn** .. 50 acs .. in Buffalo Valley on waters of Caney Fk .. 2 July 1810.
26	97	4828	**Benjamin Blackburn** .. 10 acs in Buffalo Valley .. incl place **where Robert Wallace now lives** .. 2 July 1810.
26	122	4980	**William Erwin** ase William T. Lewis .. 50 acs .. White Co .. S branch of Taylor's Cr **on which Isaac Taylor SR lives.** 25 Aug 1810.
26	124	4993	**Thomas Wilkinson** . 50 acs in Smith Co .. E side of Caney Fk on a branch which runs into sd Caney Fk below Trousdale's Ferry incl an improvement **known .. as Prater's.** 27 Aug 1810.
26	130	5022	**Richard W. Smith** .. 150 acs .. both sides of Jennings Cr .. between where **sd Smith did live and Richard Lock's.** 1 Sept 1810.
26	130	5024	**John Griffith** ase of William Clark. Enters 191 acs .. both sides of Jennings Cr. Beg at Richard W. Smith's SE corner .. incl **his improvement.** 1 Sept 1810. Removed 10 Sept 1810.
26	131	5028	**Lee Sullivan** ase of heirs of Hugh McLaughlin. Enters 640 acs .. Smith Co .. S side of Cumberland. Beg at a small beech on W boundary of Nathaniel McCanne .. W 180 poles to E boundary of a 640-ac survey by James Roulston for heirs of Wm. Sullivan dec. thence S .. Incl **the place whereon Lodwick Vaden lives.** 3 Sept 1810.

26	131	5029	**Joshua Hadley** .. 80 acs .. Smith Co .. S side of Cumberland .. on E boundary of a survey of 640 acs of heirs of William Sullivan dec. 3 Sept 1810.
26	132	5031	**William Sullivan** .. 300 acs .. Smith Co .. S side of Cumberland .. on the bank of the R .. lower corner of an entry in name of Lee Sullivan .. just above the mouth of Lodwick Vaden's Spring & opposite an old bridge. 3 Sept 1810.
26	137	5066	**James Carter** ase of Joseph Pryor. Enters 214 acs .. in conformity to his occupant Survey rtd 12 Aug 1808. On Cane Cr .. adj William King's 640-acs. 10 Sept 1810.
26	128	5067	**James Whitson** ase of John Starling. Enters 50 acs .. Cane Cr. Beg on west boundary line of James Carter's Survey of 214 acs .. 10 Sept 1810.
26	138	5069	**Jonathan Ward** ase of Joseph Pryor. 100 acs .. White Co .. on Falling Waters. Beg on William King's SE corner .. to include **his Spring and improvements. 10 Sept 1810.**
26	147	5130	**Emanuel Holmes** .. 67 acs .. Waters of Brimstone Cr .. **incl where he now lives.** 17 Sept 1810.
26	147	5133	**Emanual Holmes** .. Enters 50 acs .. Dry Cr .. 17 Sept 1810.
26	149	5143	**James Cook** Enters 40 acs .. Beg on a beech on the N side of Roaring R opposite to mouth of Blackburn's Fk .. 18 Sept 1810.
26	150	5146	**Sylvanus Fowler** ase of William Henry. 300 acs .. S side of Cumberland Beg at William Tinsley's upper corner on the R .. 20 Sept 1810.
26	157	5192	**Wilson Cage** .. Enters 16 1/4 acs .. On Indian Cr beg on E boundary of 51 acs belonging to sd Cage .. 27 Sept 1810.
26	158	5198	**James Bedford** ase of Jenkin Whiteside. 100 acs on Spring Cr. Adj William Hawkins, Asa Lynn .. **incl sd Bedford's improvement.** 28 Sept 1810.
26	159	5203	**Abraham Denton** .. 100 acs in conformity to his occupant Survey .. White Co .. N side of Caney Fk & S of the Hickory Nut Mountain. **Including his improvement and dwelling house.** 28 Sept 1810.
26	166	5248	**George W. Raymon** .. 100 acs .. Blackburn's Fk .. a small distance above the plantation **where Jno McDaniel**

now lives. 5 Oct 1810.

26	166	5249	**George W. Raymon** .. .. 40 acs .. Blackburn's Fk .. **incl McDaniel's lower field.** 5 Oct 1810.
26	168	5259	**Henry Branson** .. 640 acs .. N side of Cumberland .. adj upper corner of McClure's tract .. John Armstrong .. 6 Oct 1810.
26	169	5267	**Benjamin Blackburn** .. 50 acs .. on Roaring R. Beg at the place where Byle's S boundary and Blackburn's W boundary intersect .. to include the **improvement and 50 acs of Benjamin Blackburn.**
26	173	5288	**General Lee Nolen and Stephen Cantrell JR** ase of William Lytle and **David Golston** 13 acs .. on Roaring R beg. on William Stafford's N boundary .. to include the place Saml. Bradcut sold to Jno Stafford. 11 Oct 1810.
26	173	5289	**John Rutledge** .. on Morrison Cr of Roaring R. Beg about 15 poles SE of John Sutton's upper corner of his fence on a beech .. place where Thomas Conway now lives .. **to include plantation whereon sd. Conway and Sutton now live.** 11 Oct 1810.
26	173	5290	**John Rutledge** ase of Stephen Cantrell Jr & G. Lee Nolen. Enters 10 acs .. on Morrison's Cr of Roaring R. .. to include the improvements **whereon Curtis Williams did live.** 11 Oct 1810.
26	173	5291	**Gen. Lee Nolen & Stephen Cantrell Jr** ase heirs of John Wisdom. 25 acs .. on Indian Cr the N waters of Cumberland R. Beg on Capt Isaac Moore's N boundary .. path leading from Frederick Skaggs .. to include an improvement **made by Charles Sweazy.** 11 Oct 1810.
26	174	5299	**Simeon Putman** .. 10 acs .. N side of Bowman's Br a small distance below a large fall on sd branch. .. 12 Oct 1810.
26	175	5300	**Simeon Putman** .. 5 acs .. waters of Flynn's Cr .. to include a salt petre cave. John Bowen, Loc. 12 Oct 1810.
26	175	5303	**David Young** ase of Willis Anderson heirs. Enters 30 acs .. on Indian Cr on the S fork of sd Cr .. **incl Young's improvement.** David Young, Loc. 15 Oct 1810. Sur rtd 29 July 1813 by James Roulston, DS.
26	175	5304	**Samuel Young** .. 40 acs .. White Co .. N side of Falling Waters near the upper end of the first bottom above the mouth .. to include an improvement **by Old Mr. Colhoon** .. 15 Oct 1810.

26	175	5305	**John Rutledge** ase of Stephen Cantrell .. 15 acs .. on Roaring R on the N bank .. incl **Thomas Price's improvement.** 15 Oct 1810.
26	176	5306	**John Rutledge** .. 25 acs .. on Roaring R .. incl improvement **where Geo. Price lives.** 15 Oct 1810.
26	176	5307 and 5308	**John Rutledge** .. 15 acs and 10 acs on Spring Cr of Roaring R .. incl **Abraham Moyer's improvement.** 15 Oct 1810.
26	178	5318	**John Moore** ase of John Nichols .. 100 acs .. Cane Cr of Caney Fk .. SW corner of Moore's occupant Survey .. incl **his improvement.** 16 Oct 1810.
26	181	5339	**Thomas Passons** ase of Thomas Windsoor .. 15 acs .. on Jennings Cr .. where Peyton's and Wilson's lines intersect .. 19 Oct 1810. Stephen DeBow, Loc.
26	184	5359	**Thomas Green** .. 15 acs .. waters of Indian Cr .. beg at a Dogwood & Beech marked by Daniel Wilbourn for Hugh Stewart as NW corner .. 22 Oct 1810. Wm. Cook, Loc.
26	185	5365	**William Hix** .. 50 acs .. on Sugar Cr .. to include **Isaac Abner's** improvement. 24 Oct 1810. William Hix, Loc.
26	185	5366	**George Waddal** .. 60 acs .. on Mill Cr about a quarter of a mile above **Hambleton's old mill** .. 24 Oct 1810. George Waddal, Loc.
26	185	5367	**Thomas Scandland** .. 20 acs .. S side of Cumberland .. about a mile above mouth of Sugar Cr .. 24 Oct 1810. Thomas Scanland, Loc.
26	187	5378	**Jonathan Smith** .. 40 acs on Mill Cr about 40 poles below **Hambleton's old mill** .. 24 Oct 1810. Jonathan Smith, Loc.
26	187	5379	**John Black** .. 50 acs on Knob Cr .. north side of Cumberland at the mouth of Knob Cr. 24 Oct 1810. John Black, Loc. Removed per Black's order 9 Dec 1811.
26	187	5380	**George Waddal** .. one ac .. waters of Mill Cr .. incl a salt petre cave. 24 Oct 1810.
26	187	5381	**Bailey Butler** ase of James Cook ase of Sampson William ex. to Peter Turney, dec. .. 60 acs .. dry fork of Mill Cr .. 24 Oct 1810.
26	197	5441	**Sylvanus Fowler** .. 50 acs adj his own. .. 12 Nov 1810.
26	198	5443	**Bailey Butler** ase Thomas Dillon .. one ac .. Mill Cr .. line between Jackson and Overton Counties .. salt petre

caves formerly worked by Nathaniel Messer. 12 Nov 1810.

26 199 5452 **Moses Hardin** .. 366 acs .. waters of Brimstone Cr .. **incl Cornelias Clancey's & John Hardin's improvement.** 13 Nov 1810. Moses Hardin, Loc.

26 201 5463 **John Nichols** .. 30 acs .. N of Cumberland .. below mouth of Brimstone Cr .. adj Nichol's 457 acs. 15 Nov 1810.

26 204 5482 **Sampson Williams** ase of Richard Bean. .. 31 acs .. on Doe Cr incl place **whereon Nicholas Hail now lives.** Adj Archibald McGahan .. 17 Nov 1810. Nicholas Haile, Loc.

26 207 5499 & 5500 **Stephen Cantrell JR & G. Lee Nolen** .. 40 acs .. N side of Cumberland .. adj tract granted to Robert or Richard Fenner .. and 25 acs on Sugar Cr .. to **include Hagland's improvement.** 24 Nov 1810. Hannaniah Lincoln, Loc.

[Handwritten entries follow:]

By virtue of a Certificate warrant No 213 for 5000 acres — Enters six hundred and forty acres of land & leaving a balance of said warrant yet to satisfy of 1940 acres, in Jackson County on the head of Kinch Creek of Cumberland River. Beginning forty poles East from Edward Givens North-East corner of his tract of 640 acres, being the tract Leonard Stuff lives on. Running west then north &c for Complement.

J. C. McLemore, Locators
E. Givens

Survey & Ret'd October 24th 1810 By Edw'd Givens D.S.

By virtue of a Certificate warrant No 213 for 5000 acres — Enters two hundred and forty acres (leaving a balance of said

BUILDING NEIGHBORHOODS
From
EARLY LAND RECORDS OF TENNESSEE

RG 50 SERIES 2 - LAND ENTRIES BOOK 25 - REEL 7
1ST SURVEYOR'S DISTRICT ENTRIES - JACKSON CO FOLKS

BK	PG	NUMBER	DESCRIPTION
25	1	5543	**Phillip Thomas** .. 25 acs .. Smith Co .. East side of Caney Fk .. on John Trousdale's line .. **including Daniel Tyre's improvement.** 3 Dec 1810. Icabod Thomas, Loc. Sur rtd 10 Nov 1814.
25	8	5578	**Sampson Williams** .. 18 acs .. S side of Cumberland .. on Fund's branch joining **Nathan Kent's occupant claim** .. 10 Dec 1810. Sur rtd 26 Jan 1811.
25	9	5586	**Vinson Willis** ase of Solomon DeBow .. 100 acs .. Smith Co .. on waters of Payton's C .. his occupant survey filed 2 Sept 1808.
25	13	5608	**Abner Norris** ase of John Irwin .. 100 acs .. waters of Caney Cr and Town Cr .. **including his improvements.** 18 Dec 1810.
25	20	5639	**Gen. L. Nolen** .. 100 acs .. Morrison's Cr .. to incl Paile's improvement. 25 Dec 1810.
25	24	5658	**William Haile** ase of John Busterton. Enters 1 ac on Lacy's branch of Flynn's Cr .. to incl a salt petre cave on head waters of said Lacy's branch lately found by **John D. Brook and son.** 26 Dec 1810.
25	25	5667	**Samuel Young** .. 40 acs in White Co .. on Richard Porterfield's W boundary of 260 acs **where he now lives** thence W .. 27 Dec 1810.
25	27	5677	**Sampson Williams** .. 20 acs on Doe Cr beg 5 poles below **the Spring where John Tally formerly lived** .. 29 Dec 1810.
25	27	5678	**Sampson Williams** .. 15 acs .. on Doe Cr .. 5 poles above **where Archibald McGahan now lives** .. 29 Dec 1810.
25	27	5679	**Sampson Williams** .. 10 acs .. waters of Flynn's Cr beg on N side of Brush fork .. **including William Birdwell's improvement.** 29 Dec 1810.
25	27	5680	**Sampson Williams** .. 11-1/4 acs .. on Lacy's branch of Flynn's Cr .. excluding one ac entered in name of William Hail .. 29 Dec 1810.
25	33	5716	**Patrick Fitzgerald** one of the heirs and legatees of

Garett Fitzgerald and ase of **Jabez Fitzgerald** the other legatee .. including his occupant claim on waters of Flynn's Cr bounded on the north by **Henry McKinney** .. 3 Jan 1811. S. Williams Loc.

25	34	5717	**John Shoemake** ase of Bennet Searcy .. 10 acs on waters of Martin's Cr .. **including his improvement.** 4 Jan 1811.
25	38	5742	**John Griffith** .. 41 acs .. on Jenning's Cr .. **south of Jonas Griffith's stable** E with Ellis's line and S with Jno Wilson's line .. 10 Jan 1811.
25	38	5743	**John Payton** .. 20 acs .. on head waters of Big Trace Cr including .. a salt petre cave found by **John Scott which is now in the possession of Wm. Wakefield** .. 10 Jan 1811.
25	38	5744	**John Payton Jr** .. 130 acs .. on the dividing ridge between Trace Cr and Salt Lick Cr of Barren R. .. corner of James Martin's occupant survey .. **including said Martin's spring and improvement.** 10 Feb 1811. Wm. Wakefield.
25	39	5750	**Nathan Kent** ase of John Nichols .. 100 acs on Fund's branch including the place **whereon he now lives** .. 11 Jan 1811. S. Williams, Loc.
25	39	5751	**Nicolas Teal** .. 100 acs on a branch of Salt Lick Cr including .. **where John Teal now lives** .. 11 Jan 1811.
25	40	5753	**Samuel Moore** .. 10 acs in White Co .. on waters of Caney Fk .. to incl a large salt petre cave .. formerly **worked by Jacob Drake** and sold by said Drake to said Samuel Moore and which cave said Moore has rented to Jno James. 14 Jan 1811.
25	40	5754	**Bailey Butler** .. 90 acs on S side of Cumberland about 1-1/2 mi above mouth of Mill Cr .. **John Black's upper corner.** 14 Jan 1811. Sur rtd 19 Apr 1811 by John Murray, DS.
25	50	5817	**Isaac Midkiff** .. 25 acs .. White Co .. waters of Taylor's Cr of Caney Fk adj Alexander Irwin's 100-ac survey .. 26 Jan 1811.
25	51	5820	**Thomas Maynes** .. 5 acs .. waters of Roaring R .. 26 Jan 1811. John Bowen, Loc.
25	62	5888	**John Townsend** .. 300 acs .. White Co .. waters of Caney Fk .. on the side of the **Gum Spring Mountain**.. incl Archibald McDaniel's improvement. 15 Feb 1811.
25	62	5889	**Bartlett Gentry** .. 100 acs .. both sides of Cane Cr ..

adj 200 acs granted to Smith Hutchins .. **incl said Gentry's improvement.** 5 Feb 1811. Sur rtd 19 Sept 1812. Jas. Townsend, DS.

25 67 5914 **William Harris** ase of James Taggart .. 6 acs on McFarland's Cr .. to **incl Harris's mill and mill seats.** 11 Feb 1811. Sur rtd 20 Sept 1811 by John Murray, DS.

25 67 5915 **Zedekiah Wood** ase of James Taggart .. 12 acs on waters of Proctor's Cr .. to incl **improvement where said Wood now lives.** 11 Feb 1811. Sur rtd 20 Sept 1811 by John Murray.

25 67 5916 **Obediah Rich** ase of James Taggart .. on McFarland's Cr .. 11 Feb 1811.

25 67 5917 **William Anderson** ase of James Taggart .. 10 acs on McFarland's Cr .. 11 Feb 1811.

25 67 5918 **William Rich** ase of Samuel Jackson .. on McFarland's Cr .. **including said Rich's improvement.** 11 Feb 1811. William Peterson, Loc. Sur rtd 10 Sept 1811 by John Murray, DS.

25 67 5919 **William Rich** .. on McFarland's Cr .. **including Obediah Rich's improvement.** 11 Feb 1811.

25 67 5920 **John Peterson** .. on McFarland's Cr .. **including Joshua Prim's improvement.** 11 Feb 1811.

25 67 5921 **John Peterson** .. on the Dry fork of Mill Cr .. two poles below John Baker's field .. **including said Baker's improvements. 11 Feb 1811.**

25 69 5929 **Alexander Cook** ase of Thomas Dillon .. White Co .. south side of Caney Fk .. Jacob Drake's W boundary of land sd. Drake sold to **Samuel Denton** .. S with Denton's line .. 15 Feb 1811. Sur rtd 16 Dec 1814.

25 69 5932 **Charles Anderson** ase of heirs of Stephen Gaines. On the ridge between Martin's and Flynn's Crs a small distance above where **Thomas Brown now lives.** 19 Feb 1811.

25 75 5970 **Samuel Huff** ase of James Cook .. 100 acs Beg on a black oak about 20 poles SW of a spring on waters of Brimstone Cr on N side of Cumberland .. 1 Mar 1811. Samuel Huff, Loc. Sur rtd 15 May 1812.

25 75 5971 **Emanuel Holmes** . 50 acs .. on Brimstone Cr .. about 15 poles above **where William Ryal now lives** .. 1 Mar 1811. Emanuel Holmes.

25 81 6008 **John Rutledge** .. 20 acs .. on West fork of Roaring R ..

Moore's Spring. 4 Mar 1811.

25	87	6045	**Nicholas Haile** .. 100 acs on east fork of Doe Cr .. below where **John McClure now lives** .. 11 Mar 1811.
25	91	6080	**Solomon DeBow** .. 402 acs .. Wilson Co .. 16 Mar 1811.
25	94	6099	**John Baker ase** of John G. Blount .. 25 acs on Mill Cr .. corner of George Waddle's 60 ac entry .. 18 Mar 1811.
25	97	6119	**Jeremiah Denton** .. White Co .. on Caney Fk .. on the E boundary of 200 ac survey in name of **George W. Rayman on Gum Spring Mountain.** 21 Mar 1811. Sur rtd 13 May 1814 by Jas. Townsend, DS.
25	99	6130	**Charles Hutchins** .. White Co .. one ac .. salt petre came where he worked. 22 Mar 1811.
25	99	6131	**Abel Hutson** .. 5 ac .. Warren Co .. on the south side of Caney Fk adj Joseph Franks including Joseph Frank's canoe landing. 23 Mar 1811.
25	107	6178	**Redmund D. Barry** .. 20 acs .. waters of Indian Cr .. adj occupant survey in name of Edmund Jennings .. **including improvements where Rochester lives.** 13 Apr 1811.
25	107	6181	**Edmund Jennings** .. 196 acs on Indian Cr .. adj SW corner of Matthew Cowan's survey .. **including where the Widow Kirkendal formerly lived and the place formerly occupied by Jno Carter, dec.** 13 Apr 1811.
25	107	6182	**Edmund Jennings** .. near head of Defeated Cr ... including where **the blacksmith Settles lives.** 13 Apr 1811.
25	108	6187	**James Cook** .. S side of Dry Fk of Blackburn's Fk about a mile from Edward Robertson's .. including a salt petre cave. 15 Apr 1811.
25	108	6188	**Moses Fisk** .. 100 acs on Magnolia Ridge .. 13-mile tree made by Sampson Williams in April 1800 .. including **the place where G. Hutcherson formerly lived.** 15 Apr 1811. Entry No. 6189 by Fisk also mentioned Magnolia Ridge.
25	108	6189	**Moses Fisk** .. 50 acs .. Magnolia Ridge to incl place where **John Hutcheson settled** adj Stokeley Donalson .. 15 Apr 1811.
25	110	6203	**Hamilton Montgomery** .. S side of Cumberland on Sugar Cr about a mile above the mouth of said Cr .. where Mark Rickman's line crosses .. 19 Apr 1811

25	111	6206	**Sion Pearson** .. 10 acs on waters of Roaring R to **incl the dwelling house and spring of James Taylor.** 19 Apr 1811.
25	114	6230	**William Wakefield** 102-1/2 acs on Big Trace Cr of Barren R .. SW corner of John Davis Survey .. **including improvements made by John Glenn.** 5 May 1811.
25	124	6297	**Edward Robertson** ase of John Smith 1 ac on West fork of Roaring R on the E side including salt petre cave **where Joseph Lock, Samuel Wilkeson & Robert Wilson are now at work** .. 28 May 1811.
25	125	6306	**George Price** ase of William T. Lewis. Enters 15 acs on S side of Roaring R beg at NW corner of **Abner Lee's tract on which he now lives** .. 29 May 1811.
25	124	6308	**George Price** .. 15 acs .. north side of Roaring R .. including a small improvement **where Benj. Duglass lives.** 24 May 1811.
25	124	6309	**George Price** .. 15 acs .. on the ridge between Spring Cr and Roaring R .. **including said Price's improvement where he now lives.** 29 May 1811.
25	125	6310	**George Price** .. on the N side of Spring Cr including an excellent Sugar Camp between **where Jos. Hawkins & Thomas Price lives.** 29 May 1811.
25	128	6329	**William Doyle** .. 60 acs .. N of Cumberland running N with his line .. 31 May 1811.
25	132	6358	**Gabriel Dillard** ase of heirs of Roger Person .. 100 acs on Middle Fk of Indian Cr called Young's Br .. about 30 poles from where **William Sadler now lives** .. 6 June 1811.
25	135	6376	**Gen. L. Nolen** ase of Rodeham Holmes .. 28 acs .. N side of Cumberland on first Cr below the mouth of Jennings Cr .. 10 June 1811.
25	135	6377	**Gen. L. Nolen** .. 15 acs .. N side of Cumberland on first Cr below the mouth of Jennings Cr .. **including John Proctor's improvement.** 10 June 1811.
25	135	6378	**William Lock** .. N side of Cumberland .. including improvement **where Jos. Lock now lives.** 10 June 1811.
25	142	6428	**Samuel Henson** ase of William Christmas .. 100 acs on a head branch of Flynn's Cr .. to incl a salt petre **cave now occupied by Samuel Henson.** 18 June 1811.
25	145	6449	**William Gray** .. 10 acs .. on Roaring R .. **tract on which said Gray lives** .. 24 June 1811.

25	145	6451	**Redmond D. Barry** .. 150 acs on Jennings Cr .. N side of Cumberland .. to incl Rollins' improvement and the large spring **where Hardy Pinsley now lives** .. 24 June 1811.
25	149	6479	**Joseph Dill** .. Smith Co .. 100 acs .. in the Cove Hollow the waters of Caney Fk .. adj George Robertson .. including his improvements and in conformity with his occupant survey returned March 16th 1810. Joseph Dill, Loc. 1 June 1811.
25	150	6482	**Abraham Moyor and John Moyor** .. 2 acs on Blackburn's Fk or Roaring R .. including a salt petre cave known by .. **name of Burlason's old cave.** 2 July 1811. Andrew Hampton, Loc.
25	152	6499	**Elijah Camron** .. 100 acs .. on Cane Cr .. including improvement **where said Camron now lives.** 6 July 1811.
25	152	6500	**Andrew Hampton** .. 24 acs .. Roaring R .. adj his own. Jas. Cook, Loc. 5 July 1811.
25	152	6501	**Andrew Hampton** .. 25 acs .. on Roaring R on N side of said R .. to incl **said Hampton's improvement where he now lives.** 8 July 1811.
25	152	6502	**John Chapman** .. on Roaring R adj George Price. 6 July 1811.
25	153	6504	**Thomas Brown** .. 55 acs on Dry Fk of Flynn's Cr .. 6 July 1811.
25	153	6505	**John Burke** .. 50 acs on Bullard's Cr .. adj Moore's N line .. **to incl** .. **where said John Burke now lives.** 6 July 1811.
25	153	6506	**James Bennett** ..50 acs .. N side of Cumberland. 8 July 1811.
25	161	6560	**John Burris** .. 60 acs N side of Cumberland .. to incl vacant land between said Burris and William Dyal's lines. 7 July 1811.
25	161	6561	**John Burris** .. 5 acs on the head of a branch of Jennings Cr .. upper end of **Richard Smith's plantation** .. including a salt petre **cave worked by Benja. King.** 17 July 1811.
25	163	6574	**Thomas Mays** ase of heirs of Isa Thorn .. White Co .. north from Gum Springs and W of the old Road leading to the Gum Springs. 20 July 1811.
25	164	6579	**Thomas K. Harris** .. White Co .. on the Gum Spring

Mountain beg .. at the mouth of a salt petre cave in which Thomas Mays & William Green have been at work .. called .. "Mayes salt petre cave." 22 July 1811.

25	165	6584	**John Chapman** .. 10 acs .. on Roaring R beg at George Price's upper corner .. 25 July 1811.
25	165	6585	**John Chapman** .. 6 acs .. on waters of Roaring R beg at an elm on the E side of the Big Br running west .. south .. **including the improvement where the Widow Skeggs now lives.** 23 July 1811.
25	165	6586	**Abner Lee** on Roaring R. 23 July 1811.
25	165	6587	**John Chapman .. on Roaring R .. 23 July 1811.**
25	166	6592	**Edmund Jennings** .. 68 acs .. S side of Cumberland on both sides of a branch that runs in opposite to Williamsburg .. 24 July 1811.
25	167	6596	**John McDaniel** .. 50 acs .. on Morrison's Cr .. W of the mouth of John Sutton's Spring Br .. 25 July 1811.
25	167	6597	**John Sutton** .. on Morrison's Cr .. NE corner of John McDaniels 50 ac entry .. 25 July 1811.
25	167	6598	**John D. Brooks** .. 1 ac .. waters of Doe Cr .. to incl a salt petre cave lately found by John D. Brooks. 25 July 1811.
25	167	6599	**Archibald Dill** .. on Morrison's Cr .. beg corner of 25 ac entry of John Rutledge's **on which John Sutton now lives.** 25 July 1811.
25	168	6603	**James Cook** .. 15 acs about 1/4 mile below a small branch running into Cumberland R on the south side of the river where the road leading from Martin's Cr crosses the river to Williamsburgh .. 26 July 1811.
25	168	6604	**Sylvanus Fowler** .. 4 acs on S side of Cumberland R including 4 salt petre caves .. 26 July 1811.
25	168	6605	**Silvanus Fowler** .. 1 ac .. on S side of Cumberland .. including a salt petre cave known by the name of the "Penitentiary." 25 July 1811.
25	168	6606	**Sylvanus Fowler** .. waters of Mill Cr on a branch that runs into said Cr at or near Paul Anthony's including .. a salt petre cave formerly **worked by John Lee.** 25 July 1811.

Would you believe? Page 169 concludes with Entry Location No. 6615. Page 170 begins with Entry Location No. 5749. Entry Location No. 5749 was in Rutherford Co by Jesse Thompson and does not seem to relate to

Jackson Co. Still, if my name was Thompson, I would wonder about that entry. Next entry, still on Page 170 --

25 170 6616 **Andrew Hampton** .. Waters of Doe R (cr?) .. including a salt petre cave known as Hale's & Huffman's old cave. 1 Aug 1811.

25 171 6624 **Philip Mulkey** ase of Thomas Maynes .. N of Cumberland .. waters of Brimstone Cr .. including a salt petre cave on the point of a ridge SW from where **Joel Short formerly lived** .. 2 Aug 1811.

25 181 6697 **Joseph Lock** .. 2 acs .. on Webster's Cr incl two salt petre caves **now occupied by said Lock.** 14 Aug 1811.

25 189 6734 **Joseph Hawkins** .. 65 acs .. waters of Roaring R .. on the north side of Spring Cr of Roaring R and .. to incl said Hawkins' improvements. 23 Aug 1811.

25 189 6754 **Joseph Hawkins** .. 65 acs .. Roaring R .. north side of Spring Cr .. near where **said Hawkins now lives.** James Cook, Loc. 23 Aug 1811.

25 189 6756 **Jonas Bedford** .. 4 acs .. N side of Blackburn's Fk .. to incl a salt petre cave. 24 Aug 1811

25 190 6758 **Sampson Williams** .. 5 acs .. waters of Doe Cr. 24 Aug 1811

25 190 6759 **Simeon Putman** .. head of Doe Cr .. to incl .. **where John D. Brooks now lives.** 24 Aug 1811

25 190 6760 **Jeremiah Denton** ase of Alexander Cook ase of Thomas Dillon. 80 acs .. White Co .. on N side of Cane Fk, beg at a post oak on the S side of **Gum Spring Mountain** between the Gum Springs and Thomas McDaniel's .. N to a post oak at the foot of Gum Spring thence with said mountain N .. 24 Aug 1811.

25 190 6762 **James Harwell** .. on S side of Cumberland .. S to incl the improvement **where Russell Sullivan formerly lived.** 26 Aug 1811.

25 196 6795 **Thomas K. Harris** ase of William Lytle Sr. White Co. On Gum Spring Mountain. 30 Aug 1811

25 196 6796 **John Williamson** .. White Co .. south fork of Rutledge's Mill Cr .. including **dwelling of said Williamson** .. 30 Aug 1811.

25 198 6811 **James Taggart** ase heirs of James Blair. On N side of Cumberland on waters of Proctor's Cr beg at corner of an entry made by James Taggert. 2 Sept 1811.

25	199	6823	**Nicholas Haile** ..On Spring Cr of Roaring R below Joseph Hawkins' improvement .. including an improvement now **in the occupancy of Andrew Hampton.** 4 Sept 1811.
25	200	6830	**Andrew Hampton** .. Spring Cr of Roaring R .. 5 Sept 1811.
25	205	6865	**Valentine Van Hooser** .. 15 acs .. Jennings Cr .. Patton's S boundary including his improvements. 10 Sept 1811.
25	208	6890	**William Mumford Wilson** ase William P. Anderson .. on the ridge between the two forks of Mill Cr. 19 Sept 1811.
25	208	6891	**John Butler** .. 10 acs .. Waters of Mill Cr .. 19 Sept 1811.
25	209	6892	**Sampsom Williams** ase of William Lytle .. on Doe Cr .. including a small field **in possession of James Jones.** 19 Sept 1811.
25	216	6941	**James McCall** ase of Nicholas Hale ase Garett Fitzgerald Dec. .. 10 acs on the west fork of Doe Cr beg near Cocks (Cox's?) including the improvement and **house where said McCall now lives.** 28 Sept 1811.
25	216	6942	**Nicholas Haile** .. 5 acs on the East fork of Doe Cr .. to incl a cabin built by John McLane. 28 Sept 1811.
25	217	6943	**Simeon Putman** .. S side of Cumberland on Doe Cr .. adj James Jones .. 28 Sept 1811.
25	218	6959	**Archibald Dill** .. 5 acs on Pigeon Roost Cr near and including a salt petre cave. 2 Oct 1811.
25	223	6988	**Jacob Halfacre** ase of Abner Henley .. 25 acs .. on Morrison's Cr .. 80 poles westwardly from said Halfacer's improvement on the same ridge. 7 Oct 1811.
25	223	6989	**Jacob Halfaker** .. 25 acs .. Morrison's Cr .. west from Halfaker's improvement on the same ridge. 7 Oct 1811.
25	223	6991	**Peter Piles** .. 50 acs .. Blackburn's Fk of Roaring R .. near Thomas Wilkerson's spring .. including improvement whereon **Thomas Wilkerson now lives.** 7 Oct 1811.
25	223	6992	**Peter Piles** .. on Morrison's Cr .. to incl improvement made by George Hunter which sd Piles purchased of William Haile. 7 Oct 1811.
25	223	6993	**Peter Piles** .. Blackburn's Fk .. at the mouth of Bowman's branch .. west including David Rich's improvement. 7 Oct 1811.

25 224 6997   **Edmund Jennings** .. N side of Cumberland on Henson's Br including **John Proctor's improvements.** 8 Oct 1811.

25 224 6998   **Edmund Jennings** .. 12 acs .. S side of Cumberland about 200 yards below the Salt Lick in said R .. 9 Oct 1811.

Recall that the Salt Lick in Cumberland R is an island which, at the time, was in sight of the mouth of Martin's Cr.

25 231 7041   **Daniel Newman** ase Thomas Gloster .. White Co .. on South fork of Rutledge's Mill Cr .. where **Thomas Mays built a house** .. including the spring and school house **where John Gilpen now keeps school.** 15 Oct 1811.

25 231 7042   **James Roulston** ase of Ichabod Radley .. Smith Co .. 50 acs on East side of the Caney Fk on the first bluff above the upper corner of Armstreet Stubblefield's Survey that incls Snow Cr .. including salt petre caves .. 16 Oct 1811.

25 239 7091   **Isaac Taylor** .. on Roaring R adj large tract claimed by John Haywood **on which James Harvey settled** .. 80 poles N of the Wagon Road leading from Southwest Point to Nashville .. to incl **improvement of Leon Pearson where he now lives.** 24 Oct 1811.

25 244 7122   **Stephen DeBow** ase of Solomon DeBow .. Smith Co on the Long Fk of Barren R .. near the head of a Spring **now occupied by Stephen Marlin** .. 28 Oct 1811.

25 246 7135   **Edmund Jennings** ase James Hamilton. 49 acs .. Young's Fk of Indian Cr of Cumberland R .. 29 Oct 1811.

25 246 7140   **Redmond D. Barry** .. 20 acs .. waters of Flynn's Cr & on the horse branch .. including where **Pain now lives** .. 29 Oct 1811.

25 247   "The office of Principal Surveyor for the First District was closed on the 30th day of October 1811 in consequence of the resignation of **William Christmas** and continued closed until Monday the 25th day of November 1811 when it was opened by **John C. McLemore,** Principal Surveyor of said District."

Note: Dorothy Williams Potter, in her completely excellent Passports of Southeastern Pioneers 1770-1823 (Gateway Press, Inc. Baltimore, 1982, but buy it from DWP) following Smith and Owsley's Papers of Andrew Jackson, says:

"William Christmas was employed as surveyor by the Commissioners who laid off the city of Raleigh, North Carolina, in 1792. Later he was appointed Surveyor-General of Tennessee and in this capacity made surveys of the Military Reservation on which the North Carolina land grants were based. With his office located in Nashville, he also laid off ranges and sections for presumably the First, Second, and Third Surveyor's Districts in 1807. .. William Christmas's double-nephew, **John Christmas McLemore** became a clerk in his office in 1806 at the age of sixteen. On the death of his Uncle (1811?), McLemore succeeded to his office which he held for many years. It was said McLemore had more Tennessee land 'on the books' than any individual person at any time."

So, hidden away on Page 247, Book 25, First Surveyor's District, Early Tennessee Land Records, Record Group 50 at Tennessee State Library and Archives, an innocuous little paragraph tells us that William Christmas was not necessarily dead in late 1811 but that he **did** resign and was succeeded by John C. McLemore.

John C. McLemore will become more significant to our study of ancestors as this volume progresses. In 1811, the Creek Wars and the **War of 1812** were looming. Wars could not be fought without gun powder which required salt petre. In revisionist histories, explorers and miners of salt petre (potassium nitrate) caves become as important as political and military orators who instigated the pointing and firing of the guns.

25 251 7166 **Thomas Murrey** ase of Andrew Mitchell .. 75 acs .. on S side of Cumberland ..N side of Roaring R 24 poles east from where Cumberland and Roaring Rs come together .. William Martin's S boundary and NE corner of William Lock's Survey. 25 Nov 1811.

25 251 7167 **Thomas Murrey** ase of Andrew Mitchell .. 65 acs .. S side of the Cumberland .. Sylvanus Fowler's SW corner .. 25 Nov 1811.

25 252 7173 **James Pharres** ase of Abner Gray heir of William Leighton .. 60 acs on the S side of Cumberland Beg on the East side of the Big Br about half a mile above where **Stephen Nichols now lives** on an ash marked "J.P." thence west and south .. to incl place **where Salsberry now lives**. 27 Nov 1811. James Pharriss, Loc.

25 252 7174 **James Pharris** ase of Abner Gray heir of William Leighton .. S of Cumberland R on the Big Br .. running N and E for complement .. to incl **the improvement made by Isaac Manere**. 27 Nov 1811.

25 253 7177 **David Green** ase of John C. McLemore ase of William T. Lewis .. 15 acs on Dry fork of Mill Cr .. near improvement **where Paul Anthony lives** .. 28 Nov 1811.

25 253 7178 **Lewis Stover** .. 15 acs on Dry Fk of Mill Cr .. 28 Nov 1811.

25 255 7188 **Joseph Shaw** ase of James Taylor ase heirs of Roger Person .. 20 acs .. on James Taylor's N boundary of tract known as Hickory land. 30 Nov 1811.

25	255	7189	**Joseph Shaw** .. one ac .. on Montgomery's branch of Martin's Cr .. to incl a mill seat **where James Taylor is now building a mill** .. 30 Nov 1811.
25	255	7190	**William Dillard** ase of Gabriel Dillard .. one ac .. on the west fork of Indian Cr .. Beg at William Stephens' E corner of 50-ac tract S to Dan'l Williams line thence E for complement. 30 Nov 1811.
25	255	7191	**Greenberry Taylor** .. 10 acs on Blackburn's Fk of Roaring R .. to incl an old mill and building **formerly property of John Clary.** 30 Nov 1811.
25	259	7214	**Thomas Mays** ase of heirs of Ica (?) Thorn .. 25 acs .. White Co .. South fork of Rutledge's Mill Cr .. to incl the **house and spring where he now lives.** 6 Dec 1811.
25	262	7235	**Edward Givins** .. 50 acs ..20 poles east of the road leading from Bennett's Ferry on Cumberland to Barron Court House .. **to incl improvement made by James Moore.** 9 Dec 1811.

[Handwritten entries follow:]

West — August 4th 1812 — James Cooke D.

8587. William Huff apegree Originally of Joseph Coleman By Virtue of a certificate Warrant No 1082 issued by the Register of West Tennessee for 302 acry — Enters Twenty five acres of land in Jackson County on the North side of Cumberland River on the ridge dividing the waters of Cumberland and Barron, Beginning at a white Oak marked WH standing North East of said Huffs Spring, running West, then South &c for complement, oblong East and West — August 5th 1812 — James Cook

588 Bartholomew White apegree Originally of John Blount — By Virtue of a certificate Warrant No issued by the Commissioner of West Tennessee for ___ acry — Enters One acre of land in Smith County on the Salt Lick fork of Barron River, Beginning at a red Oak and maple on the West side of said

BUILDING NEIGHBORHOODS
From
EARLY LAND RECORDS OF TENNESSEE

RG 50 SERIES 2 - LAND ENTRY BOOK 27 - REEL 7
1ST SURVEYOR'S DISTRICT ENTRIES - JACKSON CO FOLKS

BK	PG	NUMBER	DESCRIPTION
27	4	7254	**John Lea** ase William T. Lewis .. 60 acs .. on Pine Lick Fk of Jennings Cr .. a small distance above the mouth of **Joel Short SR's Cr.** 11 Dec 1811.
27	5	7255	**Thomas K. Harris** .. 152 acs .. White Co. .. On Caney Fk beg at corner of his **gum spring tract of 640 acs** .. 12 Dec 1811.
27	5	7258	**Robert Glenn** ase of Thomas K. Harris .. 55 acs .. White Co .. adj Benjamin Hawkins's 150 acs .. 12 Dec 1811.
27	6	7259	**Reuben Purkins** .. 40 acs .. on the ridge between Hutchins Cr and Cane Cr .. adj David Norris .. 12 Dec 1811.
27	7	7264	**Robert B. Purkins** .. 80 acs .. on the ridge between Hutchins and Cane Cr .. adj David Norris. 12 Dec 1811.
27	8	7269	**John W. Mann** .. 45 acs .. Smith Co .. east side of Caney Fk near a spring that **Jesse Nichols made use of last summer** .. to incl sd spring and two improvements John W. Mann purchased of John W. Nichols and Jesse Nichols, one of the improvements sd John W. Nichols purchased of John Rowland. 12 Dec 1811.
27	10	7276	**James Ward** .. 20 acs .. waters of Indian Cr .. 3 poles above sd Ward's spring .. to incl sd Ward's improvement. 13 Dec 1811. Tyre Gentry, Loc.
27	10	7277	**John Campbell** .. 20 acs on Indian Cr of Cumberland .. eastwardly from his spring and including the improvement **whereon sd Campbell lives.** 13 Dec 1811.
27	10	7278	**John Hamby** .. 10 acs .. Waters of Indian Cr .. to incl sd Hamby's improvement. 13 Dec 1811.
27	10	7279	**Tyre Gentry** .. 30 acs .. waters of Indian Cr of Cumberland .. adj tract claimed by Samuel Young **on which Lowery lives** .. west to James Ward's line .. 13 Dec 1811.
27	11	7280	**Tyre Gentry** .. 10 acs .. waters of Indian Cr 20 poles NW from the Tan Troft Spring .. including sd spring. 13 Dec 1811.

27	12	7286	**Giles Lee** ase of James Vance .. 20 acs .. in Buffalo Valley of Indian Cr .. to incl the improvement **whereon sd Lee now lives.** 16 Dec 1811.
27	13	7288	**Hezekiah Lizenby** ase of James Vance .. 22 acs .. waters of Woolf Cr of Caney Fk .. including improvement **whereon sd Lizenby now lives.** 16 Dec 1811.
27	13	7289	**William Carter** ase of James Vance .. 22 acs .. Smith Co .. in a valley of Woolf Cr of Caney Fk below the plantation **whereon George Smith now lives** .. 16 Dec 1811.
27	13	7291	**Prettyman Jones** .. 30 acs .. in Buffalo Valley .. near James Vance's 100-ac survey .. 16 Dec 1811.
27	14	7293	**Prettyman Jones** .. 5 acs in Buffalo Valley to incl improvement made by **William Hitchcock.** 16 Dec 1811.
27	14	7294	**Prettyman Jones** .. 30 acs in Buffalo Valley .. adj **John Casey's dwelling house.** 16 Dec 1811.
27	21	7323	**Bachel Clark** .. 50 acs .. on Jennings Cr .. to incl part of Williams' improvement. 24 Dec 1811.
27	24	7339	**William Poston** .. 66 acs .. S side of Cumberland on small branch of Indian Cr of Cumberland Beg at **Matthew Cowin's NE corner** .. 31 Dec 1811.
27	25	7340	**Robert McKinley** .. 8 acs on the Pond Spring Fk of Indian Cr .. adj Widow Kirkendall's. 31 Dec 1811.
27	25	7341	**Robert McKinley** .. 8 acs on Pond Spring Fk of Indian Cr .. 31 Dec 1812. Entry No. 7342 also for Robert McKinley, same location adj his own. Same date.
27	25	7343	**Richard Clark** .. 10 acs on Indian Cr .. **whereon he now lives.** 31 Dec 1811.
27	42	7407	**John Templeton** .. 40 acs .. White Co .. waters of the Caney Fk on the west side of the **Gum Spring Mountain** near the Spicewood Cove and adj Rawley Rawl's line. 8 Jan 1812.
27	46	7422	**George Collum** ase of Prettyman Jones .. 70 acs .. Smith Co .. on Rock Springs Cr of the Caney Fk .. opposite the upper end of the first bluff below the line of Jackson Co .. to incl **sd Collum's improvement.** 10 Jan 1812.
27	46	7423	**Robert Wallace** .. 40 acs .. in Buffalo Valley .. to incl part of improvement made by **William Skiles.** 10 Jan 1812.

27	47	7424	**Robert Wallace** .. 10 acs .. Buffalo Valley .. adj his own .. to incl houses and springs **whereon Wm. Collom and Zachariah Kirkland now live.** 10 Jan 1812.
27	47	7425	**Robert Wallace** .. 18 acs .. in Buffalo Valley .. adj his own and Skiles field to incl **Skile's improvement.** 10 Jan 1812. Survey rtd 2 June 1812 by James Roulston, DS.
27	47	7426	**David Wallace** ase of Prettyman Jones .. 30 acs .. in Rock Spring Valley .. on S side of Rock Springs Cr .. including an improvement made **by Richard Reynolds.** 10 Jan 1812. (Note: James Roulston is surveyor of these entries in Buffalo Valley and on Rock Springs Cr.)
27	47	7427	**David Wallace** .. 30 acs .. on Rock Springs Cr .. to incl the improvement and spring **whereon sd Wallace now lives.** 10 Jan 1812.
27	48	7428	**Henry Carr** ase of Prettyman Jones .. 30 acs on Rock Springs Cr .. to incl a cabin **built by Thomas Smith.** 10 Jan 1812.
27	48	7429	**Thomas McGarah** ase of Prettyman Jones .. 20 acs on Rock Springs Cr .. to incl **improvement where he now lives.** 10 Jan 1812.
27	48	7430	**Reuben Harris** ase of Prettyman Jones .. 15 acs .. waters of Indian Cr .. near a dripping spring in the Dry Valley. 10 Jan 1813.
27	48	7431	**Reuben Harris** .. 15 acs .. adj his own. 10 Jan 1812.
27	49	7432	**Eake Brown** ase of Tyre Gentry .. 14 acs .. on waters of Indian Cr .. near **improvement made by Mashack Hamby** .. 11 Jan 1812.
27	49	7433	**Eake Brown** .. 6 acs .. waters of Indian Cr .. **including improvement made by Mashack Hamby.** 11 Jan 1812.
27	49	7434	**Samuel Roulston** ase of Tyre Gentry .. 10 acs .. on the road leading from Walton's Ferry to Southwest Point and about 15 miles above sd Ferry. .. including the place **whereon John Brown now lives.** 11 Jan 1812. Jas. Roulston, Loc.
27	55	7458	**John Baker** .. 10 acs .. dry fork of Mill Cr .. to incl **Paul Anthony's improvement where he now lives.** 16 Jan 1812. Ezekiel Roden, Loc.
27	55	7459	**John Baker** .. 10 acs on Hutcherson's Fk of Mill Cr. .. including **Ezekiel Roden's improvement where he now lives.** 16 Jan 1812.

27	55	7460	**John Baker** .. 10 acs .. on the dry fork of Mill Cr .. to **incl Henry Tefteller's improvement where he now lives.** 16 Jan 1812.
27	60	7478	**John Hines** ase of John C. McLemore .. 20 acs .. White Co .. on waters of Cane Cr .. adj **Jesse Williams' tract where he now lives** .. 21 Jan 1812. Isaac Hines, Loc. (Note: "Hines" is the way "Haynes" is sometimes pronounced in TN.)
27	60	7479	**William Goodwin** .. 2 acs .. Indian Cr of Caney Fk .. near his own. 21 Jan 1812.
27	60	7481	**Joshua Short** .. 65 acs .. Pine lick fork of Jennings Cr .. near mouth of Odle Cr .. 22 Jan 1812.
27	62	7490	**Hazel Sugg** .. 20 acs .. White Co .. on N side of Caney Fk adj Brown's Spring between **Garrett Fitzgerald's and Elijah Bates** .. 24 Jan 1812.
27	64	7496	**Elijah Denton** ase of William Fitzgerald .. White Co. Waters of Caney Fk .. adj **James Moore's occupant survey** .. in conformity with his occupant survey filed 18 Sept 1810. 24 Jan 1811.
27	69	7515	**Pleasant Chitwood** .. 5 acs .. on Fowler's Cave Fk of Brimstone Cr .. including a salt petre cave **found by William Quary.** 28 Jan 1812.
27	69	7516	**Bachel Clark** .. 4 acs on Fowler's cave fork of Brimstone Cr .. to incl salt petre cave **now worked by John Ryal.** 29 Jan 1812. (Note: The name "Bachel" is very legible. Locator was Vachel Clark, also very legible.)
27	71	7524	**Archibald McGahan** .. 20 acs .. on waters of Doe Cr adj tract **whereon sd McGahan now lives** ..and including improvement where he now lives. 30 Jan 1812.
27	72	7525	**Samuel Casey** .. 100 acs .. on Garrison's Lick Fk of Jennings Cr .. **including his improvement.** 30 Jan 1812.
27	72	7526	**Samuel Casey** .. 50 acs .. Garrison's Lick fork of Jenning's Cr. .. adj James Crabtree. 30 Jan 1812.
27	72	7527	**Matthias Sweasea** .. 25 acs .. On Indian Cr **north** side of Cumberland .. including his improvement **where he now lives.** 30 Jan 1812.
27	72	7528	**Nathan Haggard** .. 25 acs on west fork of Roaring R .. adj Nancy Sheppard .. **including Clary's old mill.** 30 Jan 1812.
27	80	7558	**Archibald Elliott** .. 73 acs on east side of Hutchin's

                Cr thence S to Jackson County line .. **including sd Elliott's improvement.** 5 Feb 1812.

27 81 7559 **John Young** .. 60 acs .. waters of Pigeon Roost Cr .. adj J. T. Bounds and Lovelady's .. 5 Feb 1812.

27 91 7598 **Duke Skelton** .. 2 acs .. on the road from Walton's Ferry to Southwest Point .. to incl **the Spring, Houses etc. where sd Skelton now lives.** 14 Feb 1812.

27 92 7599 **Duke Skelton** .. 2 acs on the waters of Martin's Cr to incl the Spring house etc. **where Moses Gordon now lives.** 14 Feb 1812.

27 92 7600 **Duke Skelton** .. 2 acs .. on waters of Indian Cr of Caney Fk .. to incl the spring houses etc. **where John Christy now lives.** 14 Feb 1812.

27 103 7639 **James Raulston** .. 37-1/2 acs .. Indian Cr of Cumberland .. Redmond D. Barry's SE corner of his 640 ac survey .. 22 Feb 1812.

27 103 7640 **James Roulston** .. 131 acs .. Smith Co .. on Love's branch on the east side of Caney Fk. .. including improvement **whereon William Love now lives.** 22 Feb 1812.

27 104 7641 **James Roulston** .. 150 acs .. Smith Co .. east side of Caney Fk .. where Lancaster's line crosses Caney Fk just below the mouth of Woolf Cr .. 22 Feb 1812.

27 104 7642 **James Roulston** .. 21-1/2 acs .. on a branch of Rock Springs of Caney Fk. 22 Feb 1812.

27 104 7643 **John Boyd** .. 10 acs .. head of the Rock Springs Valley .. NE corner of James Roulston's survey of 187-1/2 acs .. 22 Feb 1812.

27 104 7644 **John Boyd** .. 10 acs .. head of Rock Springs Valley. .. 5 poles S of McCager Brown's spring .. 22 Feb 1812.

27 105 7645 **James Roulston** .. 50 acs .. in Rock Springs Valley .. S side of Lancaster's road .. running up sd valley including improvement **whereon Benjamin Moody now lives.** 22 Feb 1812.

27 122 7709 **William Ridge** ase of William P. Anderson .. 3 acs .. north branch of Indian Cr of Caney Fk .. to incl a salt petre cave with a spring .. 3/4 mile above Goodwin's. 29 Feb 1812. William Ridge, Loc.

27 129 7737 **Sampson Williams** .. 66 acs .. head of the dry fork of Martin's cr .. adj his own and near **Daniel Miller's fence.** 4 Mar 1812.

27	129	7738	**Sampson Williams** .. branch of dry fork of Martin's Cr beg at a small spring above **Enoch Carter's** .. 4 Mar 1812.
27	130	7741	**James W. Smith** .. 25 acs .. second island in Cumberland above the mouth of Martin's Cr .. 5 Mar 1812.
27	138	7770	**James Bracken SR** .. 200 acs .. N side of Cumberland .. second cr that runs into sd River below Jennings Cr called Fisher's Cr .. 9 Mar 1812. Wm. Bracken, Loc. Made void 21 Mar 1814.
27	147	7804	**James Simpson** .. 20 acs .. on Morrison's Cr of Roaring R .. **above where Benjamin Johnson lives.** 14 mar 1812.
27	157	7836	**John Chism** .. 50 acs .. N side of Cumberland on south fork of Jennings Cr .. 20 Mar 1812.
27	159	7846	**William Wood** .. 41 acs .. **including place where he now lives** on west fork of Roaring R. 24 Mar 1812.
27	163	7860	**Samuel Jones** .. 50 acs .. Cave fork of Jennings Cr .. upper end of sd Jones' field .. 25 Mar 1812.
27	163	7861	**Samuel Jones** .. 25 acs .. Cave fork of Jennings Cr .. 25 Mar 1812.
27	164	7862	**Edward Hutson** .. 25 acs .. Smith Co .. both sides of Walton's Road .. adj his own **on which he now lives** .. 25 Mar 1812.
27	164	7863	**Pleasant Cheatwood** .. one ac .. Fowler's Cave fork of Brimstone Cr .. salt petre cave **at which sd Cheatwood is now at work.** 25 Mar 1812.
27	165	7866	**William Goodwin** 6 acs .. Indian Cr of Caney Fk .. to incl house, spring etc. **where sd Goodwin now lives.** 26 Mar 1812.
27	166	7869	**Bailey Butler** .. one ac .. on the first Caney branch that runs into the dry fork of Mill Cr above its mouth on the east side .. 27 Mar 1812.
27	166	7870	**Bailey Butler** .. one ac .. dry fork of Mill Cr .. including salt petre cave. 27 Mar 1812.
27	166	7871	**Bailey Butler** .. one ac .. dry fork of Mill Cr .. salt petre cave found by **sd Butler and Jas. Robertson and worked at by them and others.** 27 Mar 1812.
27	168	7878	**William Woods** .. waters of Roaring R on the road leading from Blackburn's old place to Sampson Williams'

mill .. including the improvement where sd **Woods now lives.** 30 Mar 1812.

27 168 7879 **Samuel Hunter** .. 37-1/2 acs .. waters of Pigeon Roost Cr .. including **sd Hunter's improvement.** 30 Mar 1812.

27 173 7897 **Luke Thornton JR** ase of Solomon DeBow .. 81 acs .. Smith Co .. long fork of Big Barron R .. head of a spring now **occupied by sd Luke Thornton** .. 31 Mar 1812.

27 173 7898 **James Thornton** ase of Solomon DeBow .. 10 acs .. Smith Co .. long fork of Barron R .. 31 Mar 1812.

27 174 7900 **William Kerby** .. ase of Solomon DeBow .. 10 acs .. Smith Co .. long fork of Barron R .. 31 Mar 1812.

27 174 7901 **Sampson Williams** .. 50 acs .. west fork of Roaring R .. including place where **Nimrod Dodson lately lived where Susanna Rutledge now lives** .. 31 Mar 1812.

27 175 7904 **Shadrach Bridges** .. 22 acs .. branch of Rock Springs of Caney Fk. **whereon he now lives** .. 1 Apr 1812.

27 175 7905 **James Vance** .. 90 acs .. Indian Cr of Caney Fk .. between **his saw mill and top of the hill** .. 640 ac tract sd Vance sold to John Lancaster .. to incl sd **Vance's house and mill.** 1 Apr 1812.

27 175 7906 **James Vance** .. 2-1/2 acs .. S side of Indian Cr .. Harris's Valley .. 1 Apr 1812.

27 176 7907 **Asael Buller** .. 26 acs .. waters of Hutchins Cr .. to incl improvement where **Elijah Buller now lives.** 2 Apr 1812. Wm. G. Buller, Loc.

27 176 7908 **William G. Buller** .. 12 acs .. Pigeon Roost Cr of Caney Fk .. to incl **improvement made by John Dick .. where Drury Mosley once lived.** 1 Apr 1812.

27 180 7924 **Elifees Robeson** .. one ac .. South fork of Indian Cr .. half a mile below where **a Mr. Wheeler now lives** .. 3 Apr 1812.

27 186 7945 **Stephen Langford** .. 6-1/2 acs .. Wet fork of Mill Cr .. Beg at John Baker's NW corner on George Waddle's line .. an improvement **where Joshua Gore formerly lived.** 7 Apr 1812.

Yes, Folks. The record says "wet" fork, and the 1836 map showing Civil Districts in Jackson County clearly shows a Wet Fk of Mill Cr in far north Jackson County. We suspect some frontier humor in this name, considering all the "dry" forks there were.

Here's a story for whoever may read this so-called

manuscript -- just to relieve some tedium. I, Betty Huff Bryant, live in Texas where a favorite specimen of tree is called "Live Oak." A young visiting relative asked me what kind of tree that was out in my back yard, and I casually replied "Live Oak." The visitor, being young and literal-minded, asked if live oaks ever died and, if so, then what were they called.

So I took her downtown and showed her our Treaty Oak where Sam Houston is supposed to have treated with the Indians. Some idiot whacko had chemically poisoned it as a demonstration against power or something, and is now doing prison time. The tree will partially survive, although it is a mere shadow of its former stately self. At the time I showed it to my visitor, it had all the appearance of a **dead** Live Oak. The dead parts of the famous old Live Oak have been trimmed out, carefully cured, and will be cut up into souvenirs for museums, tourists, etc. Made National news, I think.

27	187	7946	**Sylvanus Fowler** .. 4 acs .. head waters of Knob Cr of Cumberland .. salt petre cave .. **formerly called Huff's cave.** 7 Apr 1812.
27	187	7947	**Mordecai Miller** .. one ac .. waters of Mill Cr .. near Paul Anthony's including .. salt petre cave called Hutchin's old cave. **7 Apr 1812.**
27	191	7961	**Bailey Butler** .. 40 acs .. N side of Cumberland .. above **Samuel Kirkpatrick's** .. including an improvement where **Richard Gordon now lives.** 18 Apr 1812.
27	207	8016	**William Stafford** .. 5 acs .. waters of Roaring R .. to incl spring and house where **Robert Searcy formerly lived.** 25 Apr 1812.
27	207	8017	**John Stafford** .. 12 acs .. on waters of Roaring R .. adj his own to beg "on the east side of the road Rankin hawled his corn up .. to lye on both sides of sd road." 25 Apr 1812.
27	207	8018	**John Stafford** .. 12 acs .. waters of Roaring R .. including **improvement that James Rankin bought of Jesse Gentry.** 25 Apr 1812.
27	220	8068	**John McClure** .. 2 acs .. Lock's branch of Cumberland .. 4 May 1812.
27	221	8070	**Elijah Sanders** .. 20 acs .. White Co .. N side of Caney Fk. South side of the Rock Island Road about 12 poles SE of Garrett Fitzgerald's SW corner .. 5 May 1812.
27	221	8071	**Elijah Sanders** .. White Co .. S side of Caney Fk .. Elihu Sander's land **whereon he now lives.** 5 May 1812.
27	221	8072	**Thomas Shute** ase of Asa Shute .. 50 acs .. Smith Co .. East side of Caney Fk near the upper end of first large

bottom above Lancaster's Ferry .. also opposite and above a timbered island .. Beg at the first house **which is Stanton's on the Lancaster Road eastwardly from Williamson's who lives on sd Road** .. 5 May 1812.

27	227	8090	**David Young** .. 2-1/2 acs .. White Co .. on Falling Water of Caney Fk .. below sd Young's lower salt petre cave **now worked by him** .. 6 May 1812.
27	227	8091	**Shadrach Bridges** .. ase of Joseph Woolfolk .. 2 acs .. White Co .. on Falling Water .. to incl a salt petre cave .. above David Young's caves and **lately worked at by Scaggs.** 6 May 1812.
27	227	8092	**Samuel Spraggins** .. Smith Co .. references Lancaster's Ferry, the timbered island, first house on Lancaster Road eastwardly from Williamson's who lives on sd road also .. etc. 6 May 1812. Entries 8093 and 8094 are also for Samuel Spraggins with Thomas Shute as locator in the same general locale.
27	230	8100	**David Green** .. 25 acs .. Jennings Cr. ..to incl **David Dickson's houses and land** between Barry's and sd Eller's. (Or Ellis?) 7 May 1812.
27	231	8107	**John Anderson** ase of James Cook. 30 acs .. a branch of Martin's Cr running into sd creek on the N side .. so as to incl his improvement. 8 May 1812. Survey rtd 11 Oct 1815. No surveyor's name.
27	233	8111	**James Cook** .. 30 acs .. N side of Walton's Road about a quarter of a mile W of the Widow Jones .. 9 May 1812.
27	233	8112	**George Leach** .. 15 acs .. on a branch of the Cumberland .. above **Findley's Tan Yard** .. 9 May 1812.
27	233	8113	**Stephen Roberts** .. 15 acs .. on a branch of Blackburn's Fk of Roaring R on the S side of sd fork. Beg on a Maypole at Bowerman's Br below the falls .. 9 May 1812.
27	238	8130	**George Seely** .. 28 acs .. on both sides of the Falling Water of Caney Fk .. Bartlett's north boundary .. to incl **Whitaker's saw and grist mill and improvement where he now lives.** 14 May 1812.
27	241	8140	**John Payton** .. 40 acs .. head waters of Big Trace Cr including a salt petre cave found by **John Scott which was lately occupied by William Wakefield.** 18 May 1812. John Payton, Loc.
27	245	8154	**Samuel Kindall** .. one ac .. waters of Dry Cr .. to incl a salt petre cave .. 1/2 mile north of the wagon road leading from mouth of Mill Cr to **Samuel Huff's** and about 1-1/2 mile from Brimstone lick. 22 May 1812.

27	256	8194	**David Young** .. 14 acs .. on South fork of Indian Cr of Caney Fk .. 5 poles north of mouth of a cave at head of sd Young's mill pond .. his 30 acs **he now lives on** .. 2 June 1812.
27	256	8195	**David Young** .. 31 acs .. on the head of the South fork of Indian Cr .. east from the confluence of Jesse Warmack's and John Warmack's spring branches .. to incl **Jesse Warmack's improvement where he now lives.** 2 June 1812.
27	256	8196	**George Skiles** .. 25 acs .. on the Rock Spring Cr of Caney Fk .. adj his own .. 2 June 1812.
27	257	8197	**John Jones** .. 15 acs .. waters of Indian Cr .. to incl sd Jones' improvement. 2 June 1812.
27	258	8203	**Washington H. Irwin** .. 100 acs .. White Co .. waters of Taylor's Cr .. near 50 acs of **William Irwin's on which he lives.** 3 June 1812.
27	261	8212	**John Lea** .. 60 acs on Pine Lick fk of Jennings Cr .. near mouth of Odle's Cr .. to incl two improvements **whereon Joel Short SR and Joel Short JR now live.** 5 June 1812.
27	268	8240	**John Trousdale** .. 25 Acs .. Smith Co .. east side of Caney Fk. **tract where he now lives** .. near James Walton. 8 June 1812.
27	270	8247	**Thomas Gaw** .. 30 acs .. on Hutchins Cr .. east of William P. Anderson's line and including springs and **a cabin built by Abner Norris.** 8 June 1812.
27	274	8262	**Richard F. Cook** .. 25 acs .. White Co .. an improvement **whereon Nelson now lives claimed by John Trap** .. 11 June 1812.
27	274	8263	**Richard F. Cook** .. 30 acs .. branch of Cane Cr of Falling Water .. to incl an improvement made by William Guffy **now occupied by William Camron.** 11 June 1812.
27	277	8273	**James Terry** ase of Joseph Woolfolk .. 1 ac .. on Roaring R adj a 640-ac survey in name of John Ford **on which sd Terry now lives** .. 12 June 1812.
27	279	8280	**William Camron** .. 2 acs .. waters of Indian Cr of Caney Fk. A salt petre cave lately found by sd Camron .. 1 and 1/2 mile from Roland's stand and east .. 15 June 1812.
27	280	8284	**Andrew Cope** .. 45 acs .. White Co .. waters of Caney Fk on the top of **Gum Spring Mountain** .. north boundary of

40 acs in name of Morgan Briant .. 15 June 1812.

27	298	8353	**Sampson Williams** .. 640 acs .. on the dry fork of Martin's Cr .. adj John G. Blount .. 27 June 1812.
27	299	8354	**Jabez Fitzgerald** one of the legatees of Garret Fitzgerald dec. .. 11-1/4 acs .. on Trace Cr of Cumberland .. to incl **Benjamin and John Menees's improvements.** 27 June 1812.
27	303	8369	**Hosea Brown and Calvin Howell** .. 2 acs .. head branches of Indian Cr of Caney fork .. to incl salt petre cave found by sd Brown. 30 June 1812.
27	309	8394	**Richard Rose** .. 2 acs .. head waters of Pigeon Roost Cr .. 6 July 1812.
27	311	8402	**James Carter** .. 2 acs .. White Co .. north side of Cane Cr .. salt petre cave lately found by sd Carter and Hartwell Harris. 7 July 1812.
27	315	8417	**John Hudson** ase John C. McLemore .. 15 acs .. head waters of Indian Cr of Cumberland .. to incl improvement made by sd Hudson near **where he now lives.** 15 July 1812.
27	315	8418	**John Hudson** .. Smith Co .. head waters of Indian Cr .. to incl sd Hudson's house and spring **where he now lives.** 15 July 1812.
27	319	8438	**Joshua Pyron** .. 5 acs .. on War Trace Cr .. 18 July 1812.
27	321	8443	**Phillip Mulkey** .. 2 acs .. N side of Cumberland on waters of Brimstone Cr .. 20 July 1812.
27	321	8444	**Phillip Mulkey** .. 1 ac .. on waters of Brimstone Cr .. to incl a salt petre cave a half mile below sd Mulkey's old cave. 20 July 1812.
27	322	8451	**Thomas Mynes** .. 10 acs .. on Doe Cr adj Nicholas Haile. 21 July 1812.
27	322	8452	**Thomas Mynes** .. 6 acs .. on Doe Cr .. adj his own .. **where he now lives.** 21 July 1812.
27	331	8488	**Sarah Twitty** .. 8 acs .. Smith's fork of Jennings Cr .. to incl **her house and field where she now lives.** 28 July 1812. Also Entry No. 8489.
27	332	8494	**Jabez Fitzgerald** .. legatee of Garret Fitzgerald dec. .. 30 acs .. S of Cumberland on the Big Br .. incl improvement where **Jacob Reece lives.** 29 July 1812.

27	339	8523	**William Cotton** .. 15 acs in Buffalo Valley .. adj Robert Wallace .. 31 July 1812.
27	343	8535	**John Moore** .. 20 acs .. Cane Cr .. east of a spring formerly **occupied by Gabriel Choat** .. to incl improvement made by sd Choat. **1 Aug 1820.**
27	343	8536	**Thomas Gaw** .. 50 acs on Hutchins Cr .. adj William P. Anderson. 1 Aug 1812.
27	345	8543	**Edmund Jennings** .. 100 acs .. N side of Cumberland on a br .. near Micajah Duke's and near the line dividing Counties of Smith and Jackson. .. **where Matthew Patton formerly lived.** 1 Aug 1812.
27	345	8544	**David Porter and John Burk** .. 6 acs .. on Cub Cr. 1 Aug 1812.
27	345	8545	**David Porter** .. 6 acs on Cubb Cr .. 1 Aug 1812.
27	346	8546	**Edmund Jennings** .. 24 acs .. N side of Cumberland R on Henson's branch to incl first improvement on sd branch above Proctor's. 1 Aug 1812.
27	349	8561	**John Teffeteller** .. one ac .. dry fork of Mill Cr on S side of Cumberland .. 4 Aug 1812.
27	350	8563	**James Cooke and George Watts** .. 2 acs .. Cub Cr on S side of Cumberland. 4 Aug 1812.
27	350	8564	**Jonas Bedford** .. 25 acs .. on Bullard's Cr .. S side of River .. adj Moore .. to incl part of improvement where **John Burks formerly lived.** 4 Aug 1812.
27	350	8565	**Jabez Fitzgerald** .. 12 acs .. Spring Cr of Roaring R .. 4 Aug 1812.
27	352	8573	**John Stafford** .. one ac .. Blackburn's fork .. salt petre cave that Jentry and Galeon sold to Elijah Ewing. 4 Aug 1812.
27	353	8574	**William Murry** .. 50 acs .. Turkey Cr .. N side of Cumberland .. to incl his improvement. James Cook, Loc. 4 Aug 1812.
27	354	8578	**James Taylor** .. one ac .. waters of Martin's Cr .. 400 yds from improvement made by Hardy Prince. James Cook, Loc. 4 Aug 1812.
27	356	8585	**James Clements** ase of Joseph Coleman by Warrant No. 1082 .. 20 acs .. on Spring Cr of Martin's Cr .. east of John Anderson .. to incl **Clement's improvement.** 5 Aug 1812.

27 356 8586   **George Haynes** ase of Joseph Coleman by Warrant No. 1082 .. 10 acs .. north side of Knob Cr .. to incl improvement made by Henry West. 4 Aug 1812.

27 356 8587   **William Huff** ase of Joseph Coleman by Warrant No. 1082 .. 25 acs .. north side of Cumberland on the ridge dividing waters of Cumberland and Barron .. marked W H northeast of sd Huff's spring .. 5 Aug 1812.

Those three above entries, 8585, 8586, and 8587, make a significant connection. James Clements, George Haynes, and William Huff were all assignees of Joseph Coleman by Warrant No. 1082 which seems to indicate they were acquainted with each other and purchased the warrant jointly. Further, in the person of James Clements/Clemmons, the entries make a connection between folks on **Martin's Cr** and Knob Cr where Samuel Huff and Samuel Hays had their salt petre caves. William Huff's entry is on the ridge dividing Barron and Cumberland, as was Samuel Huff's; AND Leonard Huff was living at the head of Knob Cr which put him up on **that** ridge.

That's an example of the fun of building neighborhoods.

27 359 8599   **Thomas Scanland** .. one ac .. Scanland's Br .. 6 Aug 1812.

27 359 8600   **Thomas Scanland** .. 3 acs .. Scanland's Br .. salt petre cave formerly worked by Charles Elliott and lately worked by the Stacys. 6 Aug 1812.

27 361 8610   **William G. Buller** .. 2 acs .. waters of Pigeon Roost Cr .. a spring formerly made use of by John Dick and last by Drury Mosely .. 7 Aug 1812.

27 362 8615   **John Casey** .. 20 acs .. in the Buffalo Valley .. to incl Casey's improvement. 8 Aug 1812.

27 366 8627   **William G. Hutcherson** .. 20 acs .. Ward's fork of Jennings Cr .. including **where John Hutcherson now lives.** 10 Aug 1812.

27 366 8628   **John M. Watkins** .. 25 acs .. on Ward's fork of Jennings Cr .. adj William G. Hutchison .. including **where Jeremiah Bell now lives.** 10 Aug 1812.

27 366 8629   **William G. Hutchison** .. one ac .. the main fork of Jennings Cr including salt petre cave where **John Hutchison is at work now near where George Hutchison now lives.** 10 Aug 1812.

27 366 8630   **Asa Shute** .. 10 acs .. on Ward's fork of Jennings Cr .. including a field which **John Davis cultivates in corn this year .. west from where sd Davis now lives** .. 10 Aug 1812.

27	367	8631	**Asa Shute** .. 29 acs on Hunting Cr of Jennings Cr .. above the upper line of a tract **which John Wilson now lives on** .. including place where **John Brown cut house logs.** 10 Aug 1812.
27	367	8632	**Asa Shute** .. 25 acs on Ward's fork of Jennings Cr .. near entry of 25 acs in name of John M. Watkins .. 10 Aug 1812.
27	367	8633	**Asa Shute** .. more land on Ward's fork. Also Entry No. 8634 .. near William G. Hutchison including house and plantation **whereon Henry Baily now lives.** 10 Aug 1812.
27	367	8634	**Asa Shute** .. 25 acs .. Ward's Fk of Jennings' Cr .. adj his own. 10 Aug 1812.
27	369	8642	**James Vance** .. half an ac .. south fork of Indian Cr of Caney fork .. to incl a salt petre cave 3/4 mile above David Young's big spring. 11 Aug 1812.
27	369	8643	**David Young and John Young** .. ase of Henry M. Rutledge. 10 acs .. on Mine Lick Cr .. to incl two falls of water .. 11 Aug 1812.
27	370	8647	**Hannaniah Lincoln, Jesse Stacy and James Wilson** ase of John C. McLemore .. one ac .. south side of Cumberland R on Scanland's br .. 12 Aug 1812. Also Entry No. 8648.
27	370	8650	**Jesse Conway** .. 70 acs .. on Hutchins Cr .. adj William P. Anderson, to incl sd Conway's improvements. 12 Aug 1812.
27	373	8660	**James Carter, Henry Sadler and Stanton Carter** ase of Henry M. Rutledge .. 3 acs .. branch of the north fork of Martin's Cr known by name of the Spring Fk .. to incl a salt petre cave about a mile above John Anderson's .. 13 Aug 1812.
27	374	8665	**William Brassell** .. 30 acs .. on the Pine Lick fork of Jennings Cr .. to incl sd Brassell's improvement. 14 Aug 1812. Also Entry No. 8666 which was .. to incl a large spring known by name of Jerr.h Purcell's spring. 14 Aug 1812.
27	375	8667	**William Brassell** .. 6 acs .. Pine Lick fork of Jennings Cr .. to incl **sd Brassell's sugar camp.** 14 Aug 1812.
27	375	8668	**William Brassell** .. 6 acs .. Pine Lick fork .. to incl **Leml. Cherry's sugar camp.** 14 Aug 1812.
27	377	8678	**William Burns** .. 5 acs .. waters of Martin's Cr on the Big Br .. to incl sd Burn's improvement. 15 Aug 1812.

27	377	8679	**Ephraim Jones** .. 4 acs .. on the Big Br of Martin's Cr .. to incl sd Jones' improvement. 15 Aug 1812.
27	378	8680	**Martin Jones** .. 2 acs .. on the Big Br of Martin's Cr .. 120 poles below William Burns' improvement. 15 Aug 1812.
27	378	8681	**Peter Piles** .. 10 acs .. waters of Roaring R at the mouth of Ewing's and Talley's Hollow.. 15 Aug 1812.
27	380	8690	**Duke Skelton** .. 2 acs .. on the road from Walton's Ferry to Southwest point .. to incl part of a field lying east of sd Skelton's and **now occupied by him.** 17 Aug 1812.
27	380	8691	**Duke Skelton** .. 3 acs .. on the road leading from Walton's Ferry to Knoxville joining the east boundary of Skelton's 2-ac entry which **incls his house and spring extending east** .. 17 Aug 1812.
27	380	8692	**William Carter** .. 12 acs .. branch of Jennings Cr known by the name of Casey's fork .. to incl sd Carter's improvement. 17 Aug 1812.
27	381	8693	**Duke Skelton** .. 2 acs .. waters of Indian Cr of Caney Fk .. adj sd Skelton's entry which incls **John Christian's house and spring.** 17 Aug 1812.

BK	PG	NUMBER	DESCRIPTION
27	383	8704	**Samuel Casey** .. 100 acs .. Garrison's Lick fork of Jennings Cr .. to incl Casey's improvement and spring **where he now lives.** 18 Aug 1812.
27	384	8705	**Samuel Casey** .. 25 acs .. Garrison's Lick. adj his own. 18 Aug 1812.
27	392	8739	**John Miller** .. 50 acs .. White Co .. adj **tract Elisha Walling lives on** known by the name of the Gum Spring tract .. 24 Aug 1812.
27	392	8742	**Asa Shute** .. 25 acs .. on Ward's fork of Jennings Cr .. 10 poles N of John W. Watkins .. to incl Jeremiah Bell's improvement. 24 Aug 1812.
27	392	8743	**Asa Shute** .. 25 acs .. Ward's fork .. adj his own .. 24 Aug 1812. Also Entry No. 8744.
27	393	8745	**Asa Shute** .. 40 acs .. on Trace Cr .. to incl Thomas McCloud's improvement. 24 Aug 1812.
27	396	8752	**Joseph Jared** .. 20 acs .. in the Rock Spring Valley .. adj James Roulston .. 24 Aug 1812.
27	396	8753	**Joseph Jared** .. 10 acs .. in the Rock Spring Valley .. near Lancaster's road. 24 Aug 1812.
27	396	8754	**Joseph Jared** .. 5 acs .. the Rock Spring Valley .. adj his own .. including a small field cleared by Reuben Smith. 24 Aug 1812.
27	396	8755	**Henry Carr** .. 15 acs .. on north side of Rock Spring Cr .. to incl cabin **built by Thomas Smith** lying about a quarter of a mile below Jacob Farming's. 24 Aug 1812.
27	397	8756	**Henry Carr** .. 10 acs .. on Rock Spring Cr adj David Wallace .. to incl **the old school house place where Allen Harvey formerly kept school being his upper school house.** Also Entry No. 8757. 24 Aug 1812.
27	401	8774	**John Baker** .. one ac .. south side of Cumberland at head of **John Peterson's still house branch** .. to incl salt petre cave. 27 Aug 1812.
27	401	8775	**John Baker** .. one ac .. waters of dry fork of Mill Cr .. to incl a salt petre cave .. worked three or four years past by Joseph Coplin. Also Entry Nos. 8776 and 8777. 27 Aug 1812.
27	402	8778	**Stephen Langford** .. 25 acs .. west fork of Mill Cr adj George Waddle's to incl Joshua Gore's improvement **now occupied by sd Langford.** 27 Aug 1812.

27	402	8779	**Samuel Jones** .. 50 acs .. on Cave fork of Jennings Cr .. adj his own .. to incl his improvement. 28 Aug 1812.
27	403	8785	**Rhesa Crabtree** .. on Skegg's branch of Jennings Cr .. to incl the improvement **Davis Dickson now lives on.** 28 Aug 1812.
27	405	8790	**George Price** .. one and one half ac .. waters of Roaring R .. above Andrew Hampton's field and about 3/4 mile from **sd Hampton's house.** 29 Aug 1812.
27	405	8791	**George Price** .. one and one half ac .. adj his other cave. 29 Aug 1812.
27	411	8821	**George Pearce and John Lock** .. 6 acs .. between Cave fork and Piney fork of Jennings Cr .. about a mile from where **Abner Lee now lives** and nearly between Joshua Short's and sd Lee's .. 2 Sept 1812.
27	416	8838	**Samuel Mansell** .. 50 acs .. Pigeon Roost Cr .. about two hundred yards below **the Widow Buller's mill.** 3 Sept 1812.
27	416	8839	**Caleb Job** .. 50 acs .. waters of west fork of Roaring R .. adj Biles south boundary .. to incl sd Job's improvement. 3 Sept 1812.
27	417	8840	**Richard Mansell** .. 5 acs .. left hand fork of Martin's Cr .. below mouth of Gray's Hollow.. 3 Sept 1812.
27	417	8841	**Richard Mansell** .. 20 acs .. on Rush fork of Flynn's Cr 40 yards east from the **house Saml. Henson now lives in.** 3 Sept 1812.
27	417	8842	**Richard Mansell** .. 15 acs .. between Flynn's Cr and Martin's Cr .. hollow that leads to the Rush fork .. to incl the principal part of the poplar Flat. 3 Sept 1812.
27	417	8843	**Richard Mansell** .. 10 acs .. on Beason's Br of Martin's Cr .. to incl **sd Mansell's mill.** 1 Sept 1812.
27	417	8844	**Richard Mansell** .. 3 acs .. on Martin's Cr .. 3 Sept 1812.
27	422	8871	**Abel Willis, Owen Yarber and Joseph Martin** .. one ac .. on Salt Lick Br of north side of the dry fork of Mill Cr .. to incl a salt petre cave lately found by sd Yarber and Martin. 1 Sept 1812. Able Willis, Loc.

Note: General Joseph Martin died in 1808. Obviously, this is a different Joseph Martin.

27	422	8872	**Nathaniel Roden & Jesse Williams** .. one ac .. on Nathan Roden's Spring branch .. 7 Sept 1812.
27	423	8879	**Berket Kinnard** .. 27 acs .. on the west fork of Roaring R .. adj John Richmond .. to incl John Clairy's old improvement. 7 Sept 1812.
27	426	8893	**George Pearce and John Lock** .. 6 acs .. between the Cave Fork and Piney Fork of Jennings Cr about a mile NW from **where Abner Lea now live** and nearly between Josiah Short's and sd Lea's. 8 Sep 1812.
27	430	8912	**Prettyman Jones** .. 10 acs .. in Buffalo Valley .. adj Giles Lea .. to incl spring and cabin **where John McKinney now lives.** 12 Sept 1812.
27	430	8913	**Prettyman Jones** .. 2 acs .. in Buffalo Valley .. to incl a spring about a quarter of a mile nearly south from a field now **occupied by John Dowell.** 12 Sept 1812.
27	431	8914	**John Clements** .. 2 acs .. on the drafts of Buffalo Valley .. to incl a spring west from where **sd Clements now lives. 12 Sept 1812.**
27	431	8915	**John Elliott** .. 15 acs .. head of Town Cr .. to incl sd Elliott's improvement. Also Entry No. 8916. 12 Sept 1812. Both entries say "waters of Town Cr." However, No. 8915 says Jackson Co and No. 8916 says White Co.
27	434	8929	**Samuel Jones** .. 4 acs on Garrison's fork of Jennings Cr .. salt petre cave lately worked by Robert Carpender and Samuel Wilkerson about 1/4 mile above where **Samuel Hutcheson now lives.** 14 Sept 1812.
27	435	8932	**James Young** .. 14 acs .. on Pigeon Roost Cr .. adj Thomas Lovelady. 15 Sept 1812.
27	435	8933	**Eli Young** .. 40 acs .. on a branch of Hutchison's Cr .. to incl a cabin **built by Charles Arington and a field cleared by the Widow Goolsby's boys.** 15 Sept 1812.
27	435	8934	**Ephraim Lea and Thomas Wilkerson** .. 2 acs .. on Jennings Cr .. 15 Sept 1812.
27	437	8944	**Edmund Jennings** .. 20 acs .. north side of Cumberland on Henson's Br .. to incl the first improvement on sd branch above Proctor's. 15 Sept 1812.
27	438	8945	**Edmund Jennings** .. 2 acs .. on waters of Martin's Cr including salt petre cave lately found by Allen Holliday. 15 Sept 1812.

27	438	8946	**Edmund Jennings** .. 2 acs .. on waters of Martin's Cr including a salt petre cave .. found by Allen Holliday. 15 Sept 1812.
27	438	8948	**Samuel Bradcut** .. 16 acs .. on Morrison's Cr .. to incl William Crocker's improvement. 16 Sept 1812.
27	438	8949	**Samuel Bradcut** .. 4 acs .. on Rutledge's Cr of Roaring R .. adj James McNight.. 16 Sept 1812.
27	455	9026	**John C. McLemore and James Vaulx** .. 300 acs .. north side of Cumberland above the mouth of Roaring R .. Also Entry No. 9028 for 100 acs. 22 Sept 1812.
27	459	9046	**Samuel Moore** .. 2 acs .. on Brimstone Cr .. to incl salt petre cave. 24 Sept 1812.
27	464	9072	**Robert Wallace** .. 10 acs .. in Buffalo Valley .. adj his own and Prettyman Jones. 25 Sept 1812.
27	475	9126	**Edmund Jennings** .. 20 acs .. on Flynn's Cr beg at Robert Stothart's northwest corner adj Uriah Anderson. 2 Oct 1812.
27	480	9151	**John McKinney** .. 10 acs .. in Buffalo Valley adj Prettyman Jones **where he lives** .. Also Entry No. 9152 for 10 acs. 5 Oct 1812.
27	480	9154	**John McKinney** .. 5 acs .. on the ridge between John Casey's and Prettyman Jones .. 5 Oct 1812. (That's Buffalo Valley.)
27	482	9161	**Thomas Wilson** .. 20 acs .. on Pine Lick fork of Jennings Cr .. to incl **Gabriel Odle's improvement.** 6 Oct 1812.
27	483	9167	**Charles Harvey** .. 50 acs .. on Mine Lick Cr .. about a half mile above where Green Woods formerly lived near a place called the Double Springs .. 6 Oct 1812.
27	486	9179	**Martin Jones** .. 5 acs .. on the Big Br of Martin's Cr .. adj William Burns .. 8 Oct 1812.
27	486	9180	**John Shoemake** .. 8 acs .. on Shaw's branch of Martin's Cr .. to incl a small improvement made by Jordon Shoemake. 8 Oct 1812.
27	487	9188	**Peter Petre** .. one ac .. waters of Mill Cr near improvement made by William Holliday and now claimed by John Butler .. 8 Oct 1812. Levi Roden, Loc.
27	492	9215	**John McKinney** .. 20 acs .. in Buffalo Valley .. to incl sd McKinney's improvement. 13 Oct 1812.

27	493	9216	**John Garvin** .. 10 acs .. on the ridge between John Casey's and Prettyman Jones's. 13 Oct 1812. (This entry was indexed "Garrett" in the original index.)
27	493	9217	**Jonathan Reneau** .. 5 acs .. dry valley of Indian Cr above Reuben Harris's .. 14 Oct 1812.
27	493	9218	**Hezekiah Lizenby** .. 7 acs .. on the ridge between Buffalo Valley and Hurricane Cr .. 14 Oct 1812.
27	493	9219	**Prettyman Jones** .. 7 acs .. in Buffalo Valley. Also Entry No. 9220. 14 Oct 1812.
27	494	9221	**Nicholas Teal** .. 30 acs .. on Salt Lick Cr .. tract **whereon he now lives** .. to incl a still house and small improvement. 14 Oct 1812.
27	496	9235	**Thomas Butler** .. 10 acs .. on the dry fork of Mill Cr adj James William's west bounday of **the tract where he now lives** .. 15 Oct 1812.
27	497	9236	**Thomas Butler** .. 10 acs .. on dry fork of Mill Cr adj John Baker's east boundary of the tract **whereon he now lives** .. 15 Oct 1812.
27	497	9237	**John Willis** .. 8 acs .. on the dry fork of Mill Cr .. adj Nathan Roden's. 15 Oct 1812.
27	497	9238	**John Willis** .. 8 acs .. on dry fork of Mill Cr .. 15 Oct 1812.
27	497	9239	**Bailey Butler** .. 31 acs .. on west fork of Mill Cr .. on John Black's east boundary. 15 Oct 1812.
27	498	9245	**James Cook** .. 215 acs .. on Cumberland R .. on the south bank opposite mouth of Knob Cr .. 17 Oct 1812.
27	499	9246	**Caleb Short** .. 30 acs .. Joel's fork of Jennings Cr .. on John Lea's east boundary. Also Entry No. 9247. 17 Oct 1812.
27	500	9253	**James Cook** .. 50 acs .. on Knob Cr at the mouth. 19 Oct 1812.
27	501	9257	**Thomas Glenn** .. 20 acs .. on Big Trace Cr .. to incl improvement whereon **sd Glenn now lives**. 19 Oct 1812.
27	508	9289	**James Huddleston** .. 25 acs .. on Cane Cr .. near house occupied by Isaac Spivey .. to incl spring and improvement whereon **sd Spivey now lives**. 24 Oct 1812.
27	508	9290	**John C. McLemore and James Vaulx** .. 100 acs .. north side of Cumberland .. adj their own. Also Entry No. 9291. 24 Oct 1812.

27	509	9293	**John C. McLemore and James Vaulx** .. 50 acs .. on Roaring R .. adj entry **whereon John Shankle now has crops** .. 24 Oct 1812.
27	509	9294	**John C. McLemore and James Vaulx** .. 30 acs .. on Jennings Cr .. adj Tandy K. Witcher's survey .. and John Thaxton's west boundary .. to incl an improvement now occupied by Hutchison. 24 Oct 1812.
27	509	9295	**John C. McLemore and James Vaulx** .. 60 acs .. head waters of Doe Cr .. including improvements **where John D. Brooks formerly lived.** 24 Oct 1812.
27	509	9296	**John C. McLemore and James Vaulx** .. 100 acs .. on waters of War Trace Cr .. beg where Harney's north boundary line of his 7,200 ac tract crosses War Trace .. including improvements where **Old Mr. McRea now lives.** 24 Oct 1812.
27	509	9297	**John Chapman** .. 8 acs .. on Roaring R .. adj Price. 24 Oct 1812.
27	510	9298	**John Moore** .. 100 acs .. on Cane Cr .. adj his own including his improvement. 24 Oct 1812.
27	511	9303	**George Hays** .. 10 acs .. on the ridge dividing waters of Cumberland and Barron .. to incl a field cleared by **John Lea.** 27 Oct 1812. **Samuel Hays, Loc.** Made void 19 Aug 1814.
27	511	9306	**John Gess** .. 25 acs .. on Pine Lick fork of Jennings Cr .. Also Entry No. 9307. 27 Oct 1812.
27	512	9311	**David Vance** .. 20 acs .. on Dry Cr adj Emanuel Holms .. 27 Oct 1812.
27	513	9312	**Emanuel Holms** ..15 acs .. on dry creek .. adj his survey **whereon he now lives** .. 28 Oct 1812.
27	515	9327	**John Dutton** .. 10 acs .. on Brimstone Cr .. to incl improvement whereon **Lena Dutton now lives.** 30 Oct 1812. (Although this entry is clearly legibly "Dutton," it was indexed as "Dillon." Case of the famous becoming more so?)
27	515	9329	**Joshua Pyron** .. 5 acs .. waters of War Trace Cr .. to incl **Blakeman's Cabin and spring.** 31 oct 1812.
27	515	9330	**Joshua Pyron** .. 5 acs .. waters of War Trace .. to incl an old sugar camp .. near **where Zilman Pyron now lives.** 31 Oct 1812.
27	515	9331	**Joshua Pyron** .. 5 acs .. waters of War Trace Cr .. to

incl .. where Zilman Pyron now lives. 31 Oct 1812.

27	521	9352	**Joseph Ownby** .. 5 acs .. dry fork of Mill Cr .. to incl a bottom .. **where sd Ownby lives.** Also Entry Nos. 9353 and 9354. 2 Nov 1812.
27	521	9355	**James Williams** .. 10 acs .. dry fork of Mill Cr .. adj John Baker's tract **whereon he now lives** .. 2 Nov 1812.
27	522	9356	**Lewis Stover** .. 6 acs .. dry fork of Mill Cr .. 2 Nov 1812.
27	522	9361	**George Stamps** .. 9 acs .. on Rock Spring Cr adj David Wallace .. to incl sd **Stamp's improvement he now occupies.** 3 Nov 1812.
27	523	9362	**David Young** .. 2 acs .. White Co .. on Falling Water between sd Young's salt petre cave and James Vance's Cave to incl a fall in sd branch where Young gets water for the use of his cave. 3 Nov 1812.
27	523	9363	**William C. Anderson and Jordon Anderson** .. 6 acs .. on a west branch of Webster's Cr .. to incl a salt petre cave and works that **James Anderson now occupies.** 3 Nov 1812.
27	523	9364	**James Vinson** .. 15 acs .. Smith Co .. waters of Salt Lick fork of Barron R .. to incl sd Vinson's improvement .. 3 Nov 1812.

BUILDING NEIGHBORHOODS
From
EARLY LAND RECORDS OF TENNESSEE
RG 50 SERIES 2 - LAND ENTRIES BOOK 28 - REEL 8
1ST SURVEYOR'S DISTRICT ENTRIES - JACKSON CO.

BK	PG	NUMBER	DESCRIPTION
28	3	9375	**John Chism** .. 9 acs .. N of Cumberland S side of Jennings Cr .. adj his 50 ac entry .. to incl part of his improvement and sugar camp. 4 Nov 1812. John Wilson, Loc.
28	19	9424	**Burkett Kinnard** .. 15 acs .. waters of Roaring R .. to incl where **Joseph Wilson now lives.** 12 Nov 1812.
28	19	9425	**Burkett Kinnard** .. 60 acs .. Blackburn's F of Roaring R .. above spring formerly used by **Thomas Wilkerson** .. to incl said Wilkerson's old improvement. 12 Nov 1812.
28	24	9441	**Moses Beller** .. ase of James Cook of Thomas Dillon .. 15 acs .. Smith Co .. Warrant No. 1213 .. E Fk of **Williamson's Br** of Caney Fk .. Beg at a beech marked "SB" .. to incl a spring .. about 1/2 mile above Samuel Beller's. 13 Nov 1812. **Samuel Beller, Loc.**
28	24	9442	**Moses Beller** .. ase of James Cook of Thomas Dillon .. 10 acs in Jackson Co on **Dry Fk of Martin's Cr** .. to incl said Beller's improvement. 13 Nov 1812. Moses Beller, Loc.
28	25	9443	**Thomas Mordock** ase of Thomas Dillon .. 15 acs .. Mill Cr .. mouth salt petre cave in name of Peter Peter now claimed by Jno Payton. 13 Nov 1812. Tobias Mordock, Loc.
28	25	9444	**John Bussell** ase of Thomas Dillon .. 100 acs .. White Co .. waters of Caney Fk .. adj his own. 13 Nov 1812. **Samuel Beller, Loc.**
28	27	9451	**David Harbert** .. 2 acs .. south side of Martin's Cr in Homes' hollow .. to incl a spring & part of improvement **made by William Fuqua.** 14 Nov 1812.
28	27	9452	**David Harbert** .. 2 acs .. on north side of Martin's Cr near .. Cave Hollow .. including in the center of the survey a cave spring. 14 Nov 1812.
28	31	9467	**Bailey Butler** .. 40 acs .. west fork of Mill Cr .. adj his own .. to incl the bottom land . 14 Nov 1812.
28	31	9468	**Thomas Butler** .. 10 acs .. on dry fork of Mill Cr .. adj **James Williams tract he now lives on.** 16 Nov 1812.

28	32	9469	**Thomas Butler** .. 20 acs .. on the dry fork of Mill Cr .. adj his own. 16 Nov 1812.
28	32	9470	**Edmund Butler** .. 20 acs .. on Turkey Cr .. adj Bailey Butler .. 16 Nov 1812.
28	45	9518	**John Payton SR** .. 39 acs near the line of Jackson Co .. waters of Mill Cr about half a mile above **John Butler's improvement** .. to incl mouth of a salt petre came .. found by **Peter Petre** .. where there are seven furnaces now worked by a number of hands being cave John Payton JR purchased of Bailey Butler. 21 Nov 1812.
28	45	9519	**John Payton SR** .. one ac .. on Trace Cr of Big Barron R .. 30 poles a little W of N from **Nicholas' fish trap** .. 21 Nov 1812. William Arant, Loc.
28	46	9520	**Goin Morgan** .. 15-3/4 acs .. East fork of Mine Lick Cr .. to incl improvement made by said Morgan **whereon Samuel Gann formerly lived.** 21 Nov 1812.
28	46	9521	**Goin Morgan** .. 50 acs near line dividing Jackson & White Counties .. East fork of Mine Lick Cr .. to incl improvement **whereon said Morgan now lives.** 21 Nov 1812.
28	46	9522	**Goin Morgan** .. 50 acs .. Middle fork of Mine Lick Cr .. to incl improvement whereon **Hubbard Brewer now lives.** 21 Nov 1812.
28	46	9525	**Levi Rash** .. 20 acs .. waters of Roaring R .. Beg at Benjamin Blackburn's SW corner .. **to incl said Rash's Outfield.** 23 Nov 1812.
28	47	9526	**William Rash** .. 10 acs ... waters of Roaring R .. on both sides of the Walton Road and between lines of said Rash & Edmund Finn. 23 Nov 1812.
28	52	9541	**Daniel Keith** .. 20 acs .. on little Trace Cr of Barron R .. adj John Gess .. to incl improvement **whereon said Keith now lives.** 25 Nov 1812.
28	52	9542	**Daniel Keith** .. 20 acs .. waters of little Trace Cr of Barron R .. including a field **now occupied by said Keith called the Garrison field..** 25 Nov 1812.
28	52	9543	**Daniel Keith** .. 10 acs .. waters of little Trace Cr of Barron R .. adj Alexander Keith's land.. to incl said **Alexander Keith's sugar camp.** 25 Nov 1812.
28	53	9544	**Peter Petre, John C. McLemore & James Vaulx** .. 11 acs .. north fork of Mill Cr called Mordock Fk S side of Cumberland .. cave found by said Peter Petre .. 200 yds from old Woolf Pen .. 25 Nov 1812.

28	53	9545	**Jonn C. McLemore & James Vaulx** .. 100 acs .. S side of Roaring R .. SW corner of McGee's survey .. 25 Nov 1812.
28	53	9546	**John C. McLemore, Bennett Searcy & James Vaulx** .. 20 acs .. head waters of Jennings Mill Cr .. to incl three salt petre caves lately found by John Murry. 25 Nov 1812.
28	54	9547	**John C. McLemore, Bennett Searcy & James Vaulx** .. 4 acs .. N side of Cumberland .. on a south branch of Proctor's Cr .. 150 yards from the road leading from James Taggarts to the mouth of Knob Cr and about half a mile from .. where _____ Wood did live. 25 Nov 1812.
28	54	9548	**John C. McLemore & James Vaulx** .. 4 acs .. waters of Roaring R .. near the Rockhouse Cave .. & a salt petre cave .. entered in the name of George Price. 26 Nov 1812.
28	59	9564	**William McMurtry** .. one ac .. on a branch of Proctor's Cr .. to incl .. Anderson's Cave. 27 Nov 1812.
28	62	9574	**Thomas McColgan and John Rowland** .. 2 acs .. waters of Knob Cr .. to incl a salt petre cave formerly worked by _____ Murry .. on the north side. 30 Nov 1812.
28	62	9575	**James McColgan** .. one ac .. west fork of Knob Cr .. to incl salt petre cave formerly worked by **James Anderson.** 30 Nov 1812.
28	63	9576	**Thomas McColgan & John Rowland** .. one ac .. on Dry Cr. to incl salt petre cave found by said Rowland. 30 Nov 1812.
28	63	9577	**Thomas McColgan and John Rowland** .. 2 acs .. waters of Knob Cr .. to incl a cave found by said Rowland. 30 Nov 1812.
28	66	9586	**William Smith** .. 18 acs .. on a branch of Indian Cr of Caney Fk .. east side of the first branch emptying in said creek on the N side **below where James Vance now lives** .. 2 Dec 1812.
28	67	9589	**John Griffith** .. 10 acs .. Pine Lick fork of Jennings Cr .. to incl **John Bennett's house and lot.** 3 Dec 1812.
28	67	9591	**Charles Harvey** .. 35 acs .. on Mine Lick Cr .. near road leading from White Court House to Carthage .. **to incl improvement made by Green Wood.** 3 Nov 1812.
28	70	9600	**Thomas Gau** .. 50 acs .. on Hutchins' Cr .. about 20

yards below mouth of the Double Spring Br .. west to Anderson's line .. to incl said Gau's improvement. 4 Dec 1812.

28	77	9621	**Simeon Putman** .. 5 acs .. E side of Brimstone Cr .. to incl salt petre cave found by sd Putman and James Harling. 9 Dec 1812.
28	78	9625	**Bailey Butler** .. 10 acs .. west fork of Mill Cr .. Beg on Jonathon Smith's east boundary .. 9 Dec 1812.
28	79	9626	**Thomas Butler & Bailey Butler** .. 5 acs .. west fork of Mill Cr .. 9 Dec 1812.
28	84	9643	**William Ridge** .. 30 acs .. waters of Mine Lick Cr .. to incl Samuel Maxwell's improvement **whereon he now lives.** 11 Dec 1812.
28	84	9644	**William Ridge** .. 30 acs .. on Mine Lick Cr .. to incl Green Wood's improvement **whereon Hubbard Brewer now lives.** 11 Dec 1812.
28	85	9648	**William Ridge** .. 30 acs a part thereof in Jackson Co .. on the south fork of Mine (Lick?) Cr .. to incl whereon **one Hartfield now lives.** 11 Dec 1812.
28	85	9649	**William Ridge** .. 30 acs on Mine (Lick?) Cr .. **to incl improvement made by Hubbard Brewer.** 11 Dec 1812. Larkin Womack, Loc.
28	86	9650	**William Ridge** .. 30 acs .. Smith Co .. North side of Caney Fk .. above where Spice Kentling now lives .. to incl **Spice Kentling's improvement.** 11 Dec 1812.
28	86	9651	**William Ridge** .. 20 acs .. on Mine Lick Cr .. to incl improvement occupied and cultivated last Summer by Henry Brewer. **11 Dec 1812.**
28	86	9652	**William Ridge** .. 6 acs .. on a branch of Caney Fk .. on which **Col. Ralston's mill** is set and about 1-1/2 mile above same. .. to incl an improvement made by Chesley Wheeler. **11 Dec 1812.**
28	89	9661	**Caleb Longest** .. 20 acs .. Big Trace Cr of Barron R .. to incl a spring and improvement **whereon John Orsburn now lives.** 14 Dec 1812.
28	90	9663	**Riggs Pennington** .. 40 acs .. Big Trace Cr of Big Barron R .. to incl improvement **whereon John Davis now lives.** 14 Dec 1812.
28	91	9664	**Riggs Pennington** .. 20 acs .. Big Trace Cr of Big Barron .. to incl spring, house and part of improvement **whereon Richard Hall now lives.** 14 Dec 1813.

28	91	9666	**Riggs Pennington** .. 20 acs ..Big Trace Cr of Barron R .. to incl an improvement **whereon Edmund Garrison now lives.** 14 Dec 1812.
28	98	9692	**John Thomas** .. 18 acs .. Rush fork of Flynn's Cr .. to incl improvement **whereon Joseph Hyde now lives.** 18 Dec 1812. Joseph Hyde, Loc.
28	98	9693	**John Thomas** .. 7 acs .. Rush Fk of Flynn's Cr .. 18 Dec 1812.
28	102	9705	**James Vaulx** .. 160 acs .. Jennings Cr .. to incl improvement **whereon William and James Crabtree lived in 1809.** 21 Dec 1812.
28	103	9712	**William Vallance** .. 10 acs .. Indian Cr of the Caney Fk on both sides of James Roulston's Wagon Road leading from **Mark Young's to said Raulston's.** 21 Dec 1812.
28	104	9713	**William Vallance** .. 1 ac .. Indian Cr .. 21 Dec 1812.
28	104	9715	**James Vance** .. 10 acs .. forks of a Br .. of Indian Cr at **said Vance's old still house** .. 21 Dec 1812.
28	108	9728	**John Stamps** .. 10 acs .. Smith Co .. Near the mouth of Rock Springs Cr .. to incl the Cave Spring. 22 Dec 1812.
28	112	9748	**Prettyman Jones** 10 Acs .. waters of Caney Fk in Buffalo Valley. 1/4 mile above where **said Jones now lives** .. 24 Dec 1812.
28	112	9749	**Prettyman Jones** .. Buffalo Valley .. adj his own. 24 Dec 1812.
28	113	9750	**Prettyman Jones** .. Buffalo Valley .. adj his own. 24 Dec 1812.
28	118	9772	**John C. McLemore** .. Big Trace Cr of Big Barron R .. Beg .. on the point of a hill below Christian Razor's spring .. **to incl said Razor's house, spring and improvement whereon he now lives** .. 29 Dec 1812. Christian Razor, Loc.
28	118	9773	**John C. McLemore** .. Smith Co .. 10 acs .. On Lick Cr of Line Cr of Big Barron .. to incl **John Harris' spring house and improvement whereon he now lives.** 29 Dec 1812. John Harris, Loc.
28	119	9774	**John C. McLemore** .. Smith Co .. Lick Cr of Line Cr of Big Barron. Beg corner of James Glenn's occupant survey .. to incl part of improvement now occupied by John Harris. 29 Dec 1812.

28	119	9775	**John C. McLemore** .. Jackson Co .. 20 acs .. Lick Cr of Line Cr of Big Barron. to incl **Robert York's house, spring, and improvement whereon he now lives.** 29 Dec 1812.
28	119	9776	**John C. McLemore** .. Smith Co .. waters of Line Cr of Big Barron .. on Hadley's line .. to incl part of improvement now occupied by **Richard York.** 29 Dec 1812.
28	119	9777	**John C. McLemore** .. Jackson Co .. Trace Cr of Big Barron .. to incl house, spring and improvement **whereon William Osburn now lives.** 29 Dec 1812.
28	120	9778	**John C. McLemore** .. 10 acs .. Jackson Co .. Trace Cr of Big Barron .. to incl improvement occupied by Caleb Longest about half a mile from **where said Longest now lives.** 29 Dec 1812.
28	120	9779	**John C. McLemore** .. 5 acs .. Jackson Co .. Trace Cr .. to incl house, spring and improvement **whereon Caleb Longest now lives.** 29 Dec 1812.
28	120	9780	**John C. McLemore** .. 10 acs .. Jackson Co .. Trace Cr of Big Barron .. to incl sugar camp occupied last spring by John Hall near **where John Hall now lives.** 29 Dec 1812. Aron Osburn, Loc.
28	120	9781	**Marlin Gambell** .. 30 acs .. Mine Lick Cr .. near Heirs of King .. to incl Gambell's spring and improvement **whereon his family now lives.** 29 Dec 1812. (We are left to wonder where Mr. Gambell was living.)
28	121	9782	**Thomas Peterson** .. 10 acs .. West fork of Proctor's Cr .. 15 poles east of cabin built by **Zedekiah Wood** .. 29 Dec 1812.
28	121	9783	**John Taggert** .. 9 acs .. East fork of Proctor's Cr .. mouth of first hollow above improvement made by William Goforth .. 29 Dec 1812.
28	121	9784	**John Taggart** .. 3 acs .. East fork of Proctor's Cr .. improvement made by William Goforth. 29 Dec 1813. John Taggart, Loc.
28	124	9797	**Thomas Conway** .. 50 acs .. Hutchins Cr .. to incl two improvements - one made by **William Lovell and one by George Hunter** and occupied last Summer by **Samuel Moore.** 30 Dec 1812.
28	124	9798	**Thomas Conway** .. 10 acs .. waters of Pigeon Roost Cr .. to incl spring formerly claimed by Samuel Moore **being the spring said Moore now makes use of.** 30 Dec 1812.

28	126	9802	**William G. Buller** .. 3 acs .. Pigeon Roost Cr .. to incl the falls of the Long Glade Br being an excellent mill seat. 30 Dec 1812.
28	126	9804	**William G. Buller**. 10 acs .. Pigeon Roost Cr. Entry of David Buller's. 30 Dec 1812.
28	127	9810	**John C. McLemore** .. 3 acs .. Mill Cr of Cumberland .. corner of John Butler's tract **whereon he now lives** being tract he purchased of James Cooke .. to incl salt petre cave found by **David Green living in the neighborhood.** 31 Dec 1812.
28	128	9811	**John C. McLemore** .. 20 acs .. dry fk of Mill Cr .. "Beg on a Sugar tree marked M near an old pen built for salt petre works & on the bank of a br about 1/2 mile above where **Mr. Teepletter now lives** in a mountanious place running N & W for complement .. to incl the 3 salt petre caves." 31 Dec 1812. John Murry, Loc.
28	128	9813	**John C. McLemore** .. 6 acs .. dry fork of Mill Cr .. 31 Dec 1812. John Murry & David Green, Locs.
28	129	9819	**John Rogers** .. 22 acs .. Br emptying into Indian Cr at **William Sarrell's (Sarrett's?) barn** .. 31 Dec 1812.
28	130	9821	**Benjamin Blackburn** .. 5 acs .. Roaring R .. 25 poles from the **dwelling house of William Wood** .. to incl said house. 31 Dec 1812.
28	130	9822	**John C. McLemore** .. 20 acs .. On Crabtree's Cave fork of Jennings Cr .. **where Major Thornton's boundary** crosses said fork .. 1 Jan 1813.
28	131	9830	**Bennett Searcy & John C. McLemore** .. 5 acs .. on a ridge that divides the first fork of Roaring R from waters of Doe Cr .. about 1/4 mile eastwardly from where ___ **McClure now lives.** 1 Jan 1813.
28	134	9838	**Absolom Norris** .. 12 acs .. on Hutchins Cr Beg on Samuel Smith's south boundary .. on both sides of the road leading from said Norris's to Reuben Purkins's. 2 Jan 1813.
28	135	9844	**John Payton JR** .. 100 acs .. Jennings Cr .. Beg on Thomas Hutcheson's upper line .. **Samuel Crabtree's improvement where he now lives.** 5 Jan 1813.
28	136	9845	**John Peyton JR** .. 40 acs .. Jennings Cr. Beg at Thaxton's (?) corner. 5 Jan 1813.
28	136	9846	**John Peyton JR** .. 5 acs .. Mill Cr of Cumberland .. about 1/4 mile above where **John Buller now lives.** 5 Jan 1813.

28	136	9847	**John Peyton JR** .. 25 acs .. Big Trace Cr .. to incl part of improvement **whereon William Osburn now lives.** 5 Jan 1813.
28	136	9848	**John Payton JR** .. 10 acs .. Big Trace Cr .. 30 poles NW from the spring where **Caleb Longest now lives.** 5 Jan 1813.
28	137	9849	**John Payton JR** .. 20 acs .. Big Trace Cr .. 5 Jan 1813.
28	137	9852	**Samuel Pettyjohn** .. 20 acs .. Mine Lick Cr .. To incl William Taylor's improvement. 7 Jan 1813.
28	137	9853	**Samuel Pettyjohn** .. Mine Lick Cr .. to incl improvement occupied last year by Joshua Gann .. road leading to Rock Island about 1/4 mile from William Taylor's improvement. 7 Jan 1813.
28	139	9858	**Garrett Fitzgerald** .. 60 acs .. White Co .. waters of Caney Fk adj William Fitzjerald .. 7 Jan 1813.
28	139	9861	**Thomas Mays** .. White Co .. 25 acs .. near foot of the **Gum Spring Mountain** .. 7 Jan 1813.
28	140	9863	**Eli Langford** .. one ac .. Petre's Br of west fork of Mill Cr .. path leading from Peter Petre's to Bailey Butler's old works. 8 Jan 1813.
28	140	9864	**Eli Langford** .. one ac .. Mill Cr .. 8 Jan 1813.
28	140	9865	**Eli Langford** .. 1 ac .. on Mordock's Br of a West fork of Mill Cr. 8 Jan 1813.
28	140	9866	**Eli Langford** Mill Cr .. Reynold's Br .. 8 Jan 1813.
28	141	9868	**Eli Langford** .. one ac .. Petre's Br .. 8 Jan 1813.
28	144	9881	**Solomon Morgan** .. 40 acs .. Big Trace Cr .. SE corner of Riggs Pennington .. part of field **now occupied by Richard Hall.** 11 Jan 1813.
28	158	9939	**Richard Clark** .. 10 acs Waters of Indian Cr .. adj his own **where he lives** .. 20 Jan 1813.
28	158	9940	**James Terman** .. 10 acs .. waters of Indian Cr .. in a hollow below **field cleared by Zededu Humber** near where John Humber and sd Terman's lines cross .. 20 Jan 1813.
28	160	9945	**Peter Richie** .. 25 acs .. Roaring R .. to incl spring and improvement whereon **said Richie now lives.** 20 Jan 1813.

28 160 9946   **James Isham** .. 160 acs .. White Co .. Waters of Caney Fk .. near Jeremiah Denton .. to the **Gum Spring Mountain.** 20 Jan 1813.

28 161 9953   **John Redick** .. 25 acs .. Young's fork of Indian Cr .. adj William Young's tract **where he now lives** .. 21 Jan 1813.

28 162 9957   **Nathan Haggard** .. 100 acs .. west fork of Roaring R .. adj Garland Anderson's line .. to incl place where **Zoph? Jackson now lives** .. 22 Jan 1813.

Entry No. 9957 is interesting. Nathan Haggard is significant to the story of Martin's Cr as is Garland Anderson; handwriting of clerk makes "H" look like "D" crossed out.

[Handwritten land entry records follow, including entries No. 9957 for Nathan Haggard dated January 22nd 1813, and No. 9938 for John Parker dated September 15th 1814.]

BK	PG	NUMBER	DESCRIPTION
28	163	9963	**Stephen Langford** .. 5-1/2 acs .. West fork of Mill Cr .. adj Langford. 23 Jan 1813.
28	164	9964	**Eli Langford** .. south side of W fork of Mill Cr .. adj William Wilson's spring branch .. near where **William McComas now lives.** 23 Jan 1813.
28	164	9965	**Eli Langford** .. West fork of Mill Cr on Reynold's branch. Adj his own .. William Wilson's .. 23 Jan 1813.
28	167	9980	**John C. McLemore** .. 10 acs .. N side of Roaring R .. first branch above where **Thomas Gore now lives** .. a mile above where **Rutledge now lives** .. 25 Jan 1813.
28	168	9981	**John C. McLemore** .. 10 acs .. N side of Roaring R .. near Thomas Gore .. and Rutledge .. 25 Jan 1813.
28	168	9982	**John C. McLemore** .. 10 acs .. salt petre cave worked by Shankle and Mayfield. 25 Jan 1813.
28	168	9983	**John C. McLemore** .. 5 acs .. head waters of Jennings Mill Cr .. cave a man named __ Stacy has lately been opening. 25 Jan 1813.
28	168	9984	**John C. McLemore** 10 acs .. Jennings Mill Cr .. S side of Cumberland .. 25 Jan 1813.
28	169	9985	**John C. McLemore** .. West fork of Mill Cr .. near Green's old cabins .. near Payton's big cave. 25 Jan 1813
28	169	9986	**John C. McLemore** ..5 acs .. dry fork of Mill Cr. near where **Lewis Stover now lives** .. 25 Jan 1813.
28	169	9987	**John C. McLemore** .. 5 acs .. North side of dry fork of Mill Cr ..near Teefletter's **where Paul Anthony formerly lived** .. to incl a large rock house .. 24 Jan 1813.
28	170	9988	**John C. McLemore** .. 5 acs .. North side of Roaring R on the bluff of sd river opposite Stafford's field above **where sd Stafford now lives** .. salt petre cave formerly occupied by Crabtree and others .. 25 Jan 1813.
28	170	9989	**John C. McLemore** .. 5 acs .. ridge dividing East fork of Doe Cr from first branch of Roaring R .. near where **McClure now lives.** 25 Jan 1813.
28	170	9990	**John C. McLemore** .. 100 acs .. head waters of Sugar Cr .. improvement where Hillums formerly lived and **where a family by the name of Stacy now lives.** 25 Jan 1813.

28	170	9991	**John C. McLemore** .. 29 acs .. Roaring R and Spring Cr .. survey in name of Andrew Hampton .. west to Nicholas Haile .. 25 Jan 1813.
28	171	9992	**John C. McLemore** .. 50 acs .. South of Cumberland on Sugar Cr .. 25 Jan 1813.
28	171	9993	**John C. McLemore** .. 10 acs .. Roaring R and Blackburn's Fk .. cave worked by Thomas Gore and others .. 26 Jan 1813.
28	171	9994	**John Stamps** .. 1-1/2 acs .. Smith Co .. mouth of Rock Springs Cr .. to incl mouth of sd Cr. 26 Jan 1813.
28	171	9995	**John Stamps** .. Smith Co .. one ac .. opposite mouth of Rock Springs Cr .. 26 Jan 1813.
28	172	9996	**John Stamps** .. 5-1/2 acs .. Smith Co .. Rock Springs Cr .. adj his own .. 26 Jan 1813.
28	172	9999	**John C. McLemore** .. 5 acs .. South side of West fork of Mill Cr .. John Payton SR's line .. 26 Jan 1813.
28	174	10005	**John Payton SR** .. 30 acs .. South side of west fork of Mill Cr .. adj his own .. 26 Jan 1813.
28	174	10006	**John Payton SR** .. 20 acs West fork of Mill Cr .. 26 Jan 1813.
28	175	10009	**Nathaniel Glover** .. 15 acs .. East side of Caney Fk on Hurricane Cr .. 26 Jan 1813.
28	175	10010	**Nathaniel Glover** 10 acs .. ridge that divides waters of Woolf and Indian Crs .. 26 Jan 1813.
28	175	10012	**William G. Buller** .. 25 acs .. Cane Cr of Caney Fk .. **where James Morgan now lives.** 26 Jan 1813.
28	176	10013	**William G. Buller** .. 15 acs .. Cane Cr of Caney Fk .. improvement by Henry Smith .. **where Susannah Morgan now lives.** 26 Jan 1813.
28	176	10014	**William G. Buller** .. 10 acs .. Cane Cr of Caney Fk .. improvement **whereon Russell Morgan now lives.** 26 Jan 1813.
28	176	10015	**William Dodson** .. 50 acs .. Cane Cr of Caney Fk .. **improvement whereon John Morgan JR now lives.** 26 Jan 1813.
28	177	10019	**Ephraim Guffy** .. 20 acs .. Cane Cr .. incl improvement **whereon Henry Smith now lives.** 27 Jan 1813.
28	177	10020	**Ephraim Guffy** .. 55 acs .. Cane Cr of Caney fork .. the

improvement **whereon James Morgan now lives and the improvement whereon Susannah Morgan now lives.** 27 Jan 1813.

28 179 10026 **Elijah Stone** .. 25 acs .. N side of Cumberland .. Richard Smith's upper corner .. 28 Jan 1813.

28 189 10065 **Reuben Carter** .. 20 acs .. on the ridge dividing Big Trace Cr and Jennings' Cr .. to incl house, spring and improvement **whereon sd Carter now lives.** 6 Feb 1813.

28 190 10070 **Nathan Price** .. 6 acs .. Jennings Cr .. improvement where **Thompkin Odle now lives.** 6 Feb 1813.

28 191 10073 **Robert Gibson** .. 10 acs .. Indian Cr in the head of Buffalo Valley .. south side of a ridge opposite sd Gibson's field. 6 Feb 183.

28 192 10074 **Robert Gibson** .. 2 acs .. Indian Cr in the head of Buffalo Valley .. ridge **on which sd Gibson now lives.** 6 Feb 1813.

28 192 10079 **Henry McDaniel** .. 10 acs .. Waters of Indian Cr .. **where William McDaniel now lives.** 8 Feb 1813.

28 198 10103 **James Youngblood** .. 5 acs Blackburn's Fk .. **where Joseph Pippin now lives** .. 10 Feb 1813.

28 199 10106 **Lewis Stover, Joseph Ownby, Thomas Ownby, James Williams & John Tefeteller** .. 1 ac .. Dry fork of Mill (CR?) near head of sd branch .. a salt petre cave. 10 Feb 1813.

28 199 10107 **Lewis Stover & Joseph Ownby** .. 1 ac .. on Ownby's branch of the dry fork of Mill Cr .. to incl salt petre cave. 10 Feb 1813.

28 199 10108 **Thomas Ownby** .. 8 acs.. dry fork of Mill Cr .. south east corner of John Baker's line .. 10 Feb 1813.

28 207 10139 **Levi Rodden** .. White Co .. 30 acs .. south boundary of the **Gum Spring tract now belonging to Elisha Walling** .. 15 Feb 1813. Also Entry No. 10140.

28 210 10155 **Robert Anderson** .. 10 acs .. small branch of Hurricane Cr .. adj tract granted Nathl M. Cann (?) .. 16 Feb 1813.

28 212 10161 **James Isham** .. 80 acs .. White Co .. west side of Caney Fk .. SE corner of Jeremiah Denton's 80 ac survey .. to the **Gum Spring Mountain** .. 17 Feb 1813.

28 220 10194 **James Jones** .. 5-1/2 acs .. South side of Cumberland on head of north fork of a branch that runs into

Cumberland above **Sheeley's Knob** and at James G. Brehan's corner .. to incl a cave lately found by sd Jones about 200 yards from sd Brehan's. 18 Feb 1813.

28 220 10195 **John C. McLemore** .. 11-1/2 acs .. on the point of a ridge dividing East fork of Doe Cr from head of a branch of Roaring R where Shaw's old cabin stands about 1/4 mile from Nicholas Hail's corner .. 19 Feb 1813.

28 221 10196 **John C. McLemore** .. 5 acs .. north side of Roaring R .. below the Big Boil in sd river called Caney Br .. cave lately found by **John Shankle SR.** 19 Feb 1813.

28 221 10197 **John C. McLemore** .. 50 acs .. adj Hampton's 75-ac survey .. on Roaring R. 19 Feb 1813. John Murry, Loc.

28 222 10199 **John Payton SR** .. 2 acs .. south side of west fork of Mill Cr .. 19 Feb 1813.

28 222 10200 **John Payton SR** .. 2 acs .. west fork of Mill Cr .. 19 Feb 1813.

28 223 10205 **William Kerr** .. 20 ac .. waters of Cane Cr .. to incl sd Kerr's improvement **whereon he now lives.** 20 Feb 1813.

28 223 10206 **John Kerr** .. 25 acs .. waters of Cane Cr .. **to incl .. whereon he now lives.** 20 Feb 1813.

28 229 10228 **Sharp Whitley** .. 20 acs .. waters of Roaring R on the north side .. Edmund Find's north boundary .. to incl a plum orchard. 25 Feb 1813.

28 229 10231 **Jeremiah Denton** .. 122 acs .. White Co .. on Caney Fk. Beg at sd Denton's NW corner of 78-ac entry .. 25 Feb 1813.

28 245 10293 **Benjamin Blackburn** .. 50 acs .. west fork of Roaring R .. Beg where Benjamin Blackburn SR's south boundary crosses .. below David Finn's .. to incl David Finn's improvement. 3 Mar 1813.

28 247 10298 **David Rose** .. 15 acs .. dry fork of Mill Cr .. adj his own. 4 Mar 1813.

28 247 10299 **Jacob Smith** .. one ac .. south side of Mill Cr .. branch that empties into sd creek opposite **Mrs. Mitchell's.** .. 4 Mar 1813.

28 250 10310 **Fouchee Garner** .. 14 acs .. Hutchin's Cr .. about 200 yards nearly west from Samuel Hunter's improvement. 5 Mar 1813.

28 251 10311 **Fouchee Garner** .. one ac .. Hutchin's Cr .. 200 yards

below road leading from **Elizabeth Young's to Buller's mill** .. 5 Mar 1813.

28	255	10325	**Spencer Dillingham** .. 50 acs .. on a branch of Blackburn's Cr .. to incl the place **whereon sd Dillingham now lives** .. 8 Mar 1813.
28	255	10328	**Owen Yarborough** .. 5 acs .. on Hutchison's fork of dry fork of Mill Cr .. NE corner of John Baker's survey .. 8 Mar 1813.
28	256	10329	**Owen Yarborough** .. 2 acs .. fork of Hutchison's and the dry fork of Mill Cr .. John Baker's survey .. 8 Mar 1813.
28	256	10330	**Owen Yarborough** .. 4 acs .. dry fork of Mill Cr .. adj John Baker .. 8 Mar 1813.
28	256	10331	**John Baker** .. 5 acs .. dry fork of Mill Cr .. adj 35 acs in name of John Peterson .. 8 Mar 1819.
28	257	10333	**Owen Yarborough** .. 4 acs .. fork of Hutchison's and dry fork of Mill Cr .. adj John Baker. 8 Mar 1813.
28	257	10335	**John Anderson** .. 5 acs .. waters of Martin's Cr .. south side of Spring Fk of Martin's Cr .. 3/4 miles west of sd Anderson's own **place where he now lives** .. to incl a salt petre cave and a mill seat .. 9 Mar 1813. James Cook, Loc.
28	257	10336	**Nathan Haggard** .. 20 acs .. ridge at head of Thompson's branch of Flynn's Cr .. including **Joseph Wood's improvement where he now lives.** 9 Mar 1813.
28	258	10337	**Patrick Fitzgerald one of the heirs and legatees of Garrett Fitzgerald, deceased, & ase of Jabez Fitzgerald, the other legatee** .. 30 acs .. to incl the improvement whereon **Jacob Ragle now lives above George Findly's Tan yard** .. 9 Mar 1813.
28	258	10338	**Patrick Fitzgerald** .. 10 acs .. waters of Indian Cr ..on a ridge between two branches of sd Indian Cr and about 1/2 mile to the north of Walton's road .. 9 Mar 1813.
28	258	10339	**Samuel Miller** .. 20 acs .. head waters of Big Br of the dividing ridge between first mentioned branch and dry fork of Martin's Cr .. to incl improvement **whereon sd Miller now lives.** 9 Mar 1813. James Cook, Loc.
28	259	10342	**John C. McLemore** .. 11 acs .. waters of Brimstone Cr .. above Chitwood Cave .. 9 Mar 1813.
28	259	10343	**John C. McLemore** .. 5 acs .. waters of the dry fork of

Mill Cr .. Hamilton's Cave .. to incl the mouth of a large rock house called Petre Cave .. found by George Thompson. 9 Mar 1813.

28 260 10344 **John C. McLemore** .. 11 acs .. N of Cumberland on Webster's Cr .. .. 9 Mar 1813.

28 260 10345 **John C. McLemore** .. 7 acs .. south fork of dry fork of Mill Cr **where Nathaniel Roden formerly lived** .. cave found by Stover .. 9 Mar 1813.

28 260 10346 **John C. McLemore** .. 6 acs south bank of Cumberland bluff made by Shely's Knob .. 9 Mar 1813.

"Shely" was the Cherokee who lived in a cave on Roaring R and harassed traveler's on the Cumberland. See notebook/scrapbook by Molden Tayse, and her history of Jackson County, published in 1990.

28 261 10347 **John C. McLemore** .. 10 acs .. S side of Cumberland .. north fork of Sugar Cr 1/2 mile below **where some families named Stacy now live** .. a fall .. where an **old** pounding mill formerly stood .. 9 Mar 1813.

The best guess (from library table consultants) is that a pounding mill lacked wheels and gears, preceded the grinding mill, and was for the same purpose. John Murrey was the usual surveyor/locator for John C. McLemore and wrote poetic and historical land descriptions.

28 261 10348 **John C. McLemore** .. 9 acs .. north side of Cumberland .. waters of first branch that runs into Knob Cr .. below Jacob Bennett's .. a number of rock houses .. found by George Thompson. 9 Mar 1813.

28 261 10349 **John C. McLemore** .. 10 acs north side of Roaring R .. to incl a salt lick .. known as the Buffalo Lick. 9 Mar 1813.

28 262 10350 **John C. McLemore** .. 20 acs .. north fork of Sugar Cr .. a mile below **where Stacy now lives** .. 9 Mar 1813.

28 262 10351 **John C. McLemore** .. 45 acs on Spring Cr .. James Bedford's west boundary .. 9 Mar 1813.

28 262 10352 **John C. McLemore** .. 45 acs .. west fork of Roaring R .. a mill seat **near old Mr. Derosett's cabin in which he now lives** .. 9 Mar 1812.

28 263 10353 **John C. McLemore** .. 5 acs .. Jennings Mill Cr south side of Cumberland .. a mile below old cave known as "Penitentiary Cave." 9 Mar 1813.

28 263 10354 **Jacob Bennett** .. 10 acs .. north side of dividing ridge between forks of Knob Cr .. cave at the mouth of Turkey Pen branch. 10 Mar 1813.

28	264	10358	**David Griffith** .. 8 acs .. north side of Cumberland on a branch of Jennings Cr .. 10 Mar 1813.
28	264	10359	**John Griffith** .. 10 acs .. Jennings Cr .. adj his own and John Wilson's. 10 Mar 1813.
28	265	10360	**David Dickson** .. 10 acs .. Jennings Cr .. to incl sd Dickson's spring & sugar camp. 10 Mar 1813.
28	266	10364	**Thomas Lee, John Moore & Joel Moore** .. 2 acs .. south fork of McFarland's Cr .. to incl cave lately found by Thomas Lee and John Moore. 10 Mar 1813.
28	267	10368	**Raynolds Jeffers** .. 25 acs .. S side of Cumberland on Sugar Cr .. to incl improvement where **sd Jeffers now lives.** 11 Mar 1813. Hananiah Lincoln, Loc.
28	279	10415	**John Campbell** .. 50 acs .. Cain Cr .. to incl improvement **where Mark Morgan now lives.** 10 Mar 1913.
28	280	10417	**Robert Harris** .. Cane Cr a branch of Caney Fk .. SW corner of James Carter's 214-ac survey on Isaac Taylor's line. 20 Mar 1813.
28	280	10418	**Robert Harris** .. 20 acs .. Cane Cr branch of Caney Fk .. **improvement made by Robert Gentry.** 20 Mar 1813.
28	280	10419	**Joseph Jared** .. 10 acs .. Rock Springs Valley .. adj his own. 20 Mar 1813.
28	280	10420	**Joseph Jared** .. 10 acs .. waters of the Caney Fk .. Beg at 25-ac entry **where he now lives** .. 20 Mar 1813.
28	281	10422	**Joseph Jared** .. 2 acs .. waters of the Caney Fk .. point of a ridge that makes down opposite to where **John Boyd now lives.** .. 20 Mar 1813.
28	282	10426	**Andrew Ferrell** .. 4 acs .. waters of Caney Fk on a ridge **between where sd Ferrell now lives** & Son Carter's .. N boundary of John Boyd's.. 20 Mar 1813.
28	282	10427	**James Boyd** .. 3 acs .. waters of Caney Fk .. adj his own, Joseph Jared. 20 Mar 1813.
28	282	10428	**James Boyd** .. 3 acs .. east side of the Caney Fk on dividing ridge between Cumberland and Caney Fk .. to incl top of the ridge between **where sd Boyd and Joseph Jared now live.** 20 Mar 1813.
28	286	10440	**John Martin** .. 60 acs .. Flynn's Cr .. east bank of sd creek about 1/4 mile above **Wm. Thompson's mill** on sd creek .. west then south .. to incl a small improvement. 23 Mar 1813.

28	286	10441	**Champ Stanton** .. 20 acs .. on a branch of Martin's Cr on south side of sd creek .. to incl an old improvement .. 23 Mar 1813.
28	287	10443	**William Murray** .. 20 acs .. north side of Cumberland on Turkey Cr .. adj his own .. 28 Mar 1813.
28	287	10444	**Jacob Bennet** .. 10 acs .. on Knob Cr 1/2 mile above sd Bennett's .. 23 Mar 1813.
28	288	10446	**John C. McLemore** .. 25 acs .. Knob Cr .. corner to survey **whereon Jacob Bennett now lives** .. to incl sd Bennett's house and part of his improvement **where he now lives.** 23 Mar 1813.
28	288	10447	**James Markus** .. 10 acs .. north side of Cumberland .. including part of sd Markus's improvement. 28 Mar 1813. (On the filmed index, this name appears as "Marks.")
28	288	10448	**John C. McLemore** .. 20 acs .. north side of Cumberland .. 23 Mar 1813.
28	289	10452	**John C. McLemore** .. 40 acs .. west fork of Roaring R called Blackburn's Fk .. George W. Raymond's SE corner of his 40-ac survey .. 23 Mar 1813.
28	290	10453	**John C. McLemore** .. 20 acs .. Blackburn's Fk .. 23 Mar 1813.
28	290	10454	**John C. McLemore** .. 20 acs .. north side of Cumberland on Webster's Cr .. Beg where Bonner's west boundary line crosses sd Cr .. 23 Mar 1813.
28	290	10455	**John C. McLemore** .. 5 acs .. Webster's Cr .. near Joseph Lock's cave. 23 Mar 1813.
28	290	10456	**John C. McLemore** .. 5 acs .. north side of Cumberland .. headwaters of first branch that runs into sd river below Webster's Cr .. cave known as Clay Cave formerly worked by Joseph Lock and John Twitty. 23 Mar 1813.
28	291	10457	**John C. McLemore** .. 5 acs .. north side of Roaring R on Big Cr .. a cave in the bluff about 100 yards above The Hanging Rock above where **Daniel Shipman now lives.** 23 Mar 1813.
28	294	10467	**David Porter** .. 12 acs .. Cub Cr adj his own. 25 Mar 1813.
28	295	10473	**Jeremiah Denton** .. White Co .. 11 acs .. north side of Caney Fk .. on John Miller SR's SE corner of a 50-ac survey **whereon John Anderson resides** .. 25 Mar 1813.

28	298	10483	**John C. McLemore** .. 100 acs .. N side of Cumberland .. near where Lock now lives .. 26 Mar 1813.
28	301	10492	**Joseph Whitney** .. 10 acs .. McFarland's and Proctor's Crs .. to incl **sd Whitney's house** and part of his improvement. 29 Mar 1813.
28	302	10494	**Aron Ethradge** .. 26 acs .. Jennings Cr .. above John Bennett's improvement .. 30 Mar 1813.
28	302	10495	**John Giss** .. 10 acs .. mouth of the sycamore fork of Pine Lick fork of Jennings Cr .. including Giss's improvement **whereon he now lives.** 30 Mar 1813.
28	302	10496	**John Giss** .. 15 acs .. Pine Lick fork of Jennings Cr .. mouth of Sycamore fork .. 30 Mar 1813.
28	302	10497	**Sampson Williams** .. 320 acs .. Smith Co .. south side of Cumberland including place **where John Warren now lives** .. 30 Mar 1813.
28	304	10502	**Jacob Bennett** .. 50 acs .. Knob Cr .. 30 Mar 1813.
28	304	10503	**Jacob Bennett** .. one ac .. Knob Cr .. north side of main ridge between Knob Cr and Black's br .. 30 Mar 1813.
28	304	10504	**Jacob Bennett** .. 4 acs .. south side of middle fork of Knob Cr .. 30 Mar 1813.
28	307	10512	**William Ridge** .. 20 acs .. waters of Indian Cr .. 2 Apr 1813. Robert Lee, Loc.
28	307	10513	**William Ridge** .. 20 acs .. waters of Indian Cr .. **spring & improvement where Robert Lee now lives.** 2 Apr 1813. Robert Lee, Loc.
28	307	10515	**Moses Byers** .. 15 acs .. Cane Cr. to incl land where the new Walton Road crosses the Rock Island or Sparta road. 3 Apr 1813. John Moore, Loc.
28	308	10516	**Charles Harvey** .. 35 acs .. Mine Lick Cr .. adj his own. 30 Apr 1813.
28	313	10536	**Edmund Butler** .. 5 acs .. waters of Dry Cr .. to incl cave lately found by sd Butler and Archibald Wood .. 5 Apr 1813.
28	313	10538	**Samuel Moore** .. 40 acs .. Brimstone Cr .. near field occupied by Moses Swaford .. 6 Apr 1813.
28	313	10539	**Peter Miller** .. half an ac .. east side of Brimstone Cr .. to incl a salt petre cave **now worked by sd Miller.** 6 Apr 1813. Samuel Holmes, Loc.

28	314	10540	**Emanuel Holmes** .. 30 acs .. north side of Cumberland .. beg corner of John Black's 50 ac entry .. crossing Knob Cr .. 6 Apr 1813. Samuel Holmes, Loc.
28	317	10551	**David Griffith** .. 40 acs .. both sides of Pine Lick fork of Jennings Cr .. to incl his improvement. 7 Apr 1813.
28	317	10552	**Bennet Lane** .. 5 (?) acs .. Pine Lick fork of Jennings Cr .. 140 yards **below his house.** 7 Apr 1813.
28	318	10557	**Alexander Keith** .. 15 acs .. Little Trace Cr of Big Barron .. to incl .. **where John Scott now lives.** 8 Apr 1813.
28	318	10558	**Alexander Keith** .. 11 acs .. Little Trace Cr of Big Barron .. 8 Apr 1813.

BK	PG	NUMBER	DESCRIPTION
28	319	10559	**Benjamin Farmer and John Burgess** .. 2 acs .. Proctor's Cr .. near entry made by Stephen Cantrell .. 8 Apr 1813. John Burgess, Loc.
28	319	10560	**Jesse Hust (Hurt?)** .. 6 acs .. near Stephen Cantrell .. to incl improvements made by Dumis Mitchell. 8 Apr 1813. John Burgess, Loc.
28	320	10563	**John C. McLemore** .. 3 acs .. Roaring R .. cave lately found by Daniel Shipman .. east fork of Price's spring branch .. at Asa Lynn's field .. north side of Roaring .. cave **now occupied by said Shipman.** 9 Apr 1813.
28	320	10564	**John C. McLemore** .. Blackburn's Fork .. 1/4 mile from an old **school house that John McDaniel formerly taught** .. to incl cave lately found by John Shankle SR. 9 Apr 1813.
28	320	10565	**Joseph Hyde** .. 2 acs .. north side of Flynn's Cr .. Cubb Hollow .. to incl improvement **whereon said Hyde now lives.** 9 Apr 1813.
28	321	10568	**James Vinson** in Dickson Co. 10 Apr 1813. This may or may not be the James Vinson who lived on Martin's Cr in Jackson Co.
28	325	10583	**John Payne** .. 10 acs .. head of Horse Hollow of dry fork of Flynn's Cr .. near **said Payne's house** .. to incl said Payne's improvement. 13 Apr 1813. James Vinson, Loc.
28	325	10584	**James Vinson** .. 5 acs .. head of the Long Hollow or Stephen's Hollow .. dry fork of Martin's Cr .. 13 Apr 1813. James Vinson, Loc.
28	326	10585	**James Vinson** .. 10 acs .. head of Roy's branch of dry fork of Flynn's Cr .. 5 poles east from said Vinson's spring .. to incl said Vinson's improvement and sugar camp **where he now lives.** 13 Apr 1813. James Vinson, Loc.
28	326	10586	**John Ragland** .. 14 acs .. head waters of dry fork of Flynn's Cr .. to incl the improvement **where said Ragland now lives.** 13 Apr 1813.
28	329	10594	**John Myers** .. 2acs .. east side of Hampton's branch .. Roaring R .. 19 Apr 1813.
28	329	10595	**George Price** .. one ac .. Hooper's Cr of Roaring R .. to incl the Big Lick. 19 Apr 1813.
28	329	10596	**George Price** .. 10 acs .. Spring Cr waters of Roaring R

112

			.. to incl improvement **whereon John Bodely now lives.** 19 Apr 1813.
28	330	10597	**George Price** .. 10 acs .. south side of Roaring R .. at Abner Lea's SE corner .. 19 Apr 1813.
28	330	10598	**George Price** .. 5 acs .. south side of Roaring R .. near Abner Lea's. 19 Apr 1813.
28	330	10599	**John Shankle SR** .. 2 acs .. north side of Roaring R .. west side of Asa Lynn's spring branch .. cave formerly worked by John McDaniel. 19 Apr 1813.
28	332	10607	**John Sutton** .. 2 acs .. Morrison's Cr of Roaring R .. adj Sutton's Grant No. 3534 .. **19 Apr 1813.**
28	338	10625	**William Cannady** .. 8 acs .. Donohoe's branch .. waters of Defeated Cr .. Edward Jenning's east boundary .. to incl said Cannady's improvement **whereon he now lives.** 24 Apr 1813. Lakes Cannady, Loc.
28	338	10627	**John Martin** .. ase of Sampson Williams .. 50 acs .. the ridge that divides the dry fork of Martin's Cr and dry fork of Flynn's Cr .. to incl place where **John Ragland now lives.** .. 24 Apr 1813. John Martin, Loc.
28	339	10631	**Francis Wisdom** .. 10 acs .. west branch of Doe Cr .. to incl said Wisdom's improvement and the house **where he now lives.** 16 Apr 1813.
28	343	10643	**Samuel Hays and Samuel Huff** ase John C. McLemore .. 2 acs .. Cave fork of Knob Cr of Cumberland R .. on the north side of said fk .. mouth of salt petre cave formerly worked by .. Anderson who erected furnaces several years past at sd cave .. south & east .. 29 Apr 1813. Samuel Hays, Loc.
28	344	10644	**Levi Greathouse** .. 14 acs .. Proctor's Cr .. 29 Apr 1813.
28	344	10645	**Samuel Huff and Samuel Hays** ase of John C. McLemore .. 2 acres .. on a fork of Knob Cr of Cumberland .. to incl **Huff's and Givin's old salt petre cave.** 29 Apr 1813. Samuel Hays, Loc.
28	357	10692	**Gilbert Cotrell** .. 30 acs Mine lick Cr .. incl improvement **whereon Joshua Gann now lives.** 10 May 1813.
28	361	10711	**Robert Wallace** .. 14 acs .. Indian Cr of Caney Fork in the Buffalo Valley .. adj Wallace. 13 May 1813.
28	363	10718	**Josiah Conn** .. 40 acs .. White Co .. Rock Island Rd .. 3/4 miles east from Abraham Denton's .. 14 May 1813.

28	364	10723	**Caleb Longest** .. 6 acs .. east side of Big Trace Cr .. east from Aron Osburn's north east corner .. to incl part of improvement **where William Osburn lately lived.** 15 May 1813. Caleb Longest, Loc.
28	365	10724	**Caleb Longest** .. 6 acs .. west side of Big Trace Cr .. 50 yards below plantation that McCloud made .. 25 May 1813.
28	367	10733	**Thomas Usrey** .. 6 acs .. waters of Roaring R adj Edmund Finn's 100-ac occupant survey .. and Ann Dyers' 50-ac entry .. **including house and spring of Thomas Usrey.** 18 May 1813. (Mr. Usrey was indexed as "Varey" on the filmed index.)
28	372	10750	**Daniel Rose** .. one ac .. north side of Cumberland .. waters of Dry Cr .. salt petre cave formerly worked by William Murry about half a mile from Emanuel Holmes. 22 May 1813.
28	378	10770	**Philip Mulkey** .. one ac .. waters of Brimstone Cr .. near said Mulkey's salt petre cave **at present worked by Jesse Stacy** .. 25 May 1813.
28	378	10771	**Hamilton Montgomery** .. 10 acs .. south side of Cumberland .. adj his own **where he now lives** .. 25 May 1813.
28	379	10773	**John C. McLemore** .. 50 acs .. waters of Brimstone Cr .. to incl an orchard and improvement formerly occupied by Joel Short SR. 25 May 1813.
28	379	10774	**John C. McLemore** .. 50 acs .. Morrison's Cr of Roaring R .. below spring formerly **used by Matthew Tally** .. 25 May 1813.
28	379	10775	**John C. McLemore** .. 40 acs .. north side of Cumberland .. on Bonner's west boundary .. 25 May 1813.
28	380	10776	**John C. McLemore** .. 30 acs .. Bonner's corner .. north bank of Cumberland .. 25 May 1813.
28	380	10777	**John C. McLemore** .. 20 acs .. Dry Cr that runs into Blackburn's fork .. 1/4 mile above **where Garland Anderson now lives** .. 25 May 1813.
28	380	10778	**John C. McLemore** .. 20 acs .. Blackburn's Fork .. below John Bowen's mill .. 25 May 1813.
28	381	10779	**John C. McLemore** .. 10 acs .. Bowerman's Br .. W of Blackburn's fork .. on W boundary of **Stephen Roberts** 15-ac survey .. to incl large fall .. 25 May 1813.
28	384	10790	**Richard York SR** .. 20 acs .. Big Trace of Barron R ..

to incl spring, house and part of improvement where **Jesse Vinson now lives.** 27 May 1813.

28	384	10791	**John Davis** .. 40 acs .. Big Trace Cr of Barron .. to incl improvement whereon **said Davis now lives.** 27 May 1813.
28	389	10811	**Burrell Mansell** .. 2 acs .. Rush fork of Flynn's Cr .. Richard Mansell's beginning corner .. to incl the cabin **where Samuel Henson now lives.** 29 May 1813.
28	390	10812	**John C. McLemore** .. 20 acs .. dry creek of Blackburn's fork .. 29 May 1813.
28	390	10813	**John C. McLemore** .. 5 acs .. south side of Cumberland .. first branch above old Mr. Scandland .. 29 May 1813.
28	390	10814	**John C. McLemore** .. 5 acs .. south side of Cumberland on Scandland's branch .. below a cave **occupied by James Anderson** .. 29 May 1813.
28	390	10815	**John C. McLemore** .. 10 acs .. Big Cr a fork of Roaring R that runs into said river .. opposite where **Abner Lee now lives.** 31 May 1813.
28	391	10818	**Emanuel Holmes** .. 2 acs .. north side of Dry Cr .. 31 May 1813.
28	391	10819	**Emanuel Holmes** .. one ac .. Dry Cr .. 31 May 1813.
28	393	10824	**John Petty** .. 10 acs .. on the ridge between Dry fork of Martin's Cr and Roy's branch .. to incl improvement made by said John Petty. 31 May 1813.
28	393	10825	**John Petty** .. 10 acs .. Dry fork of Martin's Cr .. north side of the dry valley .. north side of the Mill Road .. to incl improvement **where said Petty now lives.** 31 May 1813.
28	393	10826	**John Martin** .. 15 acs .. Dry fork of Martin's Cr .. east boundary of Sampson Williams' 640-ac tract .. to incl part of a field **cleared by William Hough.** 31 May 1813.
28	394	10827	**John Martin** .. 15 acs .. Dry fork of Flynn's Cr .. to incl improvement where **Elijah Lemmons now lives.** 31 May 1813. (This name can be read "Simmons.")
28	394	10830	**James Kirkpatrick** .. one ac. .. Brimstone Cr .. now in the **occupancy of William Carlisle.** 1 June 1813.
28	395	10831	**James Kirkpatrick** .. one ac .. Brimstone Cr .. to incl a salt petre cave out of which a hole goes out at the top of the mountain. 1 June 1813.

28	396	10837	**James Cook** .. 2 acs .. north side of Cumberland .. Lock's Br 5 miles above mouth of Roaring R .. 2 June 1813.
28	397	10838	**Sampson Williams** .. 8 acs .. Doe Cr .. conditional line made by Archibald McGahan & Nicholas Hail .. **the tract said McGahan now lives upon.** 2 June 1813.
28	397	10839	**Sampson Williams** .. 8 acs .. Doe Cr. 2 June 1813.
28	397	10840	**Isaac Rhodes** .. 10 acs .. Indian Cr of Cumberland .. to incl improvement & spring where **Micajah Brown now lives.** .. 2 June 1813.
28	398	10842	**Ephraim Jones** .. 4 acs .. Big Br of Martin's Cr .. west side of said branch .. 2 June 1813.
28	398	10844	**Caleb Short** .. 30 acs .. Joel's Cr of Jennings Cr .. to incl **Brown's old cabin.** 2 June 1813.
28	398	10845	**Caleb Short** .. 8 acs .. Joel's Cr of Jennings Cr .. to incl part of Joel Short's improvement. 2 June 1813.
28	399	10846	**Caleb Short** .. Pine Lick fork of Jennings Cr .. on the road leading from Lock's ferry to Glasgow .. to incl James Pursley's improvement. 2 June 1813.
28	399	10849	**David Young** .. White Co .. 25 acs .. south and east from mouth of said Young's old cave .. a number of salt petre caves now occupied by James Vance. 3 June 1813.
28	403	10861	**Gabriel Benson** .. 128 acs .. Smith Co .. on a branch of the Caney Fork emptying in on the E side above Lancaster's ferry called **Williamson's Br** beginning on the south boundary of a tract in name of **Howell Tatum** and on the NE corner of **Robert Anderson's 281-ac tract,** running south with said Anderson's line .. east and south for complement to incl **where Williamson lives** at the Cave Spring on said branch and to extend on oblong east. 4 June 1813. Thomas Shute, Loc. Sur rtd 30 Apr 1814 by Jno Townsend, DS.

Entry No. 10861 is the 128 acs Shute sold to James Williamson by a deed witnessed by Samuel Huff and Benjamin Thompson, both of whom appeared in Smith County Court in November 1816 to prove the conveyance. Subsequently, William Huff is recorded as living adj James Williamson and Robert Anderson's 281 acres. That conveyance identifies Thomas Shute as being "of Rutherford County."

28	411	10892	**John Shankle** .. one ac .. waters of Price's spring branch of Roaring R .. near the horse point lately found by said Shankle. 11 June 1813.

28	415	10905	**John Williams** .. one ac .. North side of Cumberland .. Second branch below Bonner's corner .. cave lately found by said Williams. 12 June 1813.
28	415	10906	**John Kirkpatrick** .. one ac .. western branch of Webster's Cr .. to incl cave lately found by said Kirkpatrick .. below Anderson's old cave. 12 June 1813.
28	418	10914	**Thomas Butler, Francis Kendall & Amos Justice** .. 2 acs .. waters of Brimstone Cr .. first fork above Sadler's sugar camp branch .. 14 June 1813.
28	423	10933	**David Waldrop** .. 2 acs .. waters of Knob Cr .. to incl a salt petre cave worked at several years past by John Brannum & lying about 200 yards nearly east **from Huff's cave.** 16 June 1813.
28	424	10934	**David Loveall** .. one ac .. west fork of Roaring R .. to incl said Loveall's improvement. 16 June 1813.
28	424	10935	**Rasha Robertson** .. 2 acs .. south side of Roaring R .. east side of Edward Robertson's spring branch .. 16 June 1813.
28	424	10936	**Thomas Anderson** .. 2 acs .. on Roaring R .. to incl part of the field called Dyer's improvement. 16 June 1813.
28	425	10938	**Richard F. Cooke** .. 70 acs .. Cane Cr .. 18 June 1813.
28	425	10940	**William Ridge** .. 19 acs .. White Co .. north side of the road that leads from the Rock Island to White Plains 1-1/2 mile from the Rock Island .. 16 June 1813.
28	426	10942	**Jonathan Reneau & Andrew Ferrell** .. 25 acs .. Rock Spring Valley to join south boundary of **David Wallace's** 30-ac tract and north boundary of his lower 30-ac entry **whereon he now lives.** 17 June 1813.
28	429	10954	**Samuel Kirkpatrick** .. North side of Cumberland .. second branch below mouth of Webster's Cr .. 18 June 1813.
28	429	10955	**Samuel Kirkpatrick** .. 9 acs .. second branch below mouth of Webster's Cr .. to incl a cave called John Williams' .. 18 June 1813.
28	430	10956	**Samuel Kirkpatrick** .. 4 acs first branch below mouth of Webster's Cr .. 18 June 1813.
28	430	10957	**Samuel Kirkpatrick** .. 2 acs .. second branch below mouth of Webster's Cr .. to incl mouth of cave .. formerly **worked by Jonas Griffith and others.** 18 June

1813.

28	432	10963	**Jesse Gilstrap** .. one ac .. Crabtree's fork of Jennings Cr .. near the head of the school house hollow .. 21 June 1813.
28	432	10964	**Jesse Gilstrap** .. one ac .. north fork of Jennings Cr .. 21 June 1813.
28	434	10971	**Sampson Williams** .. 57 acs .. Dry fork of Martin's Cr bounded on the west by a survey of John G. Blount's and on the north by a tract of said Williams including **the place where John Martin now lives.** 22 June 1813.
28	437	10981	**David Wallace** .. 5 acs .. Rock Spring Valley .. SW corner of said Wallace's 30-ac entry **whereon he now lives** .. 24 June 1813.
28	437	10982	**David Wallace** .. 5 acs .. in the Rock Spring Valley .. his south boundary of his 30-ac entry whereon he now lives 15 poles east from his house. 24 June 1813.
28	439	10990	**John H. Martin** .. 2 acs .. head of second branch below mouth of Webster's Cr north of Cumberland. 26 June 1813.

John Martin lived on Martin's Cr. **John Lepier Martin** was first sheriff of Smith Co which included Martin's Cr at the time. Is this **John H. Martin** still another John Martin? Gen. Joseph Martin had a son named **John Calvin Martin** who traveled around this area exploring and visiting his brother, the celebrated Col. William Martin, who wrote such lovely letters to Lyman C. Draper. Other descendants of Gen. Joseph Martin lived nearby.

28	440	10993	**Samuel Wilkerson** .. 8 acs .. head waters of Bowdine's branch .. 3/4 of a mile above Esquire Bowdine's. 28 June 1813.
28	441	10994	**Peter Ritchie** .. 4 acs .. Dry Cr of Blackburn's fork. 28 June 1813.
28	441	10995	**John C. McLemore** .. 5 acs .. south side of Cumberland on a south fork of Hurricane Cr .. 28 June 1813.
28	442	11000	**John Butler** .. 20 acs .. waters of Cumberland .. on Samuel Kendall's line .. east with Black's line .. 30 June 1813. Sylvanus Fowler, Loc.
28	442	11001	**Edward Butler** .. 2 acs .. waters of Knob Cr a small distance above a .. cave formerly worked by James Moore. 30 June 1813.
28	443	11002	**Silvanus Fowler** .. 2 acs .. Cave fork of Brimstone Cr .. cave called Fowler's cave. 30 June 1813.

28	443	11003	**Silvanus Fowler** .. one ac .. Cave fork of Brimstone Cr .. to incl salt petre cave called Usary's Cave. 30 June 1813.
28	443	11004	**Silvanus Fowler** .. one ac .. Sadler's fork of Brimstone Cr .. 30 June 1813.
28	443	11005	**Silvanus Fowler** .. one ac .. on Sadler's fork of Brimstone Cr .. to incl a .. cave in the first fork of said creek above **Griggs Rock House**. 30 June 1813.
28	446	11015	**Polly Twitty** .. 15 acs .. on Indian Cr .. including **her improvement**. 3 July 1813.
28	446	11016	**Richard Lock** .. 20 acs .. Pine Lick fork of Jennings Cr .. to incl two fields of John Bennet's improvement. 3 July 1813.
28	446	11017	**Richard Lock** .. 10 acs .. Pine lick fork of Jennings Cr .. to incl a small bottom below Bennet's improvement. 3 July 1813.
28	446	11018	**Richard Lock** .. branch of dry fork of Jennings Cr .. north of John Chisolm's .. to incl said Lock's sugar camp. 3 July 1813.
28	447	11019	**Edmund Buller** .. 2 acs .. waters of Brimstone Cr .. 3 July 1813.
28	447	11020	**Edmond Buller** .. one ac .. waters of Brimstone Cr .. 5 July 1813.
28	448	11024	**Burkett Kinnard** .. 15 acs .. on Flynn's Cr .. to incl improvement at mouth of Rush Fork. 7 July 1813.
28	449	11027	**Elijah Smith** .. 3 acs .. waters of Little Hurricane .. 7 July 1813.
28	453	11042	**James Mays** .. 20 acs .. White Co .. south fork of Rutledges's mill creek .. to incl said Mays' spring & improvement. 9 July 1813.
28	453	11043	**Joseph Jared** .. 10 acs .. waters of Indian Cr of Cumberland .. to incl improvement made by John Cleavland. 9 July 1813.
28	453	11044	**Joseph Jared** .. 10 acs .. place known as Walnut Ridge. 9 July 1813.
28	454	11045	**William Jared** .. 17 acs .. Rock Springs Valley .. east corner of entry of 50 acs in name of James Roulston whereon said **Jared now lives** .. to incl a .. field cleared by said Jared. 9 July 1813.

28	457	11057	**Richard Gordan** .. 2 acs .. waters of Brimstone Cr .. north of Sadler's sugar camp .. 12 July 1813.
28	458	11060	**Peter Miller** .. 4 acs .. on **Huff's spring branch of Brimstone Cr** .. to incl .. cave occupied by said Miller. 13 July 1813.
28	458	11062	**Francis Moore, Samuel Moore, & James Cornelius** .. 2 acs .. head of Roy's branch of War Trace Cr .. 13 July 1813.
28	458	11063	**Francis Moore, Samuel Moore & James Cornelius** .. 2 acs .. Roy's branch on west fork of War Trace Cr .. 13 July 1813.
28	459	11064	**Francis Moore, Samuel Moore & James Cornelius** .. 2 acs .. head of Roy's branch .. of War Trace Cr .. 13 July 1813.
28	459	11065	**Francis Moore, Samuel Moore, James Cornelius** .. one ac .. Camp branch of Jennings's Cr .. 13 July 1813.
28	463	11080	**Major Passons & Joel Longley** .. one ac .. Smith Co .. Salt lick fork of Big Barron .. cave **now occupied by said Passons.** 16 July 1813.
28	466	11090	**James Vance** .. 72 acs .. north side of Indian Cr .. 16 July 1813.
28	466	11091	**James Vance** .. 10 acs .. south side of Indian Cr of Caney Fork .. mouth of **branch that Isaac Little lives on** .. 16 July 1813.
28	466	11092	**James Vance** .. 10 acs .. waters of Indian Cr .. a small distance above an old still house **built by Renno & Karr** to incl sd spring and still house. 16 July 1813.
28	467	11093	**James Vance** .. 10 acs .. White Co .. W side of Falling Water .. 16 July 1813.
28	467	11094	**Mark Young** .. 8 acs .. Indian Cr .. between entry of Jonathan Renno and Reuben Harris .. 16 June 1813.
28	467	11096	**Robert H. Swinney** .. 20 acs .. second branch .. north side of Cumberland .. below mouth of Webster's Cr .. to incl mouth of .. cave lately found by John Williams and now occupied by **said Swinney and John H. Martin.** 17 July 1813. (This entry appears on the filmed index as "Sweazy.")
28	473	11114	**John C. McLemore** .. 50 acs .. south side of south fork of Knob Cr .. to incl a salt petre cave .. known by the name of **Huff's Old cave** now occupied by Maj. McAlgin. (McColgan ??) 23 July 1813.

28	476	11125	**Bailey Butler** .. 20 acs .. waters of Knob Cr .. first main fork below **Huff's old cave.** 24 July 1813.
28	477	11128	**Bachel Clark** .. 46 acs .. headwaters of Bowdine's Br .. cave now occupied by Samuel Wilkerson, James Crabtree and others. 16 July 1813. Vachel Clark, Loc.
28	485	11155	**David Young** .. 8 acs .. waters of Indian Cr .. **whereon Jesse Wommack now lives.** 20 July 1813.
28	485	11156	**David Young** .. 6 acs .. waters of Indian Cr .. adj his own. 29 July 1813.
28	485	11157	**David Young** .. 2 acs .. head waters of Indian Cr .. adj his own. 29 July 1813.
28	486	11158	**John D. Brooks** .. 30 acs .. on Doe Cr .. 30 July 1813.
28	488	11164	**Henry Davenport** .. 5 acs .. on War Trace Cr .. to incl small improvement made by said Davenport & the forks of Teal's branch. 31 July 1813.
28	488	11165	**Henry Davenport** .. 5 acs .. Teal's branch .. to incl house and improvement **whereon said Davenport now lives.** 31 July 1813.
28	489	11168	**John Merrell** .. one ac .. north side of Cumberland .. Webster's Cr .. cave found by said Merrell & Alexander Montgomery. 31 July 1813.
28	489	11169	**John Merrell** .. one ac .. north side of Cumberland .. Webster's Cr .. 31 July 1813.
28	489	11170	**John Williams & Edward Kirkpatrick** .. 2 acs .. Lick fork of Brimstone Cr .. to incl cave .. a mile above Carlisle's salt petre works .. 31 July 1813.
28	489	11171	**John Williams & Edward Kirkpatrick** .. 2 acs .. Sadler's sugar camp branch of Brimstone Cr .. below a salt petre cave entered by Richard Gordan .. 31 July 1813.
28	490	11172	**John Williams and Edward Kirkpatrick** .. one ac .. west side of Sadler's sugar camp branch including a rock house .. 31 July 1813.
28	490	11173	**John Williams & Edward Kirkpatrick** .. one ac .. north side of Cumberland .. Webster's Cr .. Twitty's old cave. 31 July 1813.
28	491	11178	**Dempsy Powell** .. 75 acs .. Smith Co .. east side of Caney Fork .. adj east boundary of James Roulston .. 2 Aug 1873.

28	497	11195	**John C. McLemore** .. 5 acs .. Webster's Cr .. near Lock's cave. 7 Aug 1813.
28	497	11196	**John C. McLemore** .. 5 acs .. Webster's Cr .. Joseph Lock's old cave. 7 Aug 1813.
28	497	11197	**John C. McLemore** .. 10 acs .. north side of Cumberland .. Webster's Cr .. caves lately found by William Gibson between Martin & Swenney's Cave & the Clay Cave. 7 Aug 1813.
28	497	11198	**Ezra Bushnell** ..10 acs .. north side of Cumberland .. Clay cave fork of second branch below Webster's Cr .. to incl salt petre cave now occupied **by said Bushnell.** 7 Aug 1813.
28	506	11228	**John H. Martin** .. 15 acs .. north side of Cumberland .. below Webster's Cr .. below said Martin's & Swinney's salt petre cave .. 13 Aug 1813.
28	506	11229	**Samuel Kirkpatrick & Samuel Moore** .. 6 acs .. north side of Cumberland .. second branch below Brimstone Cr .. 13 Aug 1813.
28	507	11233	**Bachel Clark** .. 6 acs .. Fowler's cave fork of Brimstone Cr .. to incl Fowler's cave. 16 Aug 1813. Vachel Clark, Loc.
28	516	11267	**Elijah Stone & Lemuel Cherry** .. 25 acs .. head waters of middle fork of Brimstone Cr .. 20 Aug 1813.
28	517	11270	**William Smith** .. 3 acs .. Rock Springs Valley .. adj Henry Kerr .. 23 Aug 1813.
28	517	11271	**Mary Williams** .. 5 acs .. Rock Springs Cr .. north boundary of Henry Kerr's .. to incl improvement whereon **William Williams now lives.** 23 Aug 1813.
28	517	11272	**Mary Williams** .. 4 acs .. Rock Springs Valley .. east boundary of Henry Kerr. 23 Aug 1813.
28	520	11282	**Henry Allard** .. 20 acs .. Spring Cr waters of Roaring R .. James Bedford's south boundary .. **whereon Benjamin Walker now lives.** 23 Aug 1813.
28	522	11289	**Peter Roberts** .. one ac .. waters of Flynn's Cr .. to incl salt petre cave about 2 miles above Benjamin Fox's at which said Roberts and others have lately been at work .. 24 Aug 1813.
28	543	11365	**George McGibson** .. 20 acs .. Blackburn's Fork .. to incl an improvement occupied by sd McGibson. 6 Sept 1813.

BUILDING NEIGHBORHOODS
From
EARLY LAND RECORDS OF TENNESSEE
RG 50 SERIES 2 - LAND ENTRIES BOOK 29 - REEL 8
1ST SURVEYOR'S DISTRICT ENTRIES - JACKSON CO FOLKS.

BK	PG	NUMBER	DESCRIPTION
29	7	11413	**William & Edward Kirkpatrick** .. 1-1/2 acs .. Sadler's sugar camp br of Brimstone Cr .. 13 Sept 1813
29	8	11418	**Charles Broadwater** .. 10 acs .. on Martin's Cr beginning at the northwest corner of a 20-ac tract **whereon sd Broadwater now lives** .. 14 Sept 1813.
29	8	11419	**Charles Broadwater** .. 10 acs .. on Martin's Cr adj south boundary of **Caty Wilson's tract** .. to incl Caldwell's old Sugar Camp. 14 Sept 1813.
29	8	11420	**Charles Broadwater** .. 5 acs .. on Martin's Cr .. adj his own. 14 Sept 1813.
29	9	11422	**John Morgan JR** .. 50 acs .. Cane Cr .. to incl sd Morgan's improvement and spring. 15 Sept 1813. Wm. Dodson, Loc.
29	9	11423	**William Dodson** .. 10 acs .. on Martin's Cr .. adj John Shoemake's .. 10 acs **whereon he formerly lived.** 15 Sept 1813.
29	9	11424	**William Dodson** .. 20 acs .. Pigeon Roost Cr .. adj Daniel Alexander .. the military line .. 15 Sept 1813.
29	12	11438	**Eake Brown** .. 14 acs .. waters of Indian Cr .. adj his own. 17 Sept 1813.
29	12	11439	**Eake Brown** .. 20 acs .. waters of Rock Spring Valley .. about 25 yards south of the Walton Road & about 5 steps eastwardly from the path leading from **Shadrach Bridges'** into sd Road. 17 Sept 1813.

Entries numbered 11438 and 11439 were both surveyed by James Roulston who returned the surveys on 20 May 1814. Although No. 11438 does not make clear which Indian Cr is intended, 11439 does. If Mr. Roulston walked that 25 yards up to the road and crossed it, he would be on the "waters of Little Indian Cr of the Cumberland."

29	13	11444	**Elijah Shuttlesworth** .. 15 acs .. south side of Martin's Cr .. adj Owen Franklin .. due west of cabin **now occupied by John Richardson** .. 18 Sept 1813.
29	15	11450	**Champaign Stanton** .. one ac .. east side of Shaw's Br of Martin's Cr .. about 1/2 mile above the plantation whereon **John Shoemake formerly lived.** 18 Sept 1813.

123

How many local historians knew his name was "Champaign?" Champ Stanton was ase of Robert Searcy, Certificate No. 1591, as was Eake Brown on Nos. 11438 and 11439, solidly on Little Indian Creek.

29	17	11458	**Luke Mayfield** .. 2 acs .. Lick Br of Roaring R .. 1/4 mile above where **Daniel Shipman now lives.** 20 Sep 1813.
29	20	11473	**David Richie** .. 13 acs .. on Roaring R .. near mouth of Bowerman's Br .. 21 Sept 1813.
29	21	11476	**Elisha Dillard** .. Smith Co .. 26 acs .. waters of Caney Fk .. near NE corner of plantation **now occupied by William Petty** .. to incl sd plantation. 21 Sept 1813.
29	23	11486	**John R. Bryan** .. one ac .. Dry fork of Mill Cr .. to incl a salt lick .. at which **William Webb** made salt. 23 Sept 1813.
29	23	11487	**James R. Bryan** .. one ac .. Dry fork of Blackburn's fork of Roaring R .. to incl falls at the mouth of Aron Been's spring branch. 23 Sept 1813.
29	26	11498	**Heirs of John Lancaster** .. 100 acs .. Smith Co .. north side of Caney Fk. 25 Sept 1813.

Note: Other entries by heirs of John Lancaster add nothing new to history of the area i.e. no personal names mentioned as neighbors, etc.

29	29	11511	**John Young** .. 2 acs .. Pigeon Roost Cr .. adj 70-ac sur .. name of Thomas Bounds & Thomas Lovelady. 27 Sept 1813.
29	33	11528	**John Payton SR** .. 20 acs .. east side of Roaring R and on the south side of the branch **Daniel Shipman lives on.** 7 Oct 1813. Ephraim Payton, Loc.
29	40	11562	**Simeon Pennington** .. 20 acs .. headwaters of McFarlin's Cr .. near spring **now used by the Widow Combs** .. to incl sd spring. 6 Oct 1813.
29	48	11595	**Robert York** .. 5 acs .. north side of Cumberland .. 14 Oct 1813.
29	48	11596	**Marlin Young, John Osbourn & Aron Osbourn** .. 2 acs .. waters of Trace Cr .. to incl where the sd **Osbourns are now digging.** 14 Oct 1813.
29	48	11597	**Robert Elam** .. 20 acs .. west fork of Roaring R .. to incl improvement **where sd Elam now lives.** 14 Oct 1813.
29	48	11598	**William Crocker** .. 7 acs .. Morrison's Cr of Roaring R .. to incl William Hale's Sugar Camp. 14 Oct 1813. Berket Kinnard, Loc.

29	50	11605	**William Gray** .. 10 acs .. Roaring R .. adj land sd **Gray now lives on** .. 18 Oct 1813.
29	50	11607	**James Gray** .. 4 acs .. long br of Roaring R .. to incl an improvement made by **Jeremiah Brown.** 18 Oct 1813.
29	65	11673	**Robert White** .. one ac .. east fork of Lock's branch .. 30 Oct 1813.
29	66	11674	**John Murrey & John C. McLemore** .. 100 acs .. on the dividing ridge between Webster's Cr and Lock's branch .. adj Ezra Bushnell's 10-ac entry which incls his salt petre cave .. 30 Oct 1813.
29	66	11675	**Thomas Gillihan** .. 11 acs .. waters of Rock Spring Cr .. 3 poles west from branch that runs down by Shadrach Bridges' .. 30 Oct 1813.
29	66	11676	**George Collum** 10 acs .. Smith Co .. waters of Rock Spring Cr .. adj his own. 30 Oct 1813.
29	67	11681	**John C. McLemore** 10 acs .. Sadler's Sugar Camp branch of Brimstone Cr .. adj William and Edward Kirkpatrick .. 30 Oct 1813.
29	67	11682	**Ezra Bushnell** .. 20 acs .. Spring Cr waters of Roaring R .. including the falls. 30 Oct 1813.
29	68	11683	**Ezra Bushnell** .. 10 acs on Cumberland R .. the Island where **Simpson's floating mill formerly stood** .. below mouth of Jennings Cr .. 30 Oct 1813.
29	68	11684	**Ezra Bushnell** .. north side of Roaring R .. 5 acs .. on Asa Linn's branch .. to incl salt petre cave lately found by Daniel Shipman about 200 yards below John Shankle's Cave. 30 Oct 1813.
29	68	11685	**Ezra Bushnell** .. 2 acs .. north side of Cumberland .. adj Wilson & Lee .. 30 Oct 1813.
29	68	11686	**Daniel Shipman** .. 5 acs .. north side of Cumberland on Rutledge's branch .. adj Samuel Bradcut's line .. 30 Oct 1813.
29	68	11687	**James Whitson** .. 50 acs .. on Cane Cr .. adj James Whitson SR .. adj James Carter .. 1 Nov 1813.
29	71	11700	**Jacob Halfacre** .. 6 acs .. Morrison's Cr .. to incl his sugar camp. 2 Nov 1813.
29	74	11711	**James Butler & Abram Swagerty** .. 4 acs .. south side of Cumberland .. branch known as Hill's branch .. the Royal Cave .. 4 Nov 1813.

29	74	11712	**James Butler and Samuel Kirkpatrick** .. 2 acs .. on the Lick fork of Webster's Cr .. 5 Nov 1813.
29	74	11713	**Samuel Kirkpatrick & James Butler** .. 2 acs .. dry fork of Brimstone Cr .. to incl cave found by sd Kirkpatrick & Butler. 5 Nov 1813.
29	76	11721	**John Payton SR** .. 20 acs .. Lick branch of Roaring R .. near Luke Mayfield's .. 6 Nov 1813.
29	76	11724	**Archibald Scaggs** .. 20 acs .. north side of Cumberland on Indian Cr .. mouth of Mill Br .. 9 Nov 1813. (This entry is very legibly "Scaggs" in one place and "Skaggs" in another. It is indexed "Scruggs.")
29	76	11727	**John Rogers** .. 1-1/2 acs .. Hill's branch .. to incl mouths of two salt petre caves lately found by Benjamin Stacy and worked at by sd Stacy & Weaver .. 10 Nov 1813.
29	83	11753	**Yelvaton Nevell** .. 5 acs .. Smith's fork of Jennings Cr .. adj his own .. to incl the Big Spring. 17 Nov 1813.
29	83	11754	**John Williams** .. one ac .. branch of Roaring R .. south side of an old 3-notched road .. 17 Nov 1813.
29	83	11755	**John Williams** .. 2 acs .. waters of Sadler's Sugar Camp branch of Brimstone Cr .. 1/2 mile from Kirkpatrick's salt petre works. 17 Nov 1813.
29	83	11756	**John Williams** .. one ac .. Lick branch of Brimstone Cr .. 1/2 mile of Carlisle's .. 17 Nov 1813.
29	83	11757	**John Williams** .. one ac .. Lick branch of Brimstone Cr .. near Carlisle's .. 17 Nov 1813.
29	83	11758	**John Williams** .. Ditto.
29	83	11759, 11760,11761,	**John Williams** .. Ditto.
29	84	11762	**Elijah Denton** .. White Co .. 6 acs .. waters of Caney Fk .. Beg at a post oak on east boundary of his survey **whereon he lives** .. 17 Nov 1813.
29	85	11763	**Richard Lock & Silvanus Fowler** .. 4 ac .. S side of Cumberland .. to incl cave .. formerly occupied by Silvanus Fowler opposite Amos Kirkpatrick .. 17 Nov 1813.
29	90	11786	**Sampson Bridges** .. 1/2 ac .. West fork of Lick branch of Roaring R .. 25 Nov 1813.
29	90	11787	**Sampson Bridges** .. Ditto. 26 Nov 1813.

29	93	11799	**Ezra Bushnell** .. 5 acs .. second branch that puts into Cumberland R below Webster's Cr .. 30 Nov 1813.
29	93	11800	**Ezra Bushnell, John Murrey & John C. McLemore** .. 10 acs .. waters of Jennings Cr .. below Samuel Dixon's. 30 Nov 1813.
29	94	11801	**Ezra Bushnell, John Murrey & John C. McLemore** .. 5 acs .. waters of Webster's Cr .. near Lock's Cave .. known as Anderson's Old Cave .. where sd Anderson formerly made Petre. 30 Nov 1813.
29	94	11802	**Ezra Bushnell, John Murrey & John C. McLemore** .. 4 acs .. on the Ridge that divides Lock's Cave fork of Webster's Cr from the main fork .. to incl mouth of cave which Daniel Shipman and sd Bushnell's negroes attempted to open in August last. 30 Nov 1813.
29	94	11804	**Nathaniel Wood** .. 10 acs .. waters of Brimstone Cr .. to incl improvement whereon **the Widow Duncan formerly lived.** 30 Nov 1813.
29	95	11805	**John C. McLemore** .. 5 acs .. Rutledge's Cr of Roaring R about half a mile above Hardy Allerd's .. 30 Nov 1813.
29	95	11807	**Birket Kinnard** .. 20 acs .. Blackburn's fork of Roaring R .. near Benjamin Blackburn's 134-ac tract .. 30 Nov 1813.
29	95	11808	**Kinchen Pippen** .. 10 acs .. east side of Roaring R .. to incl **where John Finn lives.** 30 Nov 1813.
29	97	11817	**John Petty** .. 6 acs .. head waters of Big Br .. to incl spring and improvement made by John A. Slinger. 3 Dec 1813.
29	98	11818	**Josiah Conn** .. 10 acs .. White Co.. waters of Caney Fk .. between James Moore's and Abram Denton's .. 4 Dec 1813. Geo. Sugg, Loc.
29	98	11819	**Samuel Moore** .. 21 acs .. Pigeon Roost Cr of Falling water of Caney Fk .. to incl house, spring and improvement **where sd Moore now lives.** 6 Dec 1813.
29	98	11821	**William Ridge** .. 20 acs .. between Hutchins Cr & Pigeon Roost Cr .. about 1/4 mile west from Samuel Moore's ..6 Dec 1813.
29	103	11839	**Samuel Cunningham** .. 10 acs .. on War Trace Cr .. adj Yancy Thornton .. 7 Dec 1813.
29	105	11850	**Henry West** .. 10 acs .. waters of Brimstone Cr .. to incl house, spring and .. improvement **whereon sd West now lives.** 9 Dec 1813.

29	105	11851	**John Watson** .. 2 acs .. on the ridge between Cumberland and Barron R .. adj Little Berry Moore's spring .. to incl sd spring and house .. **whereon sd Moore now lives. 10 Dec 1813.**
29	106	11852	**Joseph Whitney** .. 10 acs .. waters of Knob Cr .. road leading from Bennett's Ferry to Glasgow .. north of James McColgin's south boundary .. tract **whereon sd Whitney now lives** .. including sd **Whitney's blacksmith's shop.** 10 Dec 1813.
29	106	11854	**Joseph Whitney** .. 6 acs .. waters of Brimstone Cr .. Beg at a beech near **Leonard Huff's spring** .. to incl sd spring and the house and .. improvement **whereon sd Huff now lives.** 10 Dec 1813.
29	108	11863	**Levin Dilling** .. 2-1/2 acs .. waters of Flynn's Cr .. on Thompson's branch on south side of the ridge .. to incl an improvement made by Peter Rust. 15 Dec 1813. Levin Dilling, Loc.
29	108	11864	**Agnes Thompson** .. 7-1/2 acs .. waters of Flynn's Cr on Thompson's Br .. to incl improvement known as .. Rush's improvement. 15 Dec 1813.
29	109	11866	**Thomas Shute** .. 100 acs .. Smith Co .. east side of Caney Fk .. near lower end of first big bottom above Lancaster's ferry .. called Pigeon Roost bottom .. mouth of a small branch near the upper end of a bluff .. up meanders of sd river .. 15 Dec 1813. Survey rtd 30 Apr 1814 by James Roulston, DS.
29	109	11867	**Thomas Shute** .. 206 acs .. Smith Co .. east side of Caney Fk .. upper corner of his 100-ac entry .. up the meanders of sd river including a house and small plantation near a spring in the river bank above the mouth of a little cr .. 15 Dec 1813.
29	114	11889	**William Ragland** .. 30 acs .. Pigeon Roost Cr .. Thomas Ridge's Corner on the military line .. 22 Dec 1813.
29	114	11890	**William G. Buller** .. 15 acs .. waters of Hutching's Cr .. Asael Buller's corner of his 26-ac entry .. 22 Dec 1813.
29	114	11891	**William G. Buller** .. 20 acs .. Hutching's Cr .. Asael Buller's corner .. 22 Dec 1813.
29	119	11917	**James Young** .. 10 acs .. waters of War Trace Cr .. near a small improvement **whereon Mrs. Parrott now lives** .. 29 Dec 1813.
29	119	11918	**James Young** .. 15 acs .. waters of War Trace .. adj

William Thomas's south east corner of his tract **whereon he now lives** .. being northwest corner of Samuel Cunningham's entry of 10 acs .. 29 Dec 1813.

29　119　11919　**James Young** .. waters of War Trace .. where Selby Harney's west boundary of 7,200-ac survey crosses sd creek .. 29 Dec 1813.

29　124　11942　**Nathaniel Moore** .. 25 acs .. near line between Jackson and Smith Cos .. south side of Cumberland R .. head of west fork of Indian Cr .. to incl sd Moore's spring and improvement. 1 Jan 1814.

29　124　11945　**James Wommack** ase of **Elisha Dillard** .. 50 acs .. line dividing Smith and Jackson Cos .. south side of Cumberland .. west fork of Indian Cr .. adj 640-ac tract of Daniel Wilburn's where the line of Lee Sullivan's 640-ac tract intersects .. 1 Jan 1814. James Wommack, Loc. Survey rtd 14 Aug 1814 by James Roulston, DS.

29　128　11964　**Benjamin Casen** .. 5 acs .. waters of Henley's Cr .. north side of Cumberland .. to incl house and improvement **where William Casen now lives.** 6 Jan 1814. James D. Henley, Loc.

29　128　11965　**Ezra Bushnell** .. 50 acs .. south side of Cumberland .. 3 or 4 miles above mouth of Roaring R .. 6 Jan 1814.

29　128　11966　**Henry Proctor** .. 12-1/2 acs.. north side of Cumberland .. first creek below Jennings Cr .. adj survey in name of Gen. L. Nolen .. Richard Smith's line .. 6 Jan 1814.

29　129　11967　**Elijah Stoner** .. 70 acs .. first branch that runs into Roaring R above mouth of sd river .. to incl an old cabin known as Shaw's Old Cabin .. 6 Jan 1814.

29　129　11968　**David Heddy** .. 5-1/2 acs .. S side of Roaring R .. Aron's branch .. to incl where **sd Heddy is now about building a house and has part of his logs cut.** 6 Jan 1814.

29　129　11969　**David Heddy** .. 10 acs .. south side of Roaring R .. forks of Aaron's branch .. including a Sugar Camp formerly worked by John Stafford. 6 Jan 1814.

29　129　11970　**John Proctor** .. 7 acs .. waters of first creek below mouth of Jennings Cr .. north side of Cumberland .. to incl part of sd Proctor's improvement. 6 Jan 1814.

29　133　11990　**Edward Lax** .. 4 acs .. dry fork of Martin's Cr .. in the hollow above John Martin's 15 acs. 10 Jan 1814.

29　133　11991　**Edward Lax** .. 5 acs .. waters of dry fork of Martin's

Cr .. Beg at a sugar tree running east then south .. so as to incl **William Huff's Sugar Camp in the dark Cave.** 10 Jan 1814. John Petty, Loc. (No indication of a survey.)

29	133	11992	**John Ragland** .. 4 acs .. dividing ridge between Flynn's and Martin's Crs .. to incl house .. whereon **sd Ragland now lives.** 10 Jan 1814.
29	135	12003	**George Templeton** .. 3 acs .. White Co .. W end of **Gum Spring Mountain** .. to incl house and improvement **whereon James Templeton now lives.** 12 Jan 1814.
29	137	12011	**Samuel Hunter** .. 3 acs .. waters of Pigeon Roost Cr .. sd Hunter's line .. to incl Hunter's peach orchard where **he now lives. 13 Jan 1814.**
29	137	12012	**Thomas Phillips** .. 21 acs .. White Co formerly Jackson .. waters of Pigeon Roost Cr .. first hollow below **where James Young now lives** .. 13 Jan 1814.
29	142	12041	**George Taylor** .. 10 acs .. first creek below Jennings Cr .. to incl the improvement **whereon he now lives.** 20 Jan 1814.
29	143	12051	**Isaac Pearce & Robert D. Pearce** .. 223 acs .. on Blackburn's fork .. 22 Jan 1814.
29	145	12067	**William Ridge** .. 20 acs .. White Co .. waters of Cane Cr .. to incl 2 saplings between Abner Norris and Reuben Purkins. 27 Jan 1814.
29	145	12068	**David Griffith** .. 10 acs .. Pine Lick fork of Jennings Cr .. to incl Bennet Lane's improvement. 28 Jan 1814.
29	145	12069	**Moses Smith** .. 10 acs .. Jennings Cr .. adj boundary of heirs of John Burress .. adj Jones Griffith's survey .. 28 Jan 1814.
29	147	12092	**James Rankin** .. 7 acs .. on Roaring R .. 3 Feb 1814.
29	149	12106	**William Lock** .. 3 acs .. south side of Cumberland .. 4 Feb 1814.
29	152	12132	**Abel Hutson** .. 25 acs .. White Co .. adj John Templeton .. 8 Feb 1814.
29	157	12168	**William Rutledge** .. 10 acs .. Blackburn's fork. to incl sd Rutledge's improvement where he is **now about to settle.** 12 Feb 1814.
29	157	12169	**William Rutledge** .. 10 acs .. Blackburn's fork .. to incl improvement **whereon Hardy Alland (?) now lives.** 12 Feb 1814.

29	160	12195	**William Lock** .. one ac .. Corner to William Walters' survey .. above where Roaring R forms junction with Cumberland .. to incl sd point. 15 Feb 1814.
29	161	12203	**James Young** .. 20 acs .. waters of War Trace .. adj his own .. to incl the improvement whereon **Cornelius Carver now lives.** 16 Feb 1814.
29	161	12205	**James Young** .. 10 acs .. branch of War Trace .. east of house **where James Ray now lives** .. 16 Feb 1814.
29	162	12206	**Matthias Hutson** .. 18 acs .. White Co .. adj survey in name of John Templeton. 17 Feb 1814.
29	166	12238, 12239, 12240, 12241	**Gabriel Benson** makes entries .. county not identified, but they are on Leeper's Lick Cr of Duck R. **Asa Shute** is Locator. 1814.
29	166	12242	**Edward Kirkpatrick & John Ryal SR** .. 2 acs .. dry fork of Brimstone Cr .. Royal's Cave. 23 Feb 1814.
29	166	12244	**John Moore** .. 20 acs .. Caney Cr .. 23 Feb 1814.
29	171	12282	**Job Morgan** .. 10 acs .. Spring Cr of Roaring R .. adj James Bedford .. 28 Feb 1814.
29	171	12283	**Job Morgan** .. 2 acs .. Spring Cr of Roaring R .. corner of tract that Jess Jones sold to John McDannel JR .. adj James Bedford .. 28 Feb 1814.
29	172	12284	**Job Morgan** .. 10 acs .. Spring Cr of Roaring R .. Ditto. 28 Feb 1814.
29	173	12293	**Simeon Putman** .. 3 acs .. west side of Lacey's branch .. near Putman's old cave .. 1 Mar 1814.
29	173	12294	**Andrew Cope** .. 39 acs .. White Co .. on top of **the Gum Spring Mountain** .. adj Cope's .. 1 Mar 1814.
29	173	12297	**Ezra Bushnell, John Murrey, Notley Wornell & John C. McLemore** .. 4 acs .. Crib Hollow waters of Roaring R .. to incl mouth of cave lately found by Wornell .. near cave now worked by John Payton SR. 2 Mar 1814.
29	179	12336	**Samuel Hodge** .. 46 acs .. Line Cr to incl improvement **where Thomas Wood now lives.** 12 Mar 1814.
29	180	12345	**Joshua Gann** .. 30 acs .. east fork of Mine Lick .. including improvement **whereon sd Gann now lives.** 14 Mar 1814.
29	180	12346	**John Payton SR** .. 39 acs .. Lick branch of Crib Hollow of Roaring R .. 14 Mar 1814.

29 187 12405 **George Skiles** .. 20 acs .. Rock Spring Valley .. 23 Mar 1814.

29 188 12406 **William Gray** .. 30 acs .. Cameron's branch of Roaring R .. adj John McGee .. to incl an improvement where **Thomas Butler now lives.** 23 Mar 1814.

29 188 12407 **Luke Mayfield & William Gray** .. 2 acs .. Crib branch of Roaring R .. to incl cave found by sd Mayfield .. 23 Mar 1814.

29 197 12481 **James Roulston** .. 20 acs .. on the road leading from Walton's Ferry to Southwest Point about 12 miles above sd Ferry .. to incl the improvement **whereon John Anderson now lives.** 8 Apr 1814.

29 198 12482 **James Vance** .. 10 acs .. waters of Indian Cr .. adj Vance's 10-ac survey which incls an old still house .. 8 Apr 1814.

29 199 12493 **Thomas Anderson** .. 10 acs .. West fork of Roaring R .. adj John Rutledge.. 12 Apr 1814.

29 199 12494 **Thomas Anderson** .. 10 acs .. 12 Apr 1814.

29 199 12495 **John Rutledge** .. 15 acs .. Blackburn's Fk .. to incl sd Rutledge's pond field. 12 Apr 1814.

What's a pond field?

29 203 12525 **Robert White** .. 18 acs .. waters of War Trace .. adj Samuel Parker .. 19 Apr 1814.

29 204 12532 **William Stafford** .. 5 acs .. adj his own. 22 Apr 1814.

29 205 12539 **Joseph Wright** .. 7 acs .. Indian Cr .. to incl improvement and spring **where John Rogers formerly lived.** 25 Apr 1814.

There is no clue in the entry as to which Indian Cr -- except it was in Jackson Co. Other entries for Wright and Rogers seem to indicate it was N of Cumberland.

29 205 12540 **James R. Bryan** .. one ac .. Brimstone Cr .. 25 Apr 1814.

29 205 12541 **James R. Bryan** .. one ac .. right hand fork of Jennings Cr .. near an old Indian grave .. 25 Apr 1814.

29 209 12563 **Duke Young** .. 2 acs .. White Co .. on Pigeon Roost Cr of Falling Water .. adj John Young .. to incl **where Duke Young now lives.** 28 Apr 1814.

29	214	12600	**James Vinson** .. 5 acs .. waters of dry fork of Martin's Cr in a hollow called The Valley adj John Petty's 10-ac entry **on which he lives.** 7 May 1814.
29	214	12601	**James Vinson** .. 10 acs .. head waters of dry fork of Martin's Cr .. to incl small spring about 1/4 mile west from **where sd Vinson lives.** 7 May 1814.
29	215	12608	**Robert B. Mitchell** .. 10 acs .. Brimstone Cr .. nearly opposite mouth of Sadler's Sugar Camp branch .. 10 May 1814.
29	218	12627	**William Ridge** .. 50 acs .. White Co .. mouth of Hutchins Cr .. adj John Crook .. Bounds and Lovelady's. 14 May 1814.
29	220	12637	**Thomas Shute** .. 260 acs .. Smith Co .. east side of Caney Fk .. adj his own and including house & plantation near to a spring in the river bank .. 16 May 1814.
29	221	12645	**Jeremiah Denton** .. 93 acs .. White Co .. Caney Fk .. adj his own .. John Miller. 17 May 1814.
29	221	12646	**Jeremiah Denton** .. 29 acs .. White Co .. Caney Fk .. adj his own .. 17 May 1814.
29	222	12650	**Sarah Twitty** .. 8 acs .. Smith's Fk of Jenning's Cr .. adj field cleared by Samuel Holcum .. 17 May 1814.
29	222	12651	**William Twitty** .. 4 acs .. North fork of Indian Cr .. to incl improvement made by James Skaggs. 17 May 1814.
29	222	12652	**William Twitty** .. 6 acs .. North Fk of Indian Cr .. adj Matthias Sweasy .. an improvement made by Sweasy. 17 May 1814.
29	225	12672	**John Bussell** .. ase of Thomas Dillon .. 16 acs .. White Co .. Caney Fk .. S side of road leading from White Plains to Rock Island .. 21 May 1814. **Samuel Bellah, Loc.**
29	225	12673	**John Bussell** .. ase of Thomas Dillon .. 15 acs .. White Co .. south side of Falling Water .. 21 May 1814. **Samuel Bellah, Loc.**
29	225	12674	and 12675 were also for John Bussell ase of Thomas Dillon but 12674 was .. 20 acs ..Smith Co .. east side of Caney Fk .. east side of Looney's branch .. to incl improvement **where ___ Smith now lives.** No. 12675 was in **Jackson Co** .. 25 acs .. Woolf pen branch of **dry fork of Martin's Cr** to incl improvement **where William Hardcastle now lives.** 21 May 1814. For both of these entries, **Samuel Bellah** was locator.

29	228	12687	**Aron Lambert** .. 128 acs .. south side of Cumberland .. adj his own and Hickman. 24 May 1814.
29	232	12714	**Abraham Myers** .. 6 acs .. Blackburn's fork .. mouth of Dry Cr .. adj John Rutledge .. 31 May 1814.
29	237	12741	**Joseph Whitney** .. 10 acs .. waters of Knob Cr .. near road leading from Bennett's Ferry to Glasgow .. adj James McColgan's .. the tract **whereon sd Whitney now lives** .. including sd Blacksmith's shop. 6 June 1814. (Does not say whose blacksmith's shop, but see Entries 11852 and 11854.)
29	237	12742	**Joseph Whitney** .. 6 acs .. waters of Brimstone Cr .. near Leonard Huff's Spring .. to incl sd spring and house .. improvement **where sd Huff now lives**. 6 June 1814.

Entries 12741 and 12742 were surveyed by John Murrey, and Sur rtd 22 Aug 1814.

29	237	12744	**Matthias Swezea** .. 5 acs .. waters of Indian Cr north side of Cumberland .. 7 June 1814.
29	238	12745	**Matthias Swezea** .. 5 acs .. North side of Cumberland .. improvement made by sd Swezea. 7 June 1814.
29	245	12788	**James Jones** .. 8 acs .. South side of Cumberland .. first branch on east side of Doe Cr .. whereon **John D. Brooks now lives** .. 17 June 1814.
29	248	12811	**Henry Moirs** .. 5 acs .. waters of Roaring R .. above **Widow Scagg's field**. 25 June 1814.
29	248	12812	**William Gray** .. 10 acs .. waters of Roaring R .. adj William Stafford .. Rutherford's branch .. to incl improvement **where John Parker now lives**. 25 June 1814.
29	250	12823	**Redmond D. Barry** .. 200 acs .. on Martin's Cr .. adj land on which William Anderson now lives .. to incl Edward Hogan's improvements and still house .. 27 June 1814.
29	251	12825	**Redmond D. Barry** .. 100 acs .. south side of Cumberland on Martin's Cr .. adj his own .. 28 Jan 1814.
29	252	12831	**Samuel Hodge** .. 14 acs .. Line Cr .. adj Hodge. 29 June 1814.
29	259	12874	**Samuel Mansell** .. 3 acs .. right hand fork of Martin's Cr .. to incl small improvement made by John Griffith. 9 July 1814.

29 259 12875 **Archibald McKaughan** .. 10 acs .. on Doe Cr .. adj Sampson Williams .. 9 July 1814.

29 259 12876 **Archibald McKaughn** .. 10 acs .. on Doe Cr .. adj Sampson Williams .. to incl sd McKaughan's field. 9 July 1814.

29 262 12888 **John Williams** .. 4 acs .. south side of Cumberland.. Penitentiary Fk of Hill's branch .. to incl cave opened by sd Williams. 12 July 1814.

29 262 12889 **John Williams** .. Ditto. 12 July 1814.

29 265 12906 **William Brassel** .. 14 acs .. Pine lick fork of Jennings Cr .. adj his own .,. 15 July 1814.

29 267 12917 **James Kerr** .. 15 acs .. waters of Hurricane Cr of Caney Fk .. to incl spring now made use of by sd Kerr. 20 July 1814.

29 269 12927 **Samuel Jenkins** .. 10 acs .. Little Trace Cr .. to incl first improvement & spring on sd cr above where **Raysor now lives**. 22 July 1814.

29 273 12949 **Daniel Keith** .. 5 acs .. waters of Little Trace of Big Barren R .. to incl sd **Keith's house, barn & spring**. 25 July 1814.

29 275 12963 **Moses Smith** .. 20 acs .. first small branch north side of Cumberland below mouth of Hensley's Cr .. adj Redmund D. Barry .. to incl improvement **where Robert Cole now lives**. 27 July 1814.

29 282 13002 **John Gresham** .. 7 acs .. near line between Jackson and White Cos on Hurricane Cr of Caney fork .. to incl Richard Moss' improvement. 4 Aug 1814.

29 285 13019 **John Butler** .. 10 acs .. west fork of Mill Cr .. adj Joseph Martin .. adj George Alexander. 5 Aug 1814.

29 285 13020 **Stephen Langford** .. 10 acs .. west fork of Mill Cr .. adj his own .. 5 Aug 1814.

29 287 13031 **Isaac Clark** .. 12 acs .. waters of Mine Lick Cr .. 8 Aug 1814.

29 290 13049 **Andrew Ferrell** .. 25 acs .. Indian Cr of Cumberland .. adj Mathew Cowan **where he now lives** .. 10 Aug 1814.

29 295 13076 **John Hines** .. 20 acs .. White Co .. waters of Taylor's Mill Cr .. adj Jesse Williams tract **where he now lives** .. 15 Aug 1814.

29 296 13082 **Levi Bozarth** .. 41 acs .. East fork of Mine Lick Cr ..

west side of cr .. to incl John Gann's SR's plantation **where sd Gann now lives** .. 15 Aug 1814.

29 301 13113 **William Rowland** .. 6 acs .. Caney Fk .. 20 feet below a spring .. to incl spring and cabin about a half mile **south of where sd Rowland lives.** 17 Aug 1814.

29 304 13129 **Levi Greathouse** .. 14 acs .. waters of Brimstone Cr .. adj Henry West .. 19 Aug 1814.

29 305 13130 **Henry West** .. 10 acs .. Brimstone Cr .. to incl house, spring and improvement where **sd West now lives.** 19 Aug 1814.

29 305 13131 **George Hays** .. 10 acs .. north side of Cumberland .. mouth of Dry creek adj John Black .. 19 Aug 1814.

29 313 13173 **John Reddick** .. 25 acs .. Young's fork of Indian Cr .. 22 Aug 1814.

29 313 13174 **John Reddick** .. 24 acs .. waters of Indian Cr .. adj Andrew Ferrell .. adj McKindley .. 22 Aug 1814.

29 313 13175 **Robert McKindley** .. 24 acs .. waters of Indian Cr .. adj Andrew Ferrell .. adj his own. 22 Aug 1814.

29 313 13176 **Robert McKindley** .. 14 acs .. Indian Cr adj his own ... 22 Aug 1814.

29 318 13197 **Elijah Stone** .. 20 acs .. Roaring R .. to incl .. Shaw's Old Cabin. 24 Aug 1814.

29 320 13211 **James McKinney** .. 4 acs .. in Buffalo Valley of Indian Cr .. Beg in the middle of sd McKinney's turnip patch .. 24 Aug 26, 1814.

29 321 13219 **James Roulston** .. 50 acs on a branch of Rock Spring Cr .. to incl .. **where Jacob Fanny now lives.** 26 Aug 1814.

29 322 13222 **Samuel Roulston** .. 49 acs .. Rock Spring Cr **where Jacob Fanny now lives** adj James Roulston's entry of 50 acs .. 27 Aug 1814. James Roulston, Loc.

29 322 13224 **Elijah Denton** .. White Co .. 6 acs on waters of Caney fork .. east of his survey **where he lives** .. 27 Aug 1814. Jeremiah Denton, Loc.

29 324 13233 **William Miller** .. 16 acs .. waters of Doe Cr .. adj Nicholas Hail .. to incl .. **where sd Miller now lives.** 27 Aug 1814.

29 324 13234 **John Lee** .. 6 acs .. on the ridge between McFarland's Cr and Proctor's Cr .. to incl .. **whereon sd Lee now**

lives. 27 Aug 1814.

29 329 13263 **John Rutledge** .. 30 acs .. Roaring R .. adj tract John Shankle bought from George Rayman & James Cook. 30 Aug 1814.

29 329 13264 **Alexander Rutledge** .. 15 acs .. waters of Roaring R .. to incl .. **where Molly Scaggs now lives.** 30 Aug 1814.

29 330 13266 **Alexander Rutledge** .. 15 acs .. Roaring R .. to incl house and field **where Thomas Gore now lives.** 30 Aug 1814.

29 330 13269 **Henry Brewer** .. 20 acs .. Mine Lick Cr .. to incl improvement made by David Miller. 31 Aug 1814.

29 330 13270 **John Crawford** .. 5 acs .. Roaring R .. adj William Gray .. to incl cabin **Widow Edwards now lives.** 31 Aug 1814.

29 332 13281 **Christian Myers** .. 30 acs .. Roaring R .. west side of Ewing's hollow near cabin **where Mrs. Goforth formerly lived** ..incl sd cabin and cabbins where **the Franklins formerly lived.** 1 Sept 1814.

29 362 13452 **Yancy Thornton** .. 46 acs .. Line Cr to incl .. **where Thomas Wood formerly lived.** 29 Sept 1814.

29 362 13453 **Yancy Thornton** .. 8 acs .. Line Cr .. adj his own .. to incl .. **where James W. Curtis now lives.** 29 Sept 1814.

29 370 13493 **Samuel Hodge** .. 114 acs .. Line Cr .. incl Thomas Wood's improvement. 6 Oct 1814.

29 370 13494 **Samuel Hodge** .. Line Cr .. adj Yancy Thornton .. 6 Oct 1814.

29 370 13495 **Samuel Hodge** .. 46 acs .. Line Cr .. adj Yancy Thornton. 6 Oct 1814.

29 373 13513 **Redmond D. Barry** .. 100 acs .. north side of Cumberland on Jennings Cr .. to incl improvement & very large spring formerly occupied by ____Rotten & **now by Hardy Pursley.** 10 Oct 1814.

29 373 13514 **Redmond D. Barry** .. north side of Cumberland .. Jennings Cr .. near field & improvement made by Fowlett (?) Pruitt .. to incl improvement made by Chisolm .. 10 Oct 1814.

29 375 13522 **James W. Smith** .. 3 acs .. south side of Cumberland .. headwaters of Martin's Cr .. 10 Oct 1814.

29 376 13528 **Adams C. Hamilton** .. 5 acs .. on Knob Cr .. **where Phillip Overturf now lives** .. 10 Oct 1814.

29 377   13536   **Benjamin Blackburn** .. 50 acs .. west fork of Roaring R .. adj Benjamin Blackburn SR .. below David Finn .. to incl **where David Finn formerly lived.** 11 Oct 1814.

BK	PG	NUMBER	DESCRIPTION

29 382 13561 **Benjamin Farmer** .. 10 acs .. waters of Proctor's Cr .. adj Zedekiah Woods .. 14 Oct 1814.

29 382 13562 **Benjamin Farmer** .. 8 acs .. waters of Proctor's Cr .. adj Zedekiah Woods .. adj Cantrell .. 14 Oct 1814.

29 384 13572 **William Wood** .. 56 acs .. west fork of Roaring R including place & improvement **where Nimrod Dotson (Dodson?) lately lived where sd Woods now lives** .. 15 Oct 1815.

29 387 13587 **Henry Brewer** .. 20 acs .. on Mine Lick Cr .. to incl improvement **where Job Franklin's Widow now lives**. 17 Oct 1814.

29 389 13599 **Samuel Hodge** .. 186 acs .. waters of Line Cr .. adj Patrick McGibbony .. to incl improvements made by Thomas Wood and a Mr. Ellis .. 19 Oct 1814.

29 390 13602 **James Clements** .. 10 acs .. Spring fork of Martin's Cr .. including Elijah Manner's (Mannear?) improvement 20 Oct 1814.

29 390 13603 **James Clemmons** .. 10 acs .. Spring fork of Martin's Cr .. to incl improvement where **sd Clemmons now lives**. 20 Oct 1814.

James Clements and James Clemmons? Both these entries were as assignee of Joseph Coleman, Certificate No. 1082. See Entries in Book 27 numbered 8585, 8586, 8587. This strengthens the knot between folks on Brimstone - Knob Crs and Martin's Cr.

29 391 13609 **William G. Buller** .. 10 acs .. Roaring R .. to incl improvement **where Richard Finn now lives**. 21 Oct 1814. A. Hollingsworth, Loc.

29 391 13610 **William G. Buller** .. 10 acs .. Cane Cr of the Caney Fk .. to incl improvement **where John Tackett formerly lived**. 21 Oct 1814.

29 391 13611 **William G. Buller** .. 5 acs .. Cane Cr of Caney Fk .. to incl improvement **where John W. Crosweight formerly lived**. 21 Oct 1814.

29 395 13630 **George Waddle** .. 60 acs .. on Mill Cr 1/4 mile above **Hamilton's old Mill** adj Joseph Martin's .. 24 Oct 1814.

29 395 13632 **Jeremiah Denton** .. White Co .. 80 acs .. south side of the **Gum Spring Mountain** .. 24 Oct 1814.

29 395 13633 **Jeremiah Denton** .. White Co .. 50 acs .. north side of Caney Fk .. adj his own. 24 Oct 1814.

29	396	13637	**Nathan Glover** .. one ac .. in Buffalo Valley .. near spring **where John Casey now lives** .. 25 Oct 1814.
29	397	13641	**James Vaulx** .. 122 acs .. on Jennings Cr .. adj Thomas Hutchison .. to incl Samuel Crabtree's improvement .. 26 Oct 1814.
29	398	13651	**Thomas Harbert & Matthew Clay** .. 10 acs .. waters of Mill Cr .. adj John Pierce .. 28 Oct 1814.
29	399	13652	**Thomas Harbert & Matthew Clay** .. 10 acs .. waters of Mill Cr .. adj their own .. 28 Oct 1814. Matthew Clay, Loc.
29	399	13653	**Thomas Harbert & Matthew Clay** .. 5 acs .. waters of Mill Cr .. 28 Oct 1814. Matthew Clay, Loc.
29	399	13654	**Thomas Harbert & Matthew Clay** .. 2 acs .. on Blackburn's Fk about one mile below **Bowen's Mill** .. 28 Oct 1814.
29	399	13655	**Thomas Harbert & Matthew Clay** .. 20 acs .. south side of main fork of Hopper's Cr .. 28 Oct 1814.
29	399	13656	**Thomas Harbert & Matthew Clay** .. Hopper's Cr adj their own. 28 Oct 1814.
29	400	13657	**Thomas Harbert & Matthew Clay** .. 10 acs .. Hopper's Cr adj their own. 28 Oct 1814.
29	400	13658	**David Young** .. 14 acs .. waters of Indian Cr .. adj his own **where he now lives** .. 28 Oct 1814.
29	400	13659	**Shadrach Bridges** .. 22 acs .. waters of Rock Spring Cr .. adj tract **sd Bridges now lives on** .. 28 Oct 1814.
29	403	13673	**John Jones** .. 5 acs .. Indian Cr of Caney Fk .. to incl an improvement made by Robert Cobb. 31 Oct 1814.
29	403	13675	**Joseph Williams** .. 20 acs .. White Co .. Pigeon Roost Cr **near the Widow Bullar's mill pond** .. to incl improvement made by Thomas Ridge. 31 Oct 1814.
29	404	13682	**Aaron Lambert** .. 52-1/2 acs .. south side of Cumberland .. adj his own .. adj Armstrong .. adj Hickman. 31 Oct 1814. Aaron Lambert SR, Loc.
29	405	13688	**David Johnson** .. 10 acs .. on Roaring R .. south bank .. adj track John Shankle bought of Cook .. 1 Nov 1814. David Johnson, Loc.
29	406	13692	**William Burns** .. 8 acs .. waters of Martin's Cr on the Big Br .. adj his own. 3 Nov 1814. Wm. Burns, Loc.

29 412 13720 **Alexander Aikman** .. 12 acs .. on the ridge between Woolf Cr & Buffalo Valley .. to incl spring & improvement **where sd Aikman formerly lived.** 7 Nov 1814. Alexander Aikman also made entry No. 13719 in Smith Co .. north side of Woolf Cr in the Sugar tree valley .. near old sugar camp made by H. Reynolds .. 7 Nov 1814.

29 412 13721 **Samuel Dixon** .. 12 acs .. east side of Jennings Cr .. adj Moses Smith .. adj John Burriss .. 7 Nov 1814.

29 420 13761 **Jeremiah Bush** .. 10 acs .. Dillard's Lick Log branch .. waters of Dillard's fork of Indian Cr .. to incl small improvement adj Bush's improvement **whereon he now lives** & line of sd Bush & William Cook .. 12 Nov 1814. James Wright, Loc.

29 420 13762 **Jeremiah Bush** .. 11 acs .. Dillard's Lick Log Br .. adj his own **whereon he now lives.** 12 Nov 1814.

29 422 13769 **Samuel Hodge** .. 50 acs .. waters of Line Cr .. adj his own. 12 Nov 1814.

29 426 13789 **John Plumley** .. 10 acs .. on Brimstone Cr .. to incl improvement **where John Dutton lives.** 14 Nov 1814. Thomas Button, Loc. (These two names, Dutton and Button, might indicate error. However, that is what the record says.)

29 428 13802 **Daniel Cherry** .. waters of Cub Run .. adj 1,000 acs granted to Tyrell & Lytle .. south from house **formerly occupied by William Shaw** .. to incl sd house. 14 Nov 1814. Daniel Cherry, Loc.

29 434 13837 **Fouchee Garner** .. one ac .. waters of Hutchins Cr .. about 200 yards below the road leading from Eli Young's to Buller's mill .. 16 Nov 1814.

29 435 13842 **Nicholas Hail** .. 20 acs .. Roaring R .. to incl improvement **where John Myers now lives.** 16 Nov 1814.

29 437 13852 **Thomas Anderson** .. 5 acs .. on Blackburn's fork of Roaring R .. 17 Nov 1814. Thomas Anderson, Loc.

29 437 13853 **Garland Anderson** .. 5 acs .. Blackburn's Fk .. mouth of Wilson's hollow .. 17 Nov 1814.

29 441 13869 **William McMurtry** .. 50 acs .. north side of Cumberland .. lower end of first cliff below mouth of Proctor's Cr .. adj Stephen Cantrell .. 19 Nov 1814. Martin McMurtry, Loc.

29 442 13878 **Joseph Jared** .. 8 acs .. on the ridge dividing waters

of Caney Fk & Cumberland .. adj tract **whereon sd Jared now lives** .. to incl a small field & peach orchard. 21 Nov 1814.

29 443 13881 **Emanuel Holmes** .. 24 acs .. waters of Brimstone Cr .. to incl house and plantation where **Samuel Meriday now lives** .. 21 Nov 1814. Em. Holmes, Loc.

29 443 13882 **Martin Jones** .. 10 acs .. on the Big Br of Martin's Cr .. to incl house and improvement where **sd Jones now lives.** 21 Nov 1814.

29 443 13883 **Martin Jones** .. 8 acs .. on Big Br of Martin's Cr .. to incl first improvement above mouth of sd branch. 21 Nov 1814. Martin Jones, Loc.

29 444 13889 **James Black** .. 20 acs .. north side of Cumberland on Black's Spring branch .. adj Edward Givins .. **on which John Black now lives** .. 21 Nov 1814. Em. Holmes, Loc.

29 444 13890 **James Bracken SR** .. 40 acs .. north side of Cumberland .. below mouth of Jennings Cr called Cub Cr formerly called Fisher's Cr .. 21 Nov 1814. Wm. Bracken, Loc.

29 445 13892 **James Bracken JR** .. 20 acs .. north side of Cumberland .. below mouth of Cub Cr .. 21 Nov 1814. Wm. Bracken, Loc.

29 447 13906 **John Gann** .. 30 acs .. south prong of Mine Lick Cr .. the plantation **whereon sd Gann now lives** .. 22 Nov 22 1814.

29 448 13907 **Sarah Twitty** .. 5 acs .. south fork of Jennings Cr .. adj Payton .. to incl improvement made by John Lee. 22 Nov 1814. John Twitty, Loc.

29 448 13909 **John McClure** .. 2 acs .. waters of Doe Cr .. to incl cave known as Haile's & Huffman's Cave. 22 Nov 1814. Thomas Mercer, Loc.

29 448 13910 **Bennet Jarvis** .. 5 acs .. north side of Cumberland .. to incl his spring & improvement. 22 Nov 1814.

29 450 13922 **James Taggart** .. 10 acs .. waters of Proctor's Cr .. adj his own .. **including sd Taggart's house.** 23 Nov 1814.

29 454 13940 **Edmund Jennings** .. 5 acs .. on the Big Br beginning on John Martin's beginning corner .. east with sd Martin's north boundary .. 24 Nov 1814. Edmund Jennings, Loc.

29 455 13944 **James Williams** .. 10 acs .. dry fork of Mill Cr .. adj John Baker that incls improvement **where Paul Anthony formerly lived** .. 25 Nov 1814.

29 456 13952 **Abraham Denton** .. 20 acs .. ridge between the headwaters of Brimstone Cr and waters of Barren R .. to incl house, spring, orchard .. **where sd Denton now lives.** 28 Nov 1814.

29 464 13993 **James Vaulx** .. 250 acs .. on Jennings Cr .. adj **where Thomas Hutcherson now lives** .. John Wilson's north boundary .. 2 Dec 1814.

29 465 13994 **James Vaulx** .. 19-3/4 acs .. east fork of Proctor's Cr .. adj 8-ac survey in name of John Taggart .. 2 Nov 1814.

29 465 13995 **James Vaulx** .. 11 acs .. east fork of Proctor's Cr .. adj John Taggart survey **on which Mayner lives .. to incl Mayner's mill** and improvement. 2 Dec 1814.

29 465 13998 **Enoch Carter** .. 10 acs .. on the Long Hollow of the Dry Fk of Martin's Cr .. adj entry in name of John Martin on the east boundary of a 640-ac tract granted to Sampson Williams .. 3 Dec 1814. Enoch Carter, Loc.

29 466 14003 **Nathaniel Mason** .. 10 acs .. Blackburn's fork of Roaring R .. to incl **where sd Mason now lives. 6 Dec 1814.**

29 467 14004 **Nathaniel Mason** .. 7 acs .. Blackburn's fork of Roaring R .. to incl sd Mason's field on the road leading from Edward Robertson's to James Bryant's. 6 Dec 1814.

29 467 14005 **David Loveall** .. 10 acs .. Blackburn's Fk .. to incl house & part of improvement **where sd Loveall now lives.** 6 Dec 1814.

29 470 14021 **Bartlett Gentry** .. 10 acs .. waters of Cane Cr .. to incl improvement made by Henry Brewer. 8 Dec 1814.

29 470 14022 **Goen Morgan** .. 25 acs .. on Mine Lick Cr .. to incl improvement **where George Sullivan now lives.** 8 Dec 1814. Robert Harris, Loc.

Additional notes to entry No. 14022, added later in the margin: Survey Ret'd. 16 May 1815. Then: "I, James Young, Sheriff of Jackson Co, do hereby transfer and assign over this entry to John Hensly having sold the same to him to satisfy a judgement that Robert Shadden obtained against Goen Morgan and Robert Harris in Circuit Court of Jackson Co, this 2nd May 1821. Signed James Young, Shff."

Then: "Made void by transfer of John Hensley attached to warrant 20 May 1824. John Lyon."

Many entries have additional information in their margins, but few are as complete as No. 14022.

29	482	14083	**James Vittito** .. 6 acs .. on the ridge between waters of Martin's and Flynn's Crs .. adj John Petty .. to incl improvement **where Ellis Payne formerly lived.** 19 Dec 1814. Enoch Carter, Loc.
29	482	14084	**Enoch Carter** .. 8 acs .. on the Dry Fk of Martin's Cr .. to incl **William Huff's old Sugar Camp in the dark Cave** .. 17 Dec 1814. Enoch Carter, Loc.
29	482	14087	**John Morrow** .. 46 acs .. an eastern branch of Brimstone Cr .. to incl improvement made by Charles & Reuben Dement. 17 Dec 1814.
29	485	14102	**Sterling May** .. 220 acs .. dividing ridge between Line Cr of Barren R and Brimstone Cr of Cumberland .. adj Edward Givins tract that **John Denton lives on** .. 19 Dec 1814.
29	486	14108	**Sarah Twitty** .. 5 acs .. south side of south fork of Jennings Cr .. adj Payton's survey **whereon Nevill & Hutchison now lives** .. 22 Dec 1814. John Murrey, Loc.
29	487	14115	**Sampson Williams** .. 299 acs .. on Martin's Cr bounded on the North by 640-ac tract granted to James Mulherin .. on the east by 640-ac tract granted to Stockley Donelson on which **William Anderson now lives** .. 23 Dec 1814.
29	488	14116	**Sampson Williams** .. 50 acs .. south side of Cumberland near head of a branch of Doe Cr .. adj tract **Nicholas Hail now lives on** .. 23 Dec 1814.
29	488	14117	**Sampson Williams** .. 23 acs .. including first island in Cumberland R above the mouth of Martin's Cr. 23 Dec 1814.
29	488	14119	**James Huddleston** .. 25 acs .. Cane Cr .. eastwardly from the house **now in the occupancy of sd Huddleston** .. to incl sd Huddleston's spring & improvement. 24 Dec 1814.
29	491	14134	**William Ridge** .. 30 acs .. on Mine Lick Cr .. to incl improvement made by Hubbard Brewer. 26 Dec 1814.
29	493	14147	**Moses Byers** .. 25 acs .. waters of Cane Cr .. adj Byers' 15-ac survey **where he now lives** .. 29 Dec 1814.
29	494	14153	**Charles Harvey** .. 50 acs .. Beg where the Walton Road crosses the west branch of Roaring R .. to incl the Stand and spring leased to James Harvey by John Haywood and **now occupied by sd Harvey's family.** 29 Dec 1814.
29	494	14154	**Tandy K. Witcher** .. 46 acs .. on Jennings Cr . adj

Stephen Maraign's .. 30 Dec 1814. Lacy Witcher, Loc.

29 495 14155 **Lacy Witcher** .. 20 acs .. on Ward's fork of Jennings Cr .. on Beckham's south boundary .. to incl Bailey's and Davis' improvements. 30 Dec 1814.

29 495 14157 **Samuel Hollinsworth** .. 6 acs .. East side of Caney Fk near line between White & Jackson Counties .. to incl spring and improvement where **Johnson Wommack now lives.** 30 Dec 1814.

29 497 14169 **James Watson** .. 8 acs .. west fork of Roaring R .. to incl .. **where sd Watson now lives.** 3 Jan 1815.

29 500 14187 **Alexander Irwin** .. 200 acs .. White Co .. Taylor's Cr .. 4 Jan 1815.

29 505 14217 **John Denton** .. headwaters of McFarland's Cr .. including Joshua Denton's improvement. 10 Jan 1815.

29 505 14218 **John Denton** .. 15 acs .. waters of Line Cr of Barren R .. tract sd Denton purchased of Wm. Givin & **on which he now lives** .. 10 Jan 1815.

29 506 14219 **Joseph Robertson** .. 25 acs .. waters of Barren R .. near spring made use of by sd Robertson .. to incl house, spring & improvement of sd Robertson. 10 Jan 1815.

29 506 14221 **James Carter** .. 2 acs .. on Mine lick Cr .. to incl a mill seat .. 10 Jan 1815.

29 508 14238 **John Brasel** .. 10 acs .. waters of Jennings Cr .. to incl Nathan Price's improvement in the Barrons. 13 Jan 1815.

29 511 14252 **Major Passons** .. 5 acs .. southeast side of Bear branch of Jennings Cr on or near John Wilson's east boundary .. to incl a spring and cabin that Richard Wilson built. 14 Jan 1815.

29 513 14261 **James Vettito** .. 6 acs .. on the ridge between waters of Martin's & Flynn's Cr .. in John Petty's west boundary .. to incl .. **where Ellis Payne formerly lived.** 16 Jan 1815. Enoch Carter, Loc.

29 513 14263 **James W. Hancock** .. 14 acs .. Rugle's branch of Cumberland R .. corner of the survey whereon **the widow Rugle formerly lived** .. 16 Jan 1815.

29 526 14337 **Heirs of Edwin Hickman** .. 320 acs .. north side of Cumberland .. near mouth of Samuel Kirkpatrick's spring branch .. 23 Jan 1815. Edwin Hickman, Loc.

29	527	14338	**Heirs of Edwin Hickman** .. Ditto.
29	530	14358	**John Wilson** .. 6 acs .. on Jennings Cr .. adj 640-ac tract granted to John Wilson & Abner Lee .. to incl a spring and improvement made by Richard Wilson. 30 Jan 1815.
29	537	14397	**Brice Collins** .. 25 acs .. north side of Cumberland .. bank of the river below mouth of Cub Cr .. adj Boulses (Bowles´ ?) corner .. 3 Feb 1815.
29	537	14398	**Brice Collins** .. north side of Cumberland .. adj Boules´s north boundary .. Cub Cr .. 3 Feb 1815.
29	538	14402	**John C. McLemore** .. 45 acs .. Blackburn´s fork of Roaring R .. 4 Feb 1815.
29	538	14403	**John Murrey & John C. McLemore** .. 100 acs .. south fork of dry fork of Hutchings fork of Mill Cr .. south of the Salt Lick on sd fork where Clay & Herbert are boring for salt water .. 4 Feb 1815.
29	538	14404	**John C. McLemore** .. 30 acs .. Pine Lick fork of Jennings Cr .. 4 Feb 1815.
29	542	14424	**John Butler** .. 10 acs .. Wet fork of Mill Cr .. adj Joseph Martin´s southeast corner .. joining George Alexander. 9 Feb 1815.
29	542	14425	**Stephen Langford** .. 10 acs .. Wet fork of Mill Cr .. adj his own. 9 Feb 1815.

BUILDING NEIGHBORHOODS
From
EARLY LAND RECORDS OF TENNESSEE
RG 50 SERIES 2 - LAND ENTRIES BOOK 30 - REEL 9
1ST SURVEYOR'S DISTRICT ENTRIES - JACKSON COUNTY FOLKS

BK	PG	NUMBER	DESCRIPTION
30	1	14484	**John McClure** .. 15 acs .. east side of Blackburn's Fork .. adj Nathan Haggard's 100-ac survey .. 14 Feb 1815. John Murrey, Loc.
30	1	14485	**John Murrey** .. 5 acs .. Anderson's branch of Blackburn's fork .. 14 Feb 1815.
30	1	14486	**John Murrey** .. 10 acs .. south fork of dry creek of Blackburn's fork .. adj his own and McLemore's .. 14 Feb 1815.
30	1	14487	**John Murrey** .. 20 acs .. south branch of Spring Cr called Woods' branch of Roaring R .. 14 Feb 1815.
30	2	14488	**John Murrey** .. 10 acs .. Roaring R near John McDaniel JR .. 14 Feb 1815.
30	2	14489	**John Murrey** .. 25 acs .. Blackburn's fork .. adj his own. 14 Feb 1815.
30	5	14511	**John Anderson** .. 50 acs .. White Co .. south of **640-ac Gum Spring tract** .. 17 Feb 1815. John Anderson, Loc.
30	6	14514	**James Carter** .. 2 acs .. on Martin's Cr .. northwest corner of tract **whereon William Anderson now lives** .. west with Charles Carter's line .. including Edward Hogan's improvement & still house. 17 Feb 1815. James Carter, Loc.
30	8	14529	**John McKinney** .. 20 acs .. Buffalo Valley .. to incl his improvement. 18 Feb 1815.
30	9	14534	**William Ridge** .. 12 acs .. waters of Mine Lick Cr .. to incl improvement where **Sally Womack used to live.** 18 Feb 1815.
30	9	14535	**William Ridge** .. 6 acs .. waters of Indian Cr .. adj David Womack's field .. to incl Womack's improvement. 18 Feb 1815.
30	10	14541	**William Molden** .. 16 acs .. on Trace Cr .. to incl part of an improvement made by Thomas McCloud. 20 Feb 1815. William Molden, Loc.
30	15	14572	**Henry Tate** .. Smith Co .. 20 acs .. north side of Caney fork .. adj John Bellah's line .. to incl a lot of

			house logs & spring that **Samuel Bellah** cut .. 23 Feb 1815. Henry Tate, Loc.
30	29	14664	**John Grant** .. 8 acs .. south fork of Jennings Cr above John Chism's. 7 March 1815. John Proctor, Loc.
30	33	14687	**John Wilson** .. 12 acs .. south side of Jennings Cr .. adj his own, Vaulx and Hutchison .. to incl part of a field made by sd Wilson. 10 Mar 1815. John Wilson, Loc.
30	33	14689	**Thomas Butler & Bailey Butler** .. 5 acs .. dry fork of Mill Cr .. 3/4 mile from Messer's (?) old cave. 10 Mar 1815. B. Butler, Loc.
30	33	14690	**Bailey Butler** .. 2 acs .. north side of Cumberland near head of Turkey Cr .. 10 May 1815.
30	39	14726	**William Williams** .. 10 acs .. dry fork of Mill Cr .. adj survey **whereon sd Williams now lives** .. 16 Mar 1815.
30	39	14727	**Ezekiel Roden** .. 20 acs .. on Hutchinson's fork of Mill Cr .. 16 Mar 1815.
30	39	14728	**Ezekiel Roden** .. 5 acs .. on Hutchinson's fork .. to incl house **where sd Roden now lives**. ..16 Mar 1815.
30	40	14732	**Robert Scantling** .. 10 acs .. Hill's branch of Cumberland .. adj his own .. 16 Mar 1815.
30	40	14733	**Thomas Ownbey** .. 3 acs .. dry fork of Mill Cr .. adj Joseph Ownbey .. 16 Mar 1815.
30	41	14737	**James Taylor** .. 8 acs .. Morrisson's Cr .. to incl field north of house **where Joseph Pryor now** lives. 17 Mar 1815.
30	41	14738	**Burkett Kinnard** .. 15 acs .. Morrisson's Cr .. to incl the **house where Joseph Pryor now lives**. 17 Mar 1815.
30	47	14774	**William Fleming & Adam Huntsman** .. 200 acs .. south side of Cumberland .. 10 poles below mouth of Kettle Cr .. east to the military line .. 21 Mar 1815. William Fleming, Loc.
30	47	14775	**William Fleming & Adam Huntsman** .. 40 acs .. adj their own. 21 Mar 1815.
30	57	14842	**Robert Bailey** .. 15 acs .. waters of Brimstone Cr .. to incl Bromnoch (?) Wilkinson's improvement. 8 Apr 1815. Noah Bennett, Loc.
30	57	14843	**Welcom Ussery** .. 15 acs .. waters of Brimstone Cr .. to

incl West's improvement. 8 Apr 1815.

30 58   14846   **Daniel Keith JR** .. 20 acs .. Little Trace Cr of Line Cr .. adj John Guest's .. to incl houses & springs .. **where Absolom and William Woods now live.** 10 Apr 1815. Daniel Keith, Loc.

30 58   14852   **Dennis Duff** .. 10 acs .. Mine Lick Cr .. to incl part of his improvement **where he now lives.** Joshua Leonard, Loc.

30 59   14858   **Shadrach Bridges** .. 20 acs .. waters of Rock Spring Cr .. adj his own. 12 Apr 1815.

30 60   14859   **Jesse Blackfan** .. 46 acs .. waters of Line Cr .. adj Yancy Thornton .. 13 Apr 1815.

30 60   14860   **Jesse Blackfan** .. 68 acs .. waters of Line Cr .. 13 Apr 1815.

30 61   14866   **James Vance** .. 20 acs .. adj his own on Pigeon Roost Br .. 14 Apr 1815.

30 62   14875   **John Gann** .. 39 acs .. east fork of Mine Lick Cr .. adj his own and **where Joshua Gann formerly lived** .. 17 Apr 1815.

30 65   14893   **Nathan Ewing** .. 15 acs .. Smith Co .. Plunkett's Cr .. adj his survey No. 6816 .. to incl a wet weather spring called by some the Rock Spring. 19 Apr 1815.

30 66   14899   **William Wheeler** .. 20 acs .. dry fork of Flynn's Cr .. to incl Smith's old improvement. 21 Apr 1815.

30 66   14900   **William Wheeler** .. dry fork of Flynn's Cr .. to incl the big spring. 21 Apr 1815. William Wheeler, Loc.

30 66   14901   **Joseph Henderson** .. 23 acs .. Dry creek of Roaring R .. east side of path leading from Jackson's to Bowen's Mill .. to incl a spring called Gibson's spring. 21 Apr 1815. Joseph Henderson, Loc.

30 67   14906   **Russell Morgan** .. 16 acs .. north side of Cane Cr of Caney Fork .. to incl improvement where **sd Morgan now lives.** 22 Apr 1815.

30 72   14943   **John McGee** .. 3 acs .. on an island in Cumberland R near the mouth of Salt Lick Cr .. to incl a salt spring on sd island. 29 Apr 1815. John McGee, Loc.

30 73   14951   **Benjamin Gist** .. 100 acs .. waters of Trace Cr .. including improvement tended by Curtis Wood **near where sd Wood now lives.** 1 May 1815. Benjamin Gist, Loc.

30	74	14954	**John Plumley** .. 20 acs .. ridge on headwaters of Brimstone Cr .. to incl **where Peter Miller formerly lived.** 2 May 1815.
30	74	14958	**Jacob A. Lane** .. 100 acs .. waters of Trace Cr .. beginning .. 40 poles south of the **house of Curtis Woods, son of Bat Woods,** running east .. 3 May 1815.
30	74	14959	**Jacob A. Lane** .. 100 acs .. waters of Trace Cr .. including house of John Gist SR **where he now lives** .. due east of house of Absalom Woods .. and a certain William Woods. 23 May 1815. Jacob A. Lane, Loc.
30	81	15000	**Jacob A. Lane** .. 101 acs .. waters of Trace Cr .. adj Benjamin Gist .. 17 May 1815.
30	83	15010	**James Carter** .. 20 acs .. White Co .. waters of Cane Cr of Falling Water adj his own **on which he lives** .. adj James Whitson's line of 200-ac tract .. 17 May 1815.
30	85	15023	**Henry West** .. 10 acs .. waters of Brimstone Cr .. to incl house .. **where sd West now lives.** 18 May 1815. John Black, Loc.
30	85	15024	**George Hays** .. 10 acs .. north side of Cumberland .. lower side of mouth of Dry Cr .. west with John Black's line .. 18 May 1815. John Black, Loc.
30	85	15025	**Levi Greathouse** .. 14 acs .. waters of Brimstone Cr .. adj Henry West's 10-ac entry .. 18 May 1815.
30	86	15031	**John Sutton** .. 6 acs .. Morrisson's Cr of Roaring R .. to incl **Jacob Halfacre's sugar camp.** 19 May 1815.
30	86	15032	**John Black** .. 20 acs .. north side of Cumberland .. where James McColgan's boundary crosses 3rd branch .. 19 May 1815.
30	86	15033	**John Black** .. north side of Cumberland .. to incl improvement made by Levi Greathouse. 19 May 1815.
30	86	15034	**Thomas Shute** .. **2,538 acs** .. south side of Cumberland .. above mouth of Well's Cr .. adj the R & Eastis & Howard on their east and with lines of other claims for complement. 19 May 1815. Thomas Shute, Loc. (BHB note: No county identified. This entry is incl herein to show that Thomas was neither a small nor merely local operator, nor was he oriented only in Jackson and Smith Counties. His entry # 15035 for 816 acs, also south side of Cumberland and adj # 15034 adj Matthews. His entry # 15036 for 440 acs adj others. Still no county identified. 19 May 1815.)
30	90	15058	**William Jared** .. 17 acs .. on the road leading from

Walton's Ferry to South West Point about 14 miles above sd Ferry including a spring known .. Pond Spring .. to incl the good pond .. 22 May 1815. James Roulston, Loc.

30	92	15071	**James Lovin** .. 6 acs .. on the ridge between Woolf Cr & Buffalo Valley .. to incl improvement **where sd Lovin now lives.** 24 May 1815.
30	95	15095	**Jeremiah Denton** .. White Co .. 13-1/2 acs .. north side of Caney Fork .. adj his own. 29 May 1815.
30	98	15110	**Redmond D. Barry** .. 100 acs .. south side of Cumberland on Martin's Cr .. adj his entry of 200 acs .. 1 June 1815.
30	99	15118	**Jesse Hust** .. 13+ acs .. north side of Cumberland .. to incl his improvement. 3 June 1815.
30	101	15128	**James Clemmons** .. 10 acs .. on the ridge between spring fork of Martin's Cr and Dry fork of Flynn's Cr .. to incl improvement made by Isaac Willoughby. 5 June 1815.
30	102	15137	**Samuel Jenkins** .. 10 acs .. Little Trace Cr .. to incl the first improvement & spring on sd creek above **where Raysor now lives.** 7 June 1815.
30	104	15149	**Benjamin Farmer** .. 8 acs .. waters of Proctor's Cr .. southeast corner of Zedekiah Woods' 12-ac survey .. 13 June 1815.
30	104	15150	**Benjamin Farmer** .. 10 acs .. Proctor's Cr .. adj his own. 13 June 1815.
30	110	15189	**Robert Cole** .. 6 acs .. Cubb Cr .. 26 June 1815.
30	110	15190	**Robert Cole** .. one ac .. Cubb Cr .. to incl house and spring **where sd Cole now lives.** 26 June 1815. Robert Cole, Loc.
30	110	15192	**William Williams** .. 5 acs .. waters of Martin's Cr .. to incl a cabin built by John Griffey. 26 June 1815. Nathan Williams, Loc.
30	117	15232	**John Hampton** .. 35 acs .. on Roaring R .. to incl improvement **where Andrew Hampton now lives.** 11 July 1815. Andrew Hampton, Loc.
30	117	15233	**Washington Hampton** .. 20 acs .. on Roaring R .. to incl improvement where **John Myers now lives.** 11 July 1815.
30	117	15234	**William Howe** .. 20 acs .. White Co .. waters of Caney fork beginning on a black oak marked W. H. 86 poles

> north of John Swindle's 20 acs .. 11 July 1815.
> **William Howe, Loc.**

Some discussion is needed here about the various spellings of the name Huff. Some folks seem to prefer the spelling "Hough" to rhyme with rough and tough. The problems with that preference are:

1. "Hough" can be thought to rhyme with "dough" as in bread, and it comes out Hoe. In the early records, Doe Cr is sometimes spelled Dowe, Dow, and Dough.

2. "Hough" can be thought to rhyme with "bough" as part of a tree, and it comes out How or Howe. One lady, wearing a name badge "Hough," was asked how she pronounced it, and she sd "How," not to rhyme with row as in a corn field but with row meaning a fight.

3. "Hough" can be thought to rhyme with "slough" as in backwater, and it comes out hue to rhyme with slew. Hue is sometimes mistaken for "Hugh" which is Hough with the "o" omitted. Careful editors or indexers then "correct" the spelling to Hughes.

4. In March 1991, I received mail addressed to "Betty Huss Bryant," because someone misread the "f's" as old style "s."

5. The old long "s" has sometimes been read "p," and the name comes out Hupp.

6. At a recent seminar, someone asked what nationality the name "Houx" was. The speaker replied that the "x" made it French. Neither he nor the questioner pronounced the name, but in my opinion, it would have to be a French spelling of Hough or Howe by a French scribe, and not necessarily the nationality of the individual. A different scribe, of Spanish (Mexican) origins, could have used the "x" for a "z" sound as in Xochimilco or the initial letter in Xerox.

7. The 1900 Census of Jackson County, TN, has several men with the given name "Hugh." The enumerator of the Martin's Creek districts consistently spelled it "Hough."

8. When asked how "Huff" can become "Howe," the answer has to be another question. How did the archaic "enow" become "enuff" illogically spelled "enough?"

Many frontier folks learned their spelling from the Bible and classic literature, some of it very old. They should be forgiven their vagaries of phonetics and spellings, but rest assured -- the name is Huff and should rhyme with buff, cuff, duff, enough, fluff, etc. including stuff but not stow. Amazing things happen when editors try to correct spellings of proper names. My own first name "Betty" exists in old records as "Bede," which is perhaps more correct phonetically. No one ever says it with "t's" except in anger or contempt.

Do not fuss about how your name was spelled 200 years ago. You are lucky to have it recorded.

30 117 15235 **Nicholas Haile** .. 20 acs .. Roaring R .. below John Myer's spring .. to incl house where **John Myers now lives.** 11 July 1815.

30 117 15236 **John C. McLemore** .. 20 acs .. on the main fork of Brimstone Cr .. east side of a large salt lick .. to incl sd lick. 11 July 1815. John Murrey, Loc.

30 117 15237 **John C. McLemore** .. 20 acs .. Jennings Cr .. between where **Samuel Casey & Old Mr. Carter now live** .. 11 July 1815.

30 118 15238 **John C. McLemore** .. 10 acs .. on the Rock House Lick branch of Jenning's Cr .. 11 July 1815.

30 118 15239 **John C. McLemore** .. 10 acs .. north branch of the south fork of Crabtree's cave fork of Jenning's Cr that runs in at Samuel Jones' .. 11 July 1815.

30 118 15240 **John C. McLemore** .. 20 acs .. south side of Cumberland .. near Williamsburgh .. 11 July 1815.

30 118 15241 **John Higdon** .. 15 acs .. waters of Roaring R .. to incl Higdon's improvement. 12 July 1815.

30 118 15242 **John Higdon** .. 4 acs .. waters of Roaring R .. to incl **where sd Higdon now lives.** 12 July 1815.

30 118 15243 **John Craig** .. 10 acs .. waters of Roaring R .. to incl where **sd Craig now lives.** 12 July 1815.

30 118 15244 **John Rutledge** .. 10 acs .. on Roaring R .. adj Jesse Davis' field .. 12 July 1815.

30 120 15250 **John C. McLemore** .. dry creek of Blackburn's fork .. 13 July 1815.

30 120 15251 **James Vaulx** .. 70 acs .. north side of Cumberland below mouth of Samuel Kirkpatrick's spring branch .. 13 July 1815.

30 123 15268 **Enoch Carter** .. 7-1/2 acs .. dry fork of Martin's Cr .. adj **tract he now lives upon** .. 18 July 1815.

30 123 15269 **John Stafford** .. 10 acs .. on Aaron's branch of Roaring R .. 18 July 1815.

30 123 15270 **John Stafford** .. 10 acs .. on Roaring R .. begins at John Johnson's northeast corner .. to incl place where **Alexander Rutledge now lives** .. 18 July 1815.

30	123	15271	**John Stafford** .. 60 acs .. adj his own .. south of a tract in name of John and William Stafford .. 18 July 1815.
30	123	15272	**Champ Staunton** .. 15 acs .. Indian Cr of Cumberland .. half mile above the **trough spring** .. to incl improvement **lately occupied by William Woods.** 18 July 1815.
30	125	15283	**Francis Anderson** .. 8-1/2 acs .. branch of Salt Lick Cr .. to incl Archibald Hair's improvement & spring **where he now lives.** 19 July 1815.
30	125	15286	**Jacob Young** .. 100 acs .. **Robertson Co** .. waters of middle fork of Red R .. adj 22-1/2 ac survey in name of John Young .. 19 July 1815. (Jacob and John Young were sons of William Young and his wife Elizabeth Huff who settled early just south of Martin's Cr. Jacob married 2) his cousin Polly Huff, presumably in Jackson Co, and they removed for a while to Robertson Co.) Survey for Entry 15286 was returned 6 Feb 1816. Entry made void 19 Mar 1819 by Jacob Young.
30	125	15287	**Enoch Carter** .. 8 acs .. dry fork of Martin's Cr .. to incl **William Huff's old sugar camp.** 19 July 1815. Certificate No. 2135. Survey rtd 17 Feb 1819. Made void 22 Apr 1824 & warrant del to Wm. W. Woodfolk he having produced a transfer from sd Carter. (See entry 15610 and compare dates of transfer to Wm. W. Woodfolk.)
30	126	15288	**Enoch Carter** .. 10 acs .. long hollow of dry fork of Martin's Cr .. northwest corner of 15-ac entry in name of John Martin on east boundary of 640-ac tract granted to Sampson Williams .. running east with Martin's line .. 19 July 1815.
30	126	15289	**Enoch Carter** .. 4 acs .. dry fork of Martin's Cr .. to incl improvement **where Susanna Carter formerly lived.** 19 July 1815.
30	128	15306	**Sally Twitty** .. 6 acs .. north side of Cumberland on Indian Cr .. between lines of Arch Skaggs and Polly Twitty .. 22 July 1815.
30	140	15378	**Jacob Galyen** .. 5 acs .. on Morrison's Cr .. waters of Roaring R .. 1 Aug 1815.
30	142	15391	**Caleb Anderson** .. 65 acs .. dry fork of Flynn's Cr .. to incl .. **where Charles Anderson now lives.** 4 Aug 1815.
30	149	15442	**John Plumley** .. 10 acs .. on Brimstone Cr .. to incl **where John Dutton lives.** 11 Aug 1815.

30	151	15459	**Bailey Butler** .. 20 acs .. south side of Brimstone Cr .. on Emanuel Home's north boundary .. 14 Aug 1815.
30	151	15461	**Emanuel Holmes** .. 8 acs .. waters of Brimstone Cr .. adj his own. 14 Aug 1815.
30	151	15462	**Russell Meredith** .. 15 acs .. waters of Brimstone Cr .. adj Emanuel Holmes .. 14 Aug 1815. Henry West, Loc.
30	152	15463	**Russell Meredith** .. 15 acs .. waters of Brimstone Cr .. near Emanuel Holmes .. 14 Aug 1815.
30	152	15464	**Russell Meredith** .. 10 acs .. head waters of Dry Cr .. near .. Benjamin Denton's old improvement .. to incl part of sd improvement. 14 Aug 1815. Henry West, Loc.
30	152	15465	**Isaac Denton** .. 15 acs .. waters of Brimstone Cr .. to incl his improvement. 14 Aug 1815.
30	152	15466	**James Taggart** .. 18 acs .. waters of Proctor's Cr .. adj his own .. 14 Aug 1815.
30	152	15467	**Philip Overturff** .. 20 acs .. north side of Cumberland .. adj Jarvis's .. and McColgin's .. 14 Aug 1815.
30	152	15468	**David Young** .. 14 acs .. waters of Indian Cr .. adj his own **where he now lives** .. 14 Aug 1815.
30	153	15469	**David Young** .. White Co .. 10 acs .. Falling Water. 15 Aug 1815.
30	156	15489	**Jordan Sullivant** .. 10 acs .. waters of Indian Cr .. the Widow Kirkland .. **where Simon Carlisle now lives** .. 17 Aug 1815.
30	156	15490	**Simon Carlisle** .. 5 acs .. waters of Indian Cr .. **whereon sd Carlisle now lives** .. 17 Aug 1815.
30	157	15498	**William Vallance** .. 11 acs .. waters of Indian Cr of Caney Fork .. to incl .. **whereon he now lives**. 18 Aug 1815.
30	158	15499	**George Skiles** .. 20 acs .. waters of Indian Cr .. to incl .. land cleared by William Vallance near **where sd Vallance now lives**. 18 Aug 1815.
30	158	15500	**John Fanning** .. 25 acs .. waters of Mine Lick .. to incl .. **whereon a Mr. Hatfield now lives**. 18 Aug 1815.
30	159	15507	**John Gambell** .. 30 acs .. Mine Lick Cr .. adj Joshua Gann .. 19 Aug 1815.
30	162	15531	**Jacob A. Lane** .. 25 acs .. adj his own .. 22 Aug 1815.

30 165 15547 **Stewart Watson** .. 6 acs .. Trace Cr of Barren .. to incl a sugar orchard **where Robert Gutherie formerly made sugar.** 26 Aug 1815.

30 167 15563 **Stephen Nicholas** .. 50 acs .. on the Big Br .. between lines of James Pharis and his own bought of Edmund Jennings .. to incl .. **whereon sd Nicholas now lives** .. 29 Aug 1815.

30 168 15567 **Henry Sadler** .. 196 acs .. on Indian Cr .. southwest corner of Matthew Cowan's survey .. including **where the Widow Kirkendall formerly lived & the place formerly occupied by John Carter.** 29 Dec 1815.

30 168 15573 **John Young** .. White Co .. 16 acs .. waters of Pigeon Roost Cr .. adj Archibald Elliott .. 31 Aug 1815.

30 170 15581 **John Peterson** .. 15 acs .. on Proctor's Cr .. adj Thomas Peterson .. 2 Sep 1815.

30 170 15582 **John Peterson** .. 10 acs .. Proctor's Cr .. adj Thomas Peterson .. 1 Sep 1815.

30 174 15610 **George Hough** ase of Tyre Gentry .. Certificate 2167 .. 30 acs .. on Indian Cr of Cumberland beginning on a white oak about 4 poles north of Samuel Young's southwest corner .. 9 Sep 1815. James Ward, Loc. Made void and certificate del. 20 Apr 1824 by order of George Hough to W. W. Woodfolk.

George Hough (Huff) is possibly the wandering husband of Susanna Huff. Back-tracking Tyre Gentry, Samuel Young, and James Ward led to Eake Brown on **Little** Indian Cr, exactly where Susanna's husband should be. That's the fun of "Building Neighborhoods."

30 175 15620 **Jesse Blackfan** .. 36 acs .. south side of Cumberland .. opposite Williamsburg .. near Sampson Williams .. 11 Sep 1815.

30 176 15626 **Adam Bordin** .. 12 acs .. Jennings Cr .. to incl **where sd Bordin now lives.** 12 Sept 1815.

30 182 15665 **John Murrey** .. 20 acs .. Jenning's Cr .. adj David Green .. Redmond D. Barry .. 19 Sept 1815.

30 182 15666 **John Murrey** .. 8 acs .. between Knob & Proctor's Crs .. adj Stephen Cantrell .. 19 Sep 1815.

30 186 15691 **John Royall** .. 20 acs .. north side of Brimstone Cr .. to incl **where Byram Bybee now lives** .. 25 Sept 1815.

30 192 15726 **George W. Martin** .. 15 acs .. south branch of Indian Cr .. adj William Dickens .. 29 Sept 1815. George W. Martin, Loc.

30	192	15727	**Aaron Whitney** .. 2 acs .. ridge beginning on a sugartree in **Samuel Hough's east boundary** .. to incl spring and house lately built by sd Whitney. 30 Sept 1815. John Plumlee, Loc.
30	192	15728	**Simeon Pennington** .. 20 acs .. McFarland's Cr .. the spring now used by the Widow Combs .. to incl .. her improvement. 30 Sept 1815. John Plumlee, Loc.
30	192	15729	**Jacob Bennett** .. 10 acs .. east fork of Proctor's Cr .. 30 Sept 1815.
30	192	15730	**Jacob Bennett** .. 10 acs .. Proctor's Cr .. 30 Sept 1815. William Goforth, Loc.
30	198	15772	**Littleton Darnald** .. 12 acs .. Hurricane branch .. 5 Oct 1815.
30	205	15820	**John Nichols** .. north side of Cumberland .. below mouth of Brimstone Cr .. adj his own. 12 Oct 1815. John Nichols, JR, Loc.
30	206	15823	**Elijah Price** .. branch of Flynn's Cr adj tract on which **Uriah Anderson now lives** .. to incl improvement made by Robert Price **where the Widow Price now lives** .. 13 Oct 1815. Elijah Price, Loc.
30	209	15846	**Joel Wilson** .. 20 acs .. north fork of Indian Cr .. to incl **where Wm. Goodwin now lives**. 19 Oct 1815. Joel Wilson, Loc.
30	211	15857	**Thomas Wilkeson** .. 5 acs .. waters of Brimstone Cr .. to incl two trunk trees cut by John Plumlee. 19 Oct 1815.
30	211	15858	**Thomas Wilkeson** .. 10 acs .. waters of Brimstone Cr .. 19 Oct 1815. Thomas Wilkeson, Loc.
30	214	15871	**Arthur Dill** .. 10 acs .. north side on Puncheon Camp Cr of Roaring R .. to incl improvement made by sd Dill. 21 Oct 1815.
30	214	15872	**Arthur Dill** .. 20 acs .. Roaring R .. to incl **where sd Dill now lives**. 21 Oct 1815.
30	214	15873	**John Sutton** .. 10 acs .. on Morrisson's Cr .. 21 Oct 1815. John Sutton, Loc.
30	214	15874	**John Sutton** .. 50 acs .. waters of Morrisson's Cr .. west side of plantation **whereon Joseph Pryor now lives** .. 21 Oct 1815.
30	221	15926	**Eli Langford & Josiah Langford** .. 50 acs .. Henderson's

branch south side of Cumberland .. north side of a mountain on James Cook's line .. to incl a field **cultivated by William Henderson.** 28 Oct 1815.

30 222 15927 **Eli Langford & Josiah Langford** .. 15 acs .. Henderson's branch .. 28 Oct 1815.

30 222 15928 **Eli Langford & Josiah Langford** .. 20 acs .. Henderson's branch .. adj their own .. 28 Oct 1815. Eli Langford, Loc.

30 224 15940 **Thomas Wood** .. 35 acs .. Little Trace Cr adj John Gist's .. to incl part of Absalom Woods' improvement. 2 Nov 1815.

30 224 15942 **Absolam Wood JR** .. waters of Trace Cr .. adj John Gist .. to incl **where sd Wood now lives.** 2 Nov 1815.

30 227 15965 **Elias Jackson** .. 8 acs .. on Rush fork of Flynn's Cr .. to incl field cleared by Samuel Henson. 7 Nov 1815.

30 227 15966 **Elias Jackson** .. 2 acs .. Rush fork of Flynn's Cr .. to incl house **where Samuel Henson now lives.** 7 Nov 1815.

30 236 16024 **William Plumley** .. 20 acs .. ridge between Line Cr and Brimstone Cr .. to incl .. **whereon sd Plumley now lives.** 15 Nov 1815.

30 237 16025 **Robert Johnson** .. 20 acs .. ridge between Cumberland and Barron R .. 1/4 mile from where John Plumley now lives. 15 Nov 1815. John Welch, Loc.

30 237 16026 **John Welch** .. 10 acs .. headwaters of Line Cr of Barren R .. to incl **whereon sd Welch now lives.** 15 Nov 1815.

30 238 16036 **Ephraim Lee & Thomas Wilkerson** .. 2 acs .. waters of Bullerd's Cr .. adj Alfred Moore .. 17 Nov 1815.

30 239 16038 **Nathan Haggard** .. 20 acs .. ridge near head of Doe Cr .. including improvement formerly made by John D. Brooks. 18 Nov 1815.

30 239 16039 **Nathan Haggard** .. 10 acs .. road leading from mouth of Roaring R to **where Stephen Roberts now lives** .. 18 Nov 1815.

30 239 16041 **Nathan Haggard** .. 2 acs .. branch of Flynn's Cr .. adj his own .. including spring and cabin where **Blackwell formerly lived.** 18 Nov 1815.

30 251 16124 **Curtis Wood** 10 acs .. Line Cr .. to incl sd Wood's spring & sugar camp. 30 Nov 1815. Thomas Wood, Loc.

30 251 16129 **Solomon Johnson** .. 5 acs .. dry fork of Mill Cr .. to

incl place known by "Turkey ??" 30 Nov 1815. Lewis Stover, Loc.

30	252	16130	**Joseph Devenport** .. 10 acs .. west fork of War Trace Cr .. above where **Ralston Ray now lives** .. 30 Nov 1815.
30	253	16140	**Robert Harris** .. 15 acs .. south fork of Mine Lick Cr .. adj Samuel Pettyjohn .. 2 Dec 1818. Robert Harris, Loc.
30	253	16141	**Robert Harris** .. 15 acs .. Mine Lick Cr .. 2 Dec 1815.
30	253	16142	**Robert Harris** .. 10 acs .. on the Mying (?) branch of Cane Cr .. above where **James Whitson JR now lives.** 2 Dec 1815.
30	253	16143	**Robert Harris** .. 30 acs .. waters of Cane Cr .. adj his own and Isaac Taylor .. 2 Dec 1815.
30	253	16144	**Robert Harris** .. 5 acs .. waters of Cane Cr .. adj his own .. 3 Dec 1815. Robert Harris, Loc.
30	254	16147	**William Wilson** .. 5 acs .. Puncheon Camp Cr of Roaring R .. to incl **where John Goforth now lives.** 2 Dec 1815. William Wilson, Loc.
30	254	16148	**William Wilson** .. 10 acs .. waters of Blackburn's fork of Roaring R .. to incl .. **where Charles Ferrell formerly lived.** 2 Dec 1815.
30	254	16149	**William Wilson** .. 5 acs .. waters of Blackburn's fork .. to incl .. **where Robert Wilson now lives.** 2 Dec 1815.
30	254	16150	**Kinchen Pippen** .. 5 acs .. waters of Martin's Cr .. 2 Dec 1815. William Wilson, Loc.
30	256	16159	**Caleb Anderson** .. 20 acs .. dry fork of Flynn's Cr .. adj Uriah Anderson .. 5 Dec 1815. Joshua Clackston, Loc.
30	258	16176	**John Gann** .. 50 acs .. north side of Cane Cr .. above James Whitson's .. 7 Dec 1815.
30	258	16180	**Isaac Halfacre** .. 10 acs .. waters of Roaring R .. to incl improvement made by Isaac Harris. 7 Dec 1815. Isaac Halfacre, Loc.
30	258	16181	**Jacob Halfacre** .. 6 acs .. Roaring R .. adj his own .. 7 Dec 1815.
30	259	16187	**Joseph Clay & Matthew Clay ase of Robert Wilson** .. 80 acs .. main fork of Hopper's Cr .. adj Thomas Harbert & Matthew Clay .. 9 Dec 1815.

30	259	16188	**Joseph Clay & Matthew Clay** .. 80 acs .. main fork of Hopper's Cr .. adj their own .. 9 Dec 1815.
30	260	16189	**Joseph Clay & Matthew Clay** .. 20 acs .. main fork of Hopper's Cr .. adj their own .. 9 Dec 1815.
30	260	16190	**Joseph Clay & Matthew Clay** .. 20 acs .. ditto.
30	260	16191	**Ditto**
30	260	16192	**Henry Carr** .. 15 acs .. branch of Blackburn's fork .. to incl **where James Youngblood formerly lived called Seguche Valey.** 11 Dec 1815. James Youngblood, Loc.
30	265	16232	**David Dixon SR** .. 4 acs .. on Wade's branch of Jenning's Cr .. adj John Murrey .. to incl .. **where Jeremiah Pursley now lives.** 14 Dec 1815.
30	266	16233	**David Dixon SR** .. 4 acs .. on Wade's branch of Jenning's Cr .. above **where Wade formerly lived** .. 14 Dec 1815.
30	266	16235	**John Temples** .. 5 acs .. ridge between Big Br and Woolf Pen branch (Martin's Cr ?) .. to incl part of land Sam Allen formerly claimed. 15 Oct 1815.
30	266	16236	**John Rutledge** .. 10 acs .. waters of Roaring R .. 15 Dec 1815.
30	266	16237	**John Temples** .. one ac .. waters of Big Br .. to incl house & spring **where Rhody Manair now lives.** 15 Dec 1815.
30	266	16238	**Alexander Rutledge** .. 15 acs .. waters of Roaring R .. to incl house & spring where **Thomas Gore now lives.** 15 Dec 1815.
30	266	16239	**Alexander Rutledge** .. 15 acs on Roaring R .. to incl .. **where Molly Scaggs now lives.** 15 Dec 1815.
30	267	16240	**John Parker** .. ase Ben McCulloch .. 20 acs .. Euen's & Talley's Hollow .. 15 Dec 1815. (The name Euens can be read as Evans, but other entries tell us it is not Evans. It is Ewing's Hollow.)
30	267	16242	**Silas Clark** .. 10 acs .. Ward's fork of Jenning's Cr .. to incl improvement made by John Davis. 15 Dec 1815.
30	267	16243	**Silas Clark** .. 3 acs .. on Jenning's Cr .. to incl .. **where Mary Hutchinson now lives.** 15 Dec 1815.
30	267	16247	**Wade Whitney** ase Ben McCulloch .. 5 acs .. waters of Brimstone Cr .. adj Plumley .. 15 Dec 1815.

30	268	16249	**William Hutson** .. 18 acs .. Jenning's Cr .. to incl **where Vachel Clark cut house logs.** 15 Dec 1815.
30	268	16250	**Obadiah Hutson** ase Asa Shute .. 8 acs .. Cave fork of Jenning's Cr .. adj Samuel Jones .. 15 Dec 1815.
30	268	16251	**Robert Carpenter** .. 10 acs .. Russell's fork of Jenning's Cr .. Thaxton's south boundary .. 15 Dec 1815.
30	273	16285	**Joshua Hall** .. 10 acs .. waters of Trace Cr .. to incl **where sd Hall now lives.** 21 Dec 1815.
30	273	16286	**John Davis** .. 10 acs .. Big Trace Cr .. adj his own 21 Dec 1815.
30	286	16369	**Solomon McCloud** .. 10 acs .. waters of Indian Cr .. to incl where ⎯⎯⎯ **Sullivan now lives.** 6 Jan 1816.
30	286	16373	**James McKinnis** .. 10 acs .. War Trace Cr .. Thomas Casity's northeast corner .. 8 Jan 1816.
30	287	16381	**Uriah Anderson** .. 100 acs .. waters of Flynn's Cr .. adj **where sd Anderson now lives** .. near Thompson's. 10 Jan 1816.
30	287	16382	**Uriah Anderson** .. 20 acs .. waters of Flynn's Cr .. adj **John Martin's 60-ac entry on Stothart's west boundary** .. 10 Jan 1816.
30	288	16383	**Uriah Anderson** .. 6 acs .. waters of Flynn's Cr .. adj Stothart's 640 ac survey .. 10 Jan 1816.
30	288	16384	**Elijah Simmons** .. 10 acs .. Flynn's Cr .. adj Matthew Anderson's 320 acs .. 10 Jan 1816.
30	288	16385	**Elijah Simmons** .. 9 acs .. between dry and main forks of Flynn's Cr .. 10 Jan 1816.
30	288	16386	**Elijah Simmons** .. 5 acs .. dry fork of Flynn's Cr .. near the low gap between Payton Anderson's and Caleb Anderson's .. 10 Jan 1816.
30	291	16413	**Rains Roberts** .. 20 acs .. waters of Roaring R .. Francis Boyles west boundary .. to incl **where Montgomery Connard now lives.** 17 Jan 1816. Rains Roberts, Loc.
30	291	16414	**Rains Roberts** .. 10 acs .. waters of Roaring R .. to incl field cleared by James Dyar. 17 Jan 1816.
30	295	16439	**Joseph Clay & Matthew Clay** .. 6 acs .. main fork of Hopper's Cr .. above where sd Clays are boring for salt water .. 22 Jan 1816.

30	302	16496	**George Stamps** .. 9 acs .. east fork of Mine Lick Cr .. 30 Jan 1816. James Davis, Loc.
30	304	16509	**Joseph Shaw** .. 20 acs .. waters of Roaring R .. near **where James Taylor now lives** .. 2 Feb 1816.
30	304	16510	**James Taylor** .. 5 acs .. east fork of Martin's Cr .. including **where William Williams now lives** 2 Feb 1816.
30	310	16549	**John Wilson** .. 6 acs .. Hunting fork of Jenning's Cr .. adj 29-ac tract entered by Ephraim Wilkinson & Catharine Wilkinson .. to incl improvement made by Charles Ferrell. 9 Feb 1816.
30	310	16550	**Rich Lock** .. 27 acs .. on Jenning's Cr .. adj John Dickson .. 9 Feb 1816.
30	312	16561	**Moses Fisk** .. 100 acs .. Blackburn's fork of Roaring R below Dillingham's and above Pierces' (Price?) .. 12 Feb 1816.
30	312	16562	**Moses Fisk** .. 50 acs .. on the high lands between Spring Cr and Roaring R .. east of the path which leads from Job Morgan's to the meeting house .. 12 Feb 1816. Moses Fisk, Loc.
30	312	16563	**Moses Fisk** .. 50 acs .. south of Spring Cr .. on the path that runs from Job Morgan's to the Race Ground .. .. westerly of McCallas .. 12 Feb 1816.
30	315	16585	**Berkett Kinnaird** .. 8 acs .. waters of Roaring R .. 23 Feb 1816.
30	315	16586	**Kinchen Pippin** .. 2 acs .. waters of Roaring R .. to incl **whereon Montgomery Kinneard now lives**. 23 Feb 1816.
30	316	16590	**Edward Lax** .. 6 acs .. on the ridge between waters of Martin's Cr & Flynn's Cr .. to incl .. **where Susanna Carter now lives**. 24 Feb 1816. Edward Lax, Loc.
30	317	16600	**Aaron Lambert** .. 100 acs .. south side of Cumberland .. 26 Feb 1816 .. Aaron Lambert JR, Loc.
30	319	16615	**Nancy Jones** .. 6 acs .. waters of Salt Lick Cr .. adj John Teels' .. 28 Feb 1816.
30	320	16619	**John Parker** .. 15 acs .. Ewing's & Talley's hollow .. east of the road leading down sd hollow & about 4 poles south of Peter Pile's south boundary .. 28 Feb 1816.
30	328	16678	**William Anderson** .. Flynn's Cr .. adj Robert Stothart on Uriah Anderson's south boundary .. 11 Mar 1816.

BK	PG	NUMBER	DESCRIPTION
30	328	16679	**William Anderson** .. 6 acs .. waters of Flynn's Cr .. 11 Mar 1816.
30	328	16680	**John Martin** .. 60 acs .. waters of Flynn's Cr .. adj Uriah Anderson .. near branch which divides Thompson's land from Uriah Anderson's **where he lives.** 11 Mar 1816.
30	330	16690	**John Murrey** .. 10 acs .. waters of Doe Cr .. adj Cox's west boundary .. Lawson's still house .. including sd still house. 14 Mar 1816. (James Young, Sheriff of Jackson Co .. sold to Settle, Whitley & Smith 2 May 1821.)
30	330	16691	**John Murrey** .. 5 acs .. south side of Cumberland .. including **where a blacksmith by the name of Hendricks now lives.** 14 Mar 1816.
30	330	16692	**John Murrey** .. west fork of Mill Cr .. adj Hickman .. east of Langford's .. 14 March 1816.
30	331	16694	**Rosanna Eakle** .. waters of Line Cr of Barren R .. adj Martin .. Rosanna Eakle's east boundary of land **whereon she now lives** .. adj Samuel Hodge. 14 Mar 1816.
30	331	16695	**Adam C. Hamilton** .. 11 acs ..south side of Cumberland .. tract .. **sd Hamilton now lives on** ..14 Mar 1816.
30	331	16696	**Robert Scanland** .. 10 acs .. south side of Cumberland adj .. Hamilton Montgomery. 14 Mar 1816.
30	331	16697	**John Murrey** .. 50 acs .. south side of Cumberland above mouth of Roaring R .. adj Aaron Lambert's 1000 ac survey .. 14 Mar 1816.
30	331	16699	**John Murrey** .. south bank of Cumberland .. adj tract **whereon the Hamiltons now live** .. 14 Mar 1816.
30	332	16700	**John Murrey** .. 10 acs .. Sugar Cr .. including falls where sd Murrey cut timber for a mill. 14 Mar 1816.
30	332	16701	**John Murrey** .. 20 acs .. Jenning's Cr .. adj Richard Lock .. 14 Mar 1816.
30	332	16703	**John Murrey** .. 4 acs .. first branch that runs into dry fork of Mill Cr .. below mouth of Hutcheson's fork **where Williams lives** .. to incl a salt petre cave. 14 Mar 1816.
30	332	16704	**John Murrey** .. 4 acs .. Jenning's Cr .. 14 Mar 1816.
30	332	16706	**John Murrey** .. 19 acs .. ridge between Sugar Cr &

			Hill's branch .. including the place **where Byram Stacy formerly lived.** 14 Mar 1816.
30	334	16721	**Gabriel Dillard** .. 4 acs .. south side of Cumberland on waters of Indian Cr .. to incl **where Park B. Swift formerly lived.** 20 Mar 1816. Benjamin Norrod, Loc.
30	338	16743	**John M. Smith** .. Wade's branch of Jenning's Cr .. adj John Murrey .. 22 Mar 1816.
30	346	16798	**Joseph Jared** .. 20 acs .. Smith Co .. east side of Caney Fork .. to incl **where Spyas (?) Kirkland formerly lived.** 1 Apr 1816.
30	347	16810	**Cornelius Carver** .. 4 acs .. southwest side of War Trace Cr .. 2 Apr 1816.
30	348	16812	**Garret Moore** .. 3 acs .. ridge between Cumberland and Barron .. near sd Moore's spring to incl .. **house wherein sd Moore now lives.** 2 Apr 1816. Noah Bennett, Loc.
30	348	16813	**Stephen Langford** .. 5 acs .. west fork of Mill Cr .. 2 Apr 1816.
30	351	16834	**Jepthah West** .. 30 acs .. between Talley's Hollow and waters of Morrisson's Cr of Roaring R .. 8 Apr 1816. Martin Langford, Loc.
30	351	16835	**Martin Langford** .. 40 acs .. head of a branch of Morrisson's Cr. 8 Apr 1816.
30	351	16836	**Jesse Allen** .. 15 acs .. east side of Morrisson's Cr .. 8 Apr 1816.
30	351	16837	**Stephen Dill** .. 5 acs .. Morrisson's Cr .. to incl a sugar camp. 8 Apr 1816.
30	353	16851	**Redmond D. Barry** .. 15 acs .. north side of Cumberland .. Pine Lick fork of Jenning's Cr .. to incl **where Christopher Long now lives.** 11 Apr 1816.
30	353	16852	**Redmond D. Barry** .. 20 acs .. south side of Cumberland .. adj his own on Martin's Cr .. 11 Apr 1816.
30	355	16864	**Ridley Roberts** .. 5 acs on Spring fork of Martin's Cr .. adj Richard Anderson's **tract where he lives** .. including strip of vacant land between sd Richard Anderson's and a 5-ac tract now called James Clement's formerly John Anderson's. 12 Apr 1816. Ridley Roberts, Loc.
30	355	16865	**Ridley Roberts** .. 10 acs on the Spring fork of Martin's Cr .. adj tract now called James Clement's formerly

			John Anderson's .. to incl strip .. between sd tract and 35-ac track **whereon James Clement's now lives** .. 12 Apr 1816. Ridley Roberts, Loc.
30	357	16877	**Robert Davis** .. 5 acs .. branch of War Trace Cr .. to incl **where Cad W. Davis now lives.** 16 Apr 1816. David Hogg, Loc.
30	363	16919	**William Rash** .. 30 acs .. on a branch of Roaring R .. to incl a field between Kinnard's & Allen's **now occupied by Wm. & Jos. Terry.** 27 Apr 1816. William Rash, Loc.
30	364	16928	**James Vinson** .. 3 acs .. Dry fork of Martin's Cr .. to incl spring & improvement made by sd Vinson. 29 Apr 1816.
30	364	16929	**John Temples** .. 6 acs.. waters of Martin's Cr .. including some Deaden Timber called Richard Anderson's Cotton patch. 29 Apr 1816.
30	364	16930	**John Temples** .. 11 acs .. waters of Martin's Cr .. including Elijah Manning's spring & improvement. 29 Apr 1816. John Temples, Loc.
30	366	16942	**Samuel Turney** .. 100 acs .. waters of Hopper's Cr .. 1 May 1816.
30	366	16943	**Madison Fisk** .. 100 acs .. to incl **John Black's old improvement.** 1 May 1816. James Turney, Loc.
30	371	16982	**James Taylor** .. 15 acs .. waters of Martin's Cr on Walton's Road .. north side of sd road .. to incl spring & improvement **where William Shaw formerly lived.** 9 May 1816.
30	371	16983	**James Dyer** .. 5 acs .. branch of west fork of Roaring R .. to incl **where sd Dyer now lives.** 9 May 1816. Joseph Wilson, Loc.
30	371	16984	**Anne Dyer** .. 20 acs .. branch of west fork of Roaring R .. to incl **where sd Anne Dyer now lives.** 9 May 1816.
30	371	16985	**Robert York** .. 15 acs .. waters of Line Cr .. including **whereon John Harris now lives.** 10 May 1816. Richard York, Loc.
30	380	17043	**James Roberts** .. 5 acs .. spring fork of Martin's Cr .. south side .. adj Ridley Roberts .. including a spring and a tract for a still house. 22 May 1816. James W. Smith, Loc.
30	382	17062	**Joseph Jared** .. 10 acs .. in the Rock Spring Valley adj John Boyd .. 23 May 1816.

| 30 | 382 | 17063 | Henry Carr .. 15 acs .. Smith Co .. east side of Caney Fork .. adj Joseph Jared .. 23 May 1816. Henry Carr, Loc.

| 30 | 382 | 17064 | James Roulston .. 50 acs .. waters of Rock Spring Cr .. adj where John Fanning now lives .. 23 May 1816. James Roulston, Loc.

| 30 | 386 | 17092 | Garrett Ford .. 10 acs .. ridge between head of dry fork of Martin's Cr & the spring fork of sd creek .. including where Isaac Willoughby now lives. 25 May 1816. Garret Ford, Loc.

| 30 | 395 | 17155 | John Brown .. 10 acs .. in Locust Hollow of dry fork of Flynn's Cr .. to incl a small improvement made by Jesse McCormack. 14 June 1816. Thos. Brown, Loc.

| 30 | 395 | 17156 | John Wheeler .. 10 acs .. adj Uriah Anderson on the Dry Fork of Flynn's Cr .. 14 June 1816.

| 30 | 395 | 17157 | Thomas Brown .. 5 acs .. Dry Fork of Flynn's Cr .. tract whereon sd Brown now lives .. 14 June 1816.

| 30 | 395 | 17158 | Thomas Brown .. one ac .. Dry Fork of Flynn's Cr .. adj his own and to incl the flat spring. 14 June 1816.

| 30 | 395 | 17161 | Elijah Simmons .. 5 acs .. waters of Flynn's Cr .. adj Charles Anderson .. 14 June 1816.

| 30 | 395 | 17162 | Elijah Simmons .. 5 acs .. Dry Fork of Flynn's Cr .. near Charles Anderson. 14 June 1816. Elijah Simmons, Loc.

| 30 | 397 | 17173 | James Roberts .. 40 acs .. Spring Fork of Martin's Cr .. adj Ridley Roberts .. 19 June 1816. Jas. W. Smith, Loc.

| 30 | 398 | 17181 | William Anderson .. 10 acs .. forks of Lick Br waters of Big Br .. 19 June 1816.

| 30 | 398 | 17182 | William Anderson .. 4 acs .. near Williamsburgh on waters of the Big Br .. adj James Pharis's 60-ac tract .. 19 June 1816.

| 30 | 398 | 17183 | William Anderson .. 4 acs .. waters of Big Br adj James Pharis. 19 June 1816.

| 30 | 398 | 17184 | William Anderson .. 2 acs .. in the low gap between Daniel Miller's & Rhoda Manier's on the head of Big Br .. 19 June 1816.

| 30 | 398 | 17185 | James W. Smith .. 3 acs .. south side of Martin's Cr .. to incl improvement made by Jo Brown & cultivated by

Thomas Tillery who resided on sd improvement in the year 1815. 19 June 1816. Jas. W. Smith, Loc.

30 401 17203 **Samuel Herrald** .. 7 acs .. Sugar Camp Hollow, south side of Flynn's Cr .. to incl spring & improvement **where sd Herrald now lives.** 21 June 1816. Benjamin Fox, Loc.

30 406 17243 **Moses Byers** .. 15 acs .. waters of Cane Cr of Caney Fork .. adj James Huddleston's 25-ac entry .. 28 June 1816. Moses Byers, Loc.

30 411 17281 **Thomas Gillihan** .. 5 acs .. waters of Little Indian Cr of Caney Fork .. including part of Moses Webb's improvement **whereon he now lives** .. 16 July 1816.

30 411 17282 **Thomas Gillihan** .. 6 acs .. waters of Indian Cr of Caney Fork .. including a small improvement made by William Goodin. 16 July 1816.

30 415 17311 **William Stafford** .. 15 acs .. south branch of Roaring R .. adj tract **sd Stafford now lives on** .. 22 July 1816.

30 419 17337 **John Plumley** .. 20 acs .. waters of Brimstone Cr .. to incl a school house where **Henry West taught school.** 27 July 1816.

30 419 17338 **John Wood** .. 4 acs .. waters of McFarlin's Cr .. to incl **where sd Wood now lives.** 27 July 1816. Noah Bennett, Loc.

30 424 17375 **Samuel Bellah** .. 30 acs .. Smith Co .. waters of Caney Fork .. adj Davis and to incl improvement **where John Smith now lives.** 1 Aug 1816. Samuel Bellah, Loc.

30 424 17376 **Richard F. Cook** .. 10 acs .. waters of Cane Cr .. adj his own. 7 Aug 1816.

30 426 17390 **Hyram Brown** .. 6 acs .. waters of Indian Cr .. near John Campbell's fence .. 5 Aug 1816. Eake Brown, Loc.

30 426 17391 **Hyram Brown** 10 acs .. waters of Indian Cr .. adj his own. 5 Aug 1816.

30 426 17392 **Eake Brown** .. 12 acs .. waters of Indian Cr .. adj his own and to incl part of Gideon Brown's Improvement. 5 Aug 1816.

30 426 17396 **Henry Sadler** .. 10 acs .. waters of Indian Cr .. adj his own 5 Aug 1816.

30 432 17441 **Charles Conway** .. 10 acs .. head waters of Flynn's Cr .. 13 Aug 1816. John Sutton, Loc.

30	433	17448	**Elijah Wheeler** .. 15 acs .. Dry fork of Flynn's Cr adj William Wheeler and James Ragland .. 15 Aug 1816.
30	433	17449	**Nathan Kent** .. 12 acs in counties of Jackson & Smith .. 15 Aug 1816. S. Williams, Loc.
30	433	17450	**Sampson Williams** .. 30 acs .. Dry fork of Martin's Cr including **where Enoch Carter now lives** .. adj John Stephen's west boundary .. 15 Aug 1816.
30	433	17451	**Sampson Williams** .. Dry fork of Martin's Cr .. adj his own and Murrey's. 15 Aug 1816.
30	433	17452	**Sampson Williams** .. 30-1/2 acs .. waters of Roaring R including .. **where James Burleson and Caleb Joab lately lived but now occupied by Edward Robertson and Thomas Anderson.** 15 Aug 1816.
30	434	17459	**James Butler & Thomas Ryal** .. 9 acs .. on Brimstone Cr .. near William Chissum's .. 19 Aug 1816.
30	440	17506	**Jepthah West** .. 25 acs .. west side of Blackburn's Fork .. to incl .. **where James Richie now lives.** 26 Aug 1816. Peter Richey, Loc.
30	440	17511	**William Wheeler** .. 10 acs .. Dry fork of Flynn's Cr .. adj his own. 27 Aug 1816.
30	441	17512	**William Wheeler** .. 5 acs .. dry fork of Flynn's Cr .. adj his own. 27 Aug 1816.
30	444	17540	**John Campbell** .. 10 acs .. waters of Indian Cr .. 2 Sept 1816.
30	444	17541	**John Campbell** .. 15 acs .. waters of Indian Cr .. 2 Sep 1816.
30	444	17542	**John Campbell** .. Ditto
30	444	17544	**John Campbell** .. 6 acs .. waters of Indian Cr .. adj Hyram Brown's 10-ac entry .. 2 Sep 1816.
30	445	17545	**Thomas Gillihan** .. 6 acs .. waters of Indian Cr adj James Turman's southeast corner .. 1 Sept 1816. Thomas Gillihan, Loc.
30	445	17546	**William Scanland** .. 20 acs .. south side of Doe Cr .. adj James McCall .. 2 Sept 1816. Dennis McCalley, Loc.
30	445	17549	**Adams C. Hamilton** .. 200 acs .. south side of Cumberland .. on the bank ..above mouth of Wallace Bickerstaff's spring branch .. adj survey in name of James Cook. 3 Sept 1816. Adams C. Hamilton, Loc.

30	445	17550	**Adams C. Hamilton** .. 5 acs .. south side of Cumberland .. to incl house and spring **where William Henderson now lives** .. 3 Sept 1816.
30	446	17556	**John Reddick** .. 25 acs .. waters of Indian Cr at southeast corner of Robert McKinley's 20-ac survey. 4 Sept 1816. Richard Moore, Loc.
30	447	17565	**John Plumley** .. 20 acs .. on the ridge between the heads of Brimstone & Knob Crs .. 7 Sept 1816. John Plumley, Loc.
30	448	17566	**John Plumley** .. 15 acs .. on Brimstone Cr .. on both sides .. to incl **where Tompkins Odle now lives.** 7 Sept 1816.
30	448	17569	**Joseph Whitney** .. 12 acs .. McFarland's Cr .. to incl **where Charles Carter now lives.** 7 Sept 1816. Aron Whitney, Loc.
30	448	17571	**Adams C. Hamilton** .. 80 acs .. south side of Cumberland on the bank .. adj his own. 9 Sept 1816. Wallis Biggerstaff, Loc.
30	449	17573	**Henry Davis** .. 10 acs .. waters of Trace Cr .. adj Jacob A. Lane .. 9 Sept 1816.
30	452	17600	**Benjamin Marr** .. 15 acs .. in the Buffalo Valley .. adj Robert Wallace .. 14 Sept 1816. Loyd Marr, Loc.
30	452	17601	**Robert Wallace** .. 5 acs .. in the Buffalo Valley .. adj Benjamin Marr's 15-ac entry. 14 Sept 1816. Robert Wallace, Loc.
30	452	17602	**Robert Wallace** .. 20 acs .. Buffalo Valley .. 14 Sept 1816.
30	453	17605	**John Anderson** .. 6 acs .. on the ridge between Richard Clack and William Young's .. 14 Sep 1816.

Apologies: It is impossible to differentiate between the handwritten Clack and Clark. In these entries by John Anderson, there are several examples of very legible "r's" which seem to indicate that the name mentioned is not Clark but Clack.

30	453	17606	**John Anderson** .. 6 acs on the ridge between Clack & Young .. 14 Sept 1816.
30	453	17607	**Samuel Young** .. 10 acs .. on a branch of Indian Cr of Cumberland ..above the improvements **whereon sd Young now lives** .. 14 Sept 1816.
30	454	17614	**David Dixon SR** .. 6 acs .. on Jenning's Cr .. adj Stephen Marion's southwest corner .. to incl **where**

Samuel Anderson now lives .. 14 Sept 1816. G. W. Dixon, Loc.

30 456 17635 **James Bowman** .. 20 acs .. head waters of McFarland's Cr .. to incl a spring known as The Big Spring. 18 Sept 1816.

30 456 17636 **Samuel Poindexter** .. 20 acs .. head waters of Proctor's Cr .. including two improvements made by Norman Norton **whereon sd Poindexter now lives.** 18 Sept 1816.

30 458 17650 **Patsy Cammorn (Cameron ?)** .. 10 acs .. waters of Indian Cr .. to incl **plantation whereon sd Patsy Cammorn now lives.** 25 Sep 1816. Pleasant Aplin, Loc.

30 458 17651 **Patsy Cammorn** .. 5 acs .. waters of Indian Cr of Caney Fork .. 25 Sept 1816. Pleasant Aplin, Loc.

30 459 17653 **Robert Page** .. 20 acs .. on the ridge between headwaters of Jenning's Cr & Trace Cr .. 25 Sep 1816. Robert Page, Loc.

30 459 17655 **Timothy Haney** .. 5 acs .. Blackburn's Fork .. to incl **spring and house where Robert Wilson now lives.** 26 Sep 1816. William Wilson, Loc.

30 459 17658 **Aaron Lambert** .. south side of Cumberland 3 or 4 miles above mouth of Roaring R .. adj his own .. 26 Sep 1816. Aaron Lambert SR, Loc.

30 469 17728 **Abraham Myers** .. 6 acs .. Talley's Hollow .. to incl John Halfacre's improvement. 10 Oct 1816. John Stafford, Loc.

30 469 17731 **John Stafford** .. south side of Roaring R .. to incl a school house & a small improvement **where Benjamin Douglass is now keeping school.** 10 Oct 1816.

30 470 17737 **William Howe** .. 20 acs .. White Co .. south side of the **Gum Spring Mountain** .. 11 Oct 1816. William Howe, Loc. Survey returned 2 Apr 1817.

30 471 17741 **Nathan Haggard** .. 20 acs .. head of Horse branch of Flynn's Cr .. to incl improvement **where the Widow Dudley now lives where John Paine formerly lived.** 12 Oct 1816. Edmund Jennings, Loc.

30 471 17743 **Aaron Lambert** .. 100 acs .. south side of Cumberland 3 miles above mouth of Roaring R .. adj 1,000 ac .. granted to sd Lambert. 12 Oct 1816. Aaron Lambert SR, Loc.

30 475 17775 **David Walker & Obediah Pinkney** .. 2 acs .. south side of Cumberland on Scantland's branch .. William Walker,

			Loc. Entry is undated, but it is between two entries dated 19 Oct 1816.
30	476	17779	**Thomas Gore** .. 2 acs .. on Rankin's branch of Roaring R .. 21 Oct 1816. Thomas Gore, Loc.
30	480	17807	**John Gamble** .. 15 acs .. on Flynn's Cr .. adj Burris and near Stotgrasses plantation. 25 Oct 1816. John Gamble, Loc.
30	481	17813	**James Davis** .. 5 acs .. White Co .. Mine Lick Cr .. corner of survey **Martin Trapp now lives on** 25 Oct 1816.
30	481	17814	**Henry Carr** .. waters of Blackburn's Fork .. adj James Youngblood. 26 Oct 1816.
30	481	17815	**William Youngblood** .. 15 acs .. waters of Blackburn's Fork .. to incl house, spring and improvement **where sd Youngblood now lives.** 26 Oct 1816.
30	481	17820	**Samuel Dixon** .. 2 acs .. west side of Jenning's Cr .. adj John Burris. 29 Oct 1816. Samuel G. Smith, Loc.
30	482	17823	**James Clements** .. 5 acs .. on Spring fork of Martin's Cr .. being on east boundary of James Roberts' 40-ac survey .. to incl a large spring. 30 Oct 1816. Jas. W. Smith, Loc.
30	487	17856	**Asa Lynn** .. 16 acs .. north side of Roaring R .. adj tract **sd Lynn now lives on** .. 13 Nov 1816.
30	487	17857	**John Murrey** .. 3 acs .. on Sugar Cr .. to incl **a stable and turnip patch** made by sd Murrey. 13 Nov 1816. John Murrey, Loc.
30	489	17876	**Elias Jackson** .. 2 acs .. on Rush fork of Flynn's Cr .. to incl a sugar orchard on top of a ridge. 19 Nov 1816. Rains Roberts, Loc.
30	490	17879	**Simeon Putman** .. 20 acs .. head waters of Flynn's Cr .. to incl **where Champ Guin now lives.** 19 Nov 1816. Rains Roberts, Loc.
30	491	17886	**Benjamin Bowman** .. 11 acs .. White Co .. adj John Mays southwest corner. 23 Nov 1816.
30	493	17900	**James Butler & Thomas Ryal** .. 9 acs .. on Brimstone Cr adj Samuel Moore's upper line. 27 Nov 1816. William Butler, Loc.
30	504	17985	**Jeremiah Denton** .. White Co .. 9 acs .. waters of main Caney Fork adj his own. 12 Dec 1816.

30	504	17986	**Hiram Brown** .. 12 acs .. waters of Indian Cr .. 13 Dec 1816. John Anderson, Loc.
30	505	18001	**John Ford** .. 15 acs .. branch of Flynn's Cr opposite **where Benjamin Ford lately lived** including place & improvement made by Samuel McCallister .. 14 Dec 1816.
30	505	18002	**John Ford** .. 12-1/2 acs .. waters of dry fork of Martin's Cr between an entry in name of Sampson Williams and one in name of John Martin .. 14 Dec 1816.
30	505	18003	**John Ford** .. 5 acs .. on a branch of Flynn's Cr including **Robert Shadden's Distillery** .. 14 Dec 1816.
30	508	18030	**James Pharis** .. 15 acs .. waters of Martin's Cr .. bounded by Carters & Millers. 18 Dec 1816. Samuel Wallace, Loc.
30	508	18033	**Hezekiah Lizenberry** .. 5 acs .. in Buffalo Valley .. near entry made by Robert Gibson. 19 Dec 1816. Ephraim Guffey, Loc.
30	509	18034	**Hezekiah Lizenberry** .. 2 acs .. in Buffalo Valley .. adj his own. 1816. Ephraim Guffey, Loc.
30	509	18037	**John Gann** .. 20 acs .. Cane Cr .. to incl Joiner Gentry's improvement **where Wm. Southwood now lives.** 20 Dec 1816.
30	511	18051	**Isaac Denton** .. 30 acs .. waters of Brimstone Cr .. including a piece of cleared land **near where sd Denton now lives.** 23 Dec 1816. John Welch, Loc.
30	511	18053	**John Plumley** .. 10 acs .. on Brimstone Cr .. to incl **a house built by Erwin West.** 25 Dec 1816.
30	527	18174	**James Condery** .. 19 acs .. fork of Trace and Line Cr .. near James Sander's south boundary. 16 Jan 1817. James Condra, Loc.

Notice: Two spellings of the same name within one entry No. 18174. Condery and Condra.

30	527	18178	**James Roberts** .. 10 acs .. between waters of Flynn's Cr and the Spring fork of Martin's Cr .. 17 Jan 1817.
30	527	18179	**James Roberts** .. 5 acs .. waters of Spring fork of Martin's Cr .. 17 Jan 1817.
30	531	18208	**John Hutchins** .. 5 acs .. on Cane Cr .. between Bartlett Gentry's and sd Hutchins lines. 28 Jan 1817. John Gann, Loc.
30	531	18209	**John Gann** .. 20 acs .. on west side of Cane Cr near

where sd Gann now lives .. 28 Jan 1817.

30 533 18223 **John Parker** .. 15 acs .. Talley's and Ewing's Hollow .. east corner to Peter Pile's 10-ac survey .. 31 Jan 1817. John Parker, Loc.

30 533 18224 **William Gray** .. 15 acs .. north side of Roaring R .. adj his own. 31 Jan 1817. James Gray, Loc.

30 533 18225 **James Gray** .. 10 acs .. Long branch of Roaring R .. to incl improvement **whereon sd Gray lives.** 31 Jan 1817.

30 533 18226 **William Stafford** .. 6 acs .. waters of Roaring R .. adj William Gray's south boundary .. where it crosses Rutherford's branch .. 31 Jan 1817.

30 533 18228 **Levi Spear** .. 40 acs .. north bank of McFarland's Cr .. to incl part of sd Spear's improvement **where he now lives that lies south of the Kentucky line.** 1 Feb 1817.

30 535 18237 **James Bennett** .. 4 acs .. on north side of Cumberland .. adj Hamilton's .. to incl **Bennett's Ferry** .. 1 Feb 1817.

30 535 18238 **Hugh Hecklin** .. 7 acs .. north side of Cumberland .. adj 640-ac tract **whereon sd Hecklin now lives** .. 1 Feb 1817. B. A. Grimes, Loc.

30 535 18239 **Macom McLarren** .. 10 acs .. on McFarland's Cr .. adj William Anderson's corner .. to incl **where sd Macom McLarren now lives.** 1 Feb 1817. William Harris, Loc.

30 535 18240 **Joel Evans** .. 4 acs .. north fork of Proctor's Cr .. to incl part of sd Evans' field. 1 Feb 1817.

30 535 18241 **Joel Evans** .. 8 acs .. north fork of Proctor's Cr .. including improvement **near where sd Evans now lives.** 1 Feb 1817. B. A. Farmer, Loc.

30 535 18242 **Thomas Lee** .. 10 acs .. on McFarland's Cr .. adj line of William Harris .. including the improvement **whereon sd Lee now lives.** 1 Feb 1817. William Harris, Loc.

30 536 18246 **Jordan Sullivent** .. 10 acs .. waters of Indian Cr of Cumberland .. 1 Feb 1817.

30 536 18247 **Hardy Pursell** .. 5 acs .. On Pine Lick fork of Jenning's Cr .. to **incl sd Hardy Pursell's house** .. 1 Feb 1817. Luke Price, Loc.

30 538 18260 **Moses Fisk** .. 100 acs .. Blackburn's fork of Roaring R .. below Dillingham's and above Pierce's. 3 Feb 1817.

30	538	18261	**Moses Fisk** .. between Spring Cr & Roaring R .. east of the path which leads from Job Morgan's to the Meeting House .. 3 Feb 1817.
30	539	18267	**Joseph Clay & Matthew Clay** .. 6-3/4 acs .. Main fork of Hopper's Cr .. above where they are now boring for salt water .. 6 Feb 1817.
30	543	18297	**John Boyd** .. 10 acs .. in Rock Spring Valley .. adj his own. 17 Feb 1817. John Boyd, Loc.
30	544	18307	**Frederick Skaggs** .. 5 acs .. on Indian Cr .. adj his own. 20 Feb 1817. Fredrick Skaggs, Loc.

BUILDING NEIGHBORHOODS
From
EARLY LAND RECORDS OF TENNESSEE
RG 50 SERIES 2 - LAND ENTRIES BOOK 31 - REEL 9
1ST SURVEYOR'S DISTRICT ENTRIES - JACKSON COUNTY FOLKS

BK	PG	NUMBER	DESCRIPTION
31	9	18385	**Gabriel Dillard** .. 10 acs ..south side of Cumberland .. 40 poles above mouth of James Harvell's spring branch .. including **where Jeremiah Dickins formerly lived.** 3 Mar 1817. James Harvill, Loc.
31	12	18405	**John Finn** .. 5 acs west fork of Roaring R .. south boundary of William S. Luty's tract .. to incl **where Richard Finn now lives.** 6 Mar 1817. Rains Roberts, Loc.
31	12	18407	**Nancy Fanning** .. 5 acs .. waters of Indian Cr .. adj Vance's north boundary .. 6 Mar 1817. John Fanning, Loc.
31	13	18411	**William Sadler** .. 5 acs .. Indian Cr of Cumberland .. adj boundary of tract **whereon he now lives.** 8 Mar 1817.
31	14	18419	**John Plumley** .. 20 acs .. waters of Brimstone Cr .. to incl **where Nancy Duncan now lives.** 8 Mar 1817. Noah Bennett, Loc.
31	15	18427	**Adams C. Hamilton** .. 8 acs .. south side of Cumberland adj his own. 10 Mar 1817.
31	15	18428	**Adams C. Hamilton** .. 5 acs .. south side of Cumberland .. on the dry branch .. adj his own. 10 Mar 1817.
31	17	18435	**John Sadler** .. 10 acs .. adj his own. 12 Mar 1817. Henry McDonald, Loc.
31	17	18436	**John McDonald** .. 5 acs .. adj Daniel Wilburn .. west fork of Indian Cr .. 13 Mar 1817. Henry McDonald, Loc.
31	37	18575	**Jonas Griffith** .. 15 acs .. waters of Jenning's Cr adj tract granted to John Griffith. 2 Apr 1817. Jonas Griffith, Loc.
31	40	18595	**James W. Smith** .. 34-1/2 acs .. south side of Cumberland immediately below where road leading from James Roberts to Williamsburgh intersects sd R at the place called Salt Lick Ford .. 12 Apr 1817. Jas. W. Smith, Loc.
31	40	18599	**William Woodfolk** .. 8 acs .. north side of Cumberland .. just above Mark Holloman's Ferry landing .. 15 Apr

1817. Wm. Woodfolk, Loc.

31	40	18600	**William Woodfolk** .. 10 acs .. between lines of Selby Harney & Francis Graves & joining Thomas Woodward's north boundary .. 15 Apr 1817.
31	41	18601	**William Woodfolk** .. 10 acs .. north side of Cumberland .. adj Lt. Williams and joining Nicholas Teel's south boundary. 15 Apr 1817.
31	41	18602	**William Woodfolk** .. 9 acs .. Smith Co. Several other entries in Smith Co.
31	45	18632	**Edward Fitzpatrick** .. 5 acs .. headwaters of Blackburn's fork.. to incl **where Burns' family lived** .. and on both sides of main Road from Carthage to Knoxville. 21 Apr 1817. Edward Fitzpatrick, Loc.
31	52	18683	**James Pharis** .. 11-1/2 acs .. on the Big Br nearly opposite Williamsburgh joining **the tract he now lives upon** .. north 46 poles to a sugar tree near his turnip patch. 28 Apr 1817. James Pharis, Loc.
31	52	18684	**James Pharis** .. 30 acs .. on Big Br nearly opposite town of Williamsburgh joining tract of 68 acs in name of Stephen Nicholas .. 28 Apr 1817.
31	57	18715	**Joseph Nevill** .. 4 acs .. south side of Smith's fork of Jenning's Cr .. adj Yelveston Nevill .. 7 May 1817. Samuel Griffith, Loc.
31	59	18735	**James Young, Sampson Williams, & Armstreet Stubblefield** .. 32 acs .. on Mill fork of Brimstone Cr .. above the Brimstone Lick .. 12 May 1817.
31	59	18736	**James Young, Sampson Williams, & Armstreet Stubblefield** .. 80 acs .. on Brimstone Cr .. corner of tract **James Short now lives upon** .. 12 May 1817.
31	59	18737	**James Young, Sampson Williams, & Armstreet Stubblefield** .. 90 acs .. Brimstone Cr .. near James Short. 12 May 1817.
31	59	18738	**James Young, Sampson Williams & Armstreet Stubblefield** .. 80 acs .. on Brimstone Cr .. adj tract **where Abraham Denton now lives** .. 12 May 1817.
31	60	18742	**William Rhea** .. 35 acs .. White Co .. waters of Town Cr .. adj entry in name of John Trapp .. 13 May 1817.
31	62	18753	**Joshua Pyron** .. 5 acs .. on War Trace Cr .. to incl improvement Pyron purchased of Hutchenson. 16 May 1817.

31	62	18754	**Joshua Pyron** .. 5 acs .. Smith Co .. on War Trace .. 16 May 1817.
31	62	18760	**Levi Spear** .. 8 acs .. McFarland's Cr .. on the State Line to incl old improvement made by sd Spear. 17 May 1817. John Murrey, Loc.
31	63	18761	**Malcom McLarren** .. 10 acs .. McFarland's Cr .. adj William Anderson's .. to incl part of sd McLarren's improvement. 17 May 1817.
31	63	18762	**William Key** .. 10 acs .. waters of Trace Cr .. the trace **whereon sd Key now lives** .. 17 May 1817.
31	63	18763	**John Murrey** .. 15 acs .. on Plumley's Mill fork of Brimstone Cr .. 17 May 1817.
31	65	18778	**John C. McLemore** .. 50 acs .. on Fowler's Cave fork of Brimstone Cr .. near Pleasant Cheatwood's salt petre works .. 21 May 1817.
31	65	18779	**John C. McLemore** .. 29 acs .. on Brimstone Cr .. John Plumley's northwest corner .. 21 May 1817.
31	65	18782	**John C. McLemore** .. 20 acs .. south side of Cumberland southwest 50 poles from the Big Salt Lick in sd R near Williamsburgh .. to incl sd lick. 22 May 1817. Made void 11 Mar 1822.
31	65	18783	**John C. McLemore** .. 25 acs .. on Dry Cr of Blackburn's fork .. .. 22 May 1817.
31	66	18786	**Samuel A. Moore** .. 40 acs .. White Co .. waters of the Caney fork in a cove of **The Gum Spring Mountain** .. adj corner of George W. Rayman's boundary .. 27 May 1817. Denton Moore, Loc.
31	68	18803	**Reuben Carter** .. 4 acs .. on Garrison fork of Jenning's Cr between Samuel Casey's & Wm. Carter's lines .. 2 June 1817. Reuben Carter, Loc.
31	76	18870	**John Burk** .. 17 acs .. waters of Cub Cr .. Henley's southwest corner .. Brackin's north boundary .. 30 June 1817. John Burk, Loc.
31	79	18893	**George White** .. 9 acs .. waters of the Big Br adj Pharis and Stephen Nichols. 5 July 1817.
31	80	18894	**George White** .. 10 acs .. waters of Dry fork of Martin's Cr .. to incl **Moses Bellew's old sugar camp.** 5 July 1817. (Note: Because the name "Bellew" does not seem to be a Martin's Cr name, we suspect an error in this record. Moses Bellah/Belar made entries on Martin's Cr.)

31	80	18895	**George White** .. one ac .. waters of the Big Br including spring near Edward Lax's in the head of the hollow leading down to Wm. (Mrs.?) Hardcastle's. 5 July 1817.
31	81	18910	**Thomas Shute** .. 50 acs .. on War Trace Cr .. 12 July 1817.
31	84	18927	**Garret Ford** .. 25 acs .. on Big Br .. nearly opposite Williamsburgh including **where Stephen Nicholas now lives** between James Pharis entries .. 25 July 1817. **P. Pharis, Loc.**

Who was P. Pharis? No Pharis name with a first initial "P" has been encountered. (Dec 1991)

31	87	18957	**Silas Clark** .. 13 acs .. on Ward's fork of Jenning's Cr .. to incl **where sd Clark now lives**. 4 Aug 1817.
31	92	18995	**John Rutledge** .. 10 acs .. on Blackburn's fork .. adj Edmund Sutton's line. 16 Aug 1817. Andrew Hampton, Loc.
31	93	18996	**Washington Hampton** .. 4-1/2 acs .. south side of Roaring R .. to incl Abraham Myer's old Sugar Camp. 16 Aug 1817.
31	98	19041	**Allen Hollady** .. 3 acs .. branch of War Trace Cr .. between Buffalo Spring & James Bellew's old camping ground. 1 Sep 1817. Allen Hollady, Loc. (This is the correct neighborhood for James Bellew judging from later land records.)
31	102	19071	**Thomas Butler & Bailey Butler** .. 5 acs .. wet fork of Mill Cr .. 13 Sept 1817. B. Butler, Loc.
31	104	19087	**Arthur Dill** .. 8 acs .. on Blackburn's fork .. adj Henry McDaniel's corner on Edmund Sutton's line .. 20 Sept 1817.
31	104	19088	**Arthur Dill** .. 2 acs .. on Blackburn's fork .. 20 Sep 1817. Martin Langford, Loc.
31	104	19089	**Arthur Dill** .. 10 acs .. Blackburn's fork .. to incl an improvement. 20 Sept 1817.
31	106	19099	**John C. McLemore** .. 20 acs .. Blackburn's fork .. 23 Sept 1817.
31	106	19100	**John Chapman** .. 10 acs .. north side of Roaring R .. adj entry in name of John Higdon granted to sd Chapman. 23 Sept 1819. John Chapman, Loc.

31	108	19117	**Zachariah Grace** .. 5 acs .. north side of Martin's Cr .. 29 Sept 1817. Zachariah Grace, Loc.
31	121	19223	**Brice Collins** .. 25 acs .. head branch of Hensley's Cr .. 28 Oct 1817. James D. Henley, Loc.
31	124	19247	**Thomas Pack** .. one ac .. waters of Jenning's Cr .. to incl sd Pack's spring. 6 Nov 1817. Thos. Pack, Loc.
31	124	19248	**Willie Carter** .. one ac .. headwaters of Jenning's Cr .. to incl sd Carter's spring. 6 Nov 1817. Thos. Pack, Loc.

Note: Page 126, containing Entry Nos. 19262 - 19269, is followed by Page 127 which contains two entries for John Rutledge obviously misnumbered. They are numbered 19470 and 19471 but then are followed by 19272, 19273, etc. Whether or not these incorrect numbers were used for surveys and further identification is still unknown. The documents supporting the entries may have been correct, and only the registrations misnumbered.

31	127	19470/19270	**John Rutledge** .. 10 acs .. waters of west fork of Roaring R .. adj Edward Robertson's .. 24 Nov 1817. Walter Robinson, Loc.
31	127	19471/19271	**John Rutledge** .. 10 acs .. west fork of Roaring R .. to incl **where John Jackson now lives.** 24 Nov 1817.
31	127	19272	**Walter Robertson** .. 6 acs .. west fork of Roaring R .. between Edward Robertson's & John Rutledge's. 24 Nov 1817.
31	127	19273	**Walter Robertson** .. 4 acs .. west fork of Roaring R .. on Edward Robertson's Spring branch about half a mile below his spring .. 24 Nov 1819.
31	127	19274	**Walter Robertson** .. 10 acs .. Roaring R .. to incl improvement made by William Jackson. 24 Nov 1817.
31	140	19377	**William Woodfolk** .. 20 acs .. north side of Cumberland .. just above Mark Holloman's Ferry Landing .. 19 Dec 1819.
31	145	19414	**William Carter** .. 7 acs .. waters of Jenning's Cr .. 2 Jan 1818. William Carter, Loc.
31	146	19429	**David Hogg** .. 12 acs .. waters of War Trace .. adj Thomas Cassady. 5 Jan 1818. David Hogg, Loc.
31	152	19480	**Andrew Hampton** .. 3 acs .. Roaring R .. adj William Hampton's 50-ac tract .. 16 Jan 1818. Andrew Hampton, Loc.

31	155	19501	**John Murrey** .. 10 acs .. dry fork of Mill Cr .. to incl a spring and old improvement formerly **occupied by the Widow Black.** 21 Jan 1818. John Murrey, Loc.
31	155	19502	**John Murrey** .. 10 acs .. dry fk of Mill Cr .. old improvement **formerly occupied by John Black.** 21 Jan 1818.
31	155	19503	**John Murrey** .. 5 acs .. on the ridge between forks of Sugar Cr .. to incl two springs near where sd Murrey cut timber for his mill .. 21 Jan 1818.
31	155	19504	**John Murrey** .. 5 acs .. on Sugar Cr .. adj Thomas Hill's line .. 21 Jan 1818.
31	155	19505	**John Murrey** .. 5 acs .. headwaters of Hopper's Cr of Roaring R .. including spring and foundation of an old cabin on Fisk's road. 21 Jan 1818.
31	155	19506	**John Murrey** .. 5 acs .. waters of north fork of Sugar Cr .. to incl a **cabin built by Byram Stacy** 21 Jan 1818.
31	155	19507	**John Murrey** .. 5 acs .. on Sugar Cr between where **sd John Murrey & Thomas Hill now live** .. to incl a woolf pen. 21 Jan 1818.
31	155	19508	**John Murrey** .. 5 acs .. head of north fork of Mill fork of Sugar Cr .. 21 Jan 1818.
31	156	19509	**John Murrey** .. 5 acs .. on Sugar Cr .. between Thomas Hill's & James Hagland's surveys. 21 Jan 1818.
31	156	19510	**John Murrey** .. 5 acs .. Sugar Cr .. adj 10-ac survey in name of Hamilton Montgomery .. 21 Jan 1818.
31	156	19511	**John C. McLemore** .. headwaters of north fork of Sugar Cr .. to incl part of a sugar orchard above **where Byram Stacy now lives.** 22 Jan 1818.
31	158	19526	**John Temple** .. 11 acs .. waters of the Big Br .. to incl house and improvement **where Lucinda Hardcastle now lives.** 28 Jan 1818. John Temples, Loc.

Note: One Lewis Hardcastle is reported to have settled early on Martin's Cr. He has not surfaced in the records except as descendants named children in his honor. "Lucy" Hardcastle appears on the 1820 census and in later tax records. She has been misread as "Luey."

31	158	19527	**John Temples** .. 6 acs .. on the Big Br .. to incl Price's sugar camp on top of a ridge. 28 Jan 1818.
31	167	19602	**William Buckner** .. 20 acs .. south side of Roaring R near John Stafford's .. to incl a spring in Aaron's old

field. 18 Feb 1818. William Buckner, Loc.

31 168 19605 **Burkett Kinnard** .. 5 acs .. waters of Roaring R .. adj Rains Roberts .. to incl **where Montgomery Kinnard now lives.** 18 Feb 1818.

31 168 19606 **Burkett Kinnard** .. 4 acs .. waters of Martin's Cr .. to incl part of Kinchen Pippen's field. 18 Feb 1818. Burkett Kinnard, Loc.

31 168 19607 **Montgomery Kinnard** .. 15 acs .. waters of Roaring R .. to incl sd Kinnard's improvement. 18 Feb 1818.

31 170 19622 **William Scanlan** .. 20 acs .. head of Bullerd's Cr .. 23 Feb 1818. Jno G. Park, Loc.

31 172 19639 **John Baker** .. 10 acs .. dry fork of Mill Cr .. southwest from Gabriel Baker's spring house .. to incl Gabriel Baker's improvement. 27 Feb 1818. Lewis Stover, Loc.

31 172 19640 **Jesse Williams** .. 3 acs .. dry fork of Mill Cr .. adj entry in name of Thomas Ownby .. 27 Feb 1818.

31 172 19643 **William Buckner** .. 10 acs .. south side of Roaring R .. Rutherford's branch .. 27 Feb 1818.

31 172 19644 **William Buckner** .. 10 acs .. south side of Roaring R .. 27 Feb 1818.

31 173 19647 **Lewis Stover** .. 6 acs .. dry fork of Mill Cr .. adj his own. 27 Feb 1818. Lewis Stover, Loc.

31 173 19651 **Kinchen Pippen** .. 5 acs .. head waters of Martin's Cr .. to incl spring & peach orchard at Champ Guin's old place. 28 Feb 1818.

31 176 19676 **James Vinson** .. 15 acs .. Dry fork of Martin's Cr .. adj his own 10-ac survey nearly west of the school house where **Elrod formerly kept school** .. west to James Pharis's line. 5 Mar 1818. James Vinson, Loc.

31 177 19677 **James Vinson** .. 15 acs .. on the head of Roy's branch of dry fork of Flynn's Cr .. northeast corner of sd Vinson's 10 ac survey .. 5 Mar 1818.

31 178 19687 **Henry Moss** .. 20 acs .. waters of Line cr .. to incl spring and house **where sd Moss now lives.** 9 Mar 1818.

31 178 19688 **Archibald Plumley** .. 15 acs .. on Dry Cr .. to incl a sugar camp **occupied by Joseph Whitney.** 9 Mar 1818. James Moss, Loc.

31 178 19691 **John Anderson** .. 10 acs .. waters of Indian Cr of Caney

Fk near the Walton Road .. to incl **where sd Anderson now lives.** 10 Mar 1818.

31 178 19692 **John Campbell** .. 6 acs .. near the line between White & Jackson Counties on the ridge .. 10 Mar 1818. John Campbell, Loc.

31 181 19716 **William Jared JR** .. 5 acs .. on Walton's Road adj place **where he now lives** .. 18 Mar 1818.

31 181 19717 **William Jared JR** .. 5 acs .. on Walton's Road .. 18 Mar 1818.

31 189 19773 **Wallace Bickerstaff** .. 10 acs .. north side of Cumberland .. adj General Lee Nolen's corner .. 8 Apr 1818. Jacob Bennett, Loc.

31 198 19840 **John C. McLemore & James Vaulx** .. 300 acs .. north side of the Cumberland .. 4 May 1818.

31 201 19867 **Thomas Shute** .. 200 acs .. on War Trace Cr .. 15 May 1818.

31 201 19868 **Thomas Shute** .. 140 acs .. on War Trace. adj his own. 15 May 1818.

31 205 19897 **Redmond D. Barry** .. 82-1/2 acs .. waters of Indian Cr .. southwest corner of tract sold by sd Barry to John & William Sadler .. 25 May 1818.

31 209 19934 **Greenberry Taylor** .. 5 acs .. on Indian Cr .. south side of the Walton Road.. adj Samuel Watkins' field .. 9 June 1818. James Taylor, Loc.

31 236 20156 **Joseph Shaw** .. 62 acs .. east side of Shaw's branch of Martin's Cr .. crossing sd Cr .. to incl **where James McKinley now lives.** 6 Aug 1818.

31 236 20157 **Joseph Wright** .. 7 acs .. waters of Indian Cr of Cumberland to incl **where sd Wright now lives.** 6 Aug 1818.

31 237 20159 **Charles Devenport** .. one ac .. branch of War Trace .. to incl **where sd Devenport now lives** .. 10 Aug 1818.

31 237 20163 **Samuel G. Smith** .. 20 acs .. Dry fork of Martin's Cr .. adj Sampson Williams' 66 acs .. 10 Aug 1818. J. W. Smith, Loc.

31 252 20282 **Willis Pippin** .. 5 acs .. on Bowerman's branch of Roaring R .. to incl a salt petre cave found by Zachariah Roberts & sd Pippin. 31 Aug 1818.

31 253 20291 **Joseph Shaw** .. 10 acs .. waters of Martin's Cr .. east

side of Harris Hollow .. to incl Harris' old improvement. 3 Sept 1818. Wm. Rowland, Loc.

| 31 | 253 | 20292 | **Joseph Shaw** .. 10 acs .. waters of Martin's Cr .. adj his own. 3 Sept 1818.

| 31 | 253 | 20293 | **Joseph Shaw** .. 10 acs .. waters of Martin's Cr .. begin at Liles northwest corner .. 3 Sept 1818.

| 31 | 253 | 20294 | **William Rowland** .. 10 acs .. waters of Indian Cr of Cumberland .. adj his 37 acs **where Wm. Elrod now lives** .. 3 Sept 1818.

| 31 | 253 | 20295 | **William Rowland** .. 20 acs .. waters of Indian Cr of Cumberland adj his own **that William Elrod now lives on** .. 3 Sept 1818.

| 31 | 259 | 20342 | **John Anderson** .. 8 acs .. on the Walton Road .. to incl field cultivated this year by Abisha Cannon and to adjoin the .. tract **where sd Cannon now lives.** 21 Sept 1818. John Anderson, Loc.

| 31 | 266 | 20407 | **John Ryal** .. 5 acs .. north side of Cumberland .. west from John Nichols northeast corner to to **incl sd Ryal's house.** 6 Oct 1818. John Ryal, Loc.

| 31 | 272 | 20450 | **William Gibson** .. 8 acs .. headwaters of Doe Cr .. adj Thomas Davidson's line .. 22 Oct 1818. Jepthah West, Loc.

| 31 | 272 | 20451 | **William Gibson** .. 5 acs .. waters of Roaring R .. including **John Goforth's improvement.** 22 Oct 1818.

| 31 | 272 | 20452 | **Jepthah West** .. 2 acs .. Bowerman's branch of Blackburn's fork ..to incl a sugar camp. 22 Oct 1818.

| 31 | 273 | 20457 | **Joshua Leonard** .. 10 acs .. on Mine Lick Cr .. to incl **where sd Leonard now lives.** 23 Oct 1818. Joshua Stone, Loc.

| 31 | 282 | 20513 | **John G. Park & James Tilford** .. 50 acs .. south side of Cumberland on the bank .. nearly opposite upper end of first Island below Williamsburgh .. 14 Nov 1818. John G. Park, Loc.

| 31 | 286 | 20538 | **William Clark** .. 5 acs .. on Indian Cr of the Caney Fk .. to incl **where John Smith now lives.** 21 Nov 1818. Wm. Clark, Loc.

| 31 | 286 | 20539 | **William Clark** .. 2 acs .. Indian Cr of Caney Fk .. adj his own. 21 Nov 1818.

| 31 | 286 | 20540 | **Tenah Gill** .. one ac .. Indian Cr of Caney Fk .. to incl Samuel Walker's upper sugar camp. 21 Nov 1818.

31	286	20541	**Tenah Gill** .. 4 acs .. Indian Cr of the Caney Fk .. to incl Samuel Walker's lower sugar camp. 21 Nov 1818. Wm. Clark, Loc.
31	289	20562	**Hardy Pursell** .. 5 acs .. on Brimstone Cr .. adj John Nichols .. 28 Nov 1818.
31	291	20579	**Patsy Cameron** .. 10 acs .. waters of Indian Cr of the Caney Fk .. 5 Dec 1818. Alexander Blair, Loc.
31	291	20580	**Patsy Cameron** .. 5 acs .. Indian Cr of Caney Fk .. adj her own. 5 Dec 1818.
31	294	20599	**David Newman** .. 75 acs .. headwaters of Martin's Cr .. about 1/4 mile north from Kinchen Pippin. 10 Dec 1818. David Newman, Loc.
31	297	20621	**James Tilford** .. 10 acs .. south side of Cumberland .. adj Tilford & Parks .. 26 Dec 1818. James Tilford, Loc.
31	297	20623	**James Tilford & John G. Park** .. 20 acs .. south side of Cumberland .. adj their own where they are now boring for salt water. 26 Dec 1818.
31	300	20644	**James Goolsby** .. 10 acs .. beginning at a white oak near a place called the Double Springs .. to incl sd springs. 6 Jan 1819. James Goolsby, Loc.
31	300	20645	**James Goolsby** .. 5 acs .. near an improvement made by Wade Goolsby. 6 Jan 1819.
31	300	20646	**William Harper** .. 2 acs .. on a fork of Martin's Cr .. to incl a mill seat. 6 Jan 1819.
31	301	20653	**Nathaniel Mason** .. 13 acs .. west fork of Roaring R .. to incl a field cleared by James Bruington. 13 Jan 1819. Nathaniel Mason, Loc.
31	302	20659	**Zachariah Roberts** .. 4 acs .. Bowerman's branch of Roaring R .. adj Willis Pipkins .. to incl a salt petre cave found by sd Roberts & James Pryor. 15 Jan 1819.
31	303	20670	**John Temple** .. Dry fork of Martin's Cr .. to incl **where Nathan Allen now lives**. 19 Jan 1819. Richard Clark, Loc.
31	303	20671	**John Temple** .. 7 acs .. waters of the Big Br adj James Pharis .. 19 Jan 1819.
31	303	20672	**John Temple** .. 5 acs .. southwest side of dry fork of Flynn's Cr .. adj Wheeler's south boundary .. 19 Jan 1819.

31	303	20673	**John Temple** .. one ac .. northeast side of dry fork of Flynn's Cr .. 19 Jan 1819.
31	304	20674	**John Richardson** .. 8 acs .. near head of the Dry fork of War Trace Cr .. Harney's west boundary .. to incl part of sd Richardson's improvement. 19 Jan 1819. John Richardson, Loc.
31	304	20679	**John C. McLemore** .. 150 acs .. north side of Cumberland .. adj Wilsons and Collins. 20 Jan 1819.
31	306	20695	**John Murrey** .. 10 acs .. waters of Doe Cr .. adj Uriah Anderson and James Jones. 25 Jan 1819.
31	306	20696	**Robert F. Sweeney** .. 20 acs .. waters of Doe Cr .. 25 Jan 1819. Wm. Lock, Loc.
31	306	20697	**John Murry** .. 10 acs .. waters of Doe Cr .. adj Cox...the Mercer field .. 25 Jan 1819.
31	307	20698	**John Murrey** .. 10 acs .. waters of Doe Cr .. between Thomas Hardin's and Glover's. 25 Jan 1819.
31	307	20699	**John Murrey** .. 10 acs .. waters of Doe Cr .. **where Lawson lives** .. 25 Jan 1819.
31	307	20700	**John Murrey** .. 10 acs .. Doe Cr .. adj Uriah Anderson's entry that incls the mouth of Doe Cr .. 8 ac tract entered in name of James Jones .. 25 Jan 1819.
31	307	20701	**John Murrey** .. 10 acs .. Doe Cr.. adj Brehon's south boundary .. Cox's .. 25 Jan 1819. (Recorded twice. Once out of sequence.)
31	312	20735	**Henry Sadler** .. one ac .. Smith Co .. east side of Caney Fk .. above mouth of Rock Spring .. to incl a spring between mouth of Rock Spring & Indian Cr .. 5 Feb 1819.
31	317	20775	**Peter Smith** ase of Tandy Shumake .. 20 acs .. west fork of Russell's Mill Cr adj his own and Swearingham .. 18 Feb 1819. P. Smith, Loc.
31	320	20792	**David Richie** .. 8 acs .. Roaring R .. adj Peter Piles .. including house **where sd Richie now lives**. 25 Feb 1819. David Richie, Loc.
31	320	20793	**James Richie** .. 2 acs .. Roaring R .. to incl Robert Wilson's old sugar camp. 25 Feb 1819.
31	320	20794	**Alexander Rutledge** .. 5 acs .. Dyer's branch of Roaring R .. adj Rains Roberts .. 25 Feb 1819. Jepthah West, Loc.

31	320	20795	**Alexander Rutledge** .. 5 acs .. Dry branch of Roaring R .. to incl a small field called Joseph Wilson's. 25 Feb 1819.
31	320	20796	**Sterling Harris** .. 2 acs .. Bowerman's Br of Blackburn's Fk. 25 Feb 1819.
31	320	20797	**Sterling Harris** .. 5 acs .. on the ridge opposite David Richie's .. west side of Blackburn's Fk. 25 Feb 1819.
31	320	20798	**Sterling Harris** .. Bowerman's Br .. 25 Feb 1819.
31	322	20814	**Thomas Scanland, James Hogland, Robert Jennings & David Hogland** .. 5 acs .. branch of Sugar Cr that empties in at James Hogland's .. 2 Mar 1819.
31	322	20815	**Thomas Scanland** .. 5 acs .. south side of Cumberland .. **whereon Robert Jennings now lives** .. 2 Mar 1819.
31	322	20816	**James Hogland** .. 3 acs .. Sugar Cr .. adj Reynolds Jeffrey's lower corner .. 2 Mar 1819.
31	323	20819	**David Heddy** .. 10 acs .. waters of Doe Cr .. adj Cox and Sweeney. 3 Mar 1819. William Lock, Loc.
31	323	20820	**David Heddy** .. 5-1/2 acs .. Doe Cr .. adj his own. 3 Mar 1819.
31	325	20837	**William Woodfolk** .. 21 acs .. north side of Cumberland .. west boundary of Nathaniel Williamson's 2,560 ac tract .. near a small branch of Fund's Br. 8 Mar 1819.
31	325	20839	**James W. Smith** .. 24 acs .. adj Joseph Shaw's 62-1/2 ac entry on east side of Shaw's branch of Martin's Cr .. 8 Mar 1819.
31	325	20840	**James W. Smith** .. 6 acs .. head waters of Indian Cr above the Trough Spring .. Samuel Enoch's north boundary .. 8 Mar 1819.
31	325	20841	**James W. Smith** .. 21 acs .. head waters of Indian Cr .. Samuel Enoch's east boundary 8 Mar 1819.
31	331	20883	**Moses Attleberry** .. north side of Cumberland .. near James McColgin's. 6 Apr 1819. Moses Attleberry, Loc.
31	332	20889	**Robert Thompson** .. 5 acs .. waters of Flynn's Cr .. to incl **where Benjamin Burchett now lives**. 12 Apr 1819. Robert Thompson, Loc.
31	332	20890	**Robert Thompson** .. on waters of Flynn's Cr .. adj his own. 12 Apr 1819.

31	333	20898	**John Murrey** .. 4 acs .. south side of Cumberland .. at James G. Brehon's corner .. 17 Apr 1819.
31	333	20899	**John Murrey** .. Doe cr .. improvement where Lawson formerly lived. 17 Apr 1819.
31	333	20900	**John Murrey** .. 10 acs .. Doe Cr .. 17 Apr 1819.
31	341	20953	**William Wheeler** .. 20 acs .. dry fork of Flynn's Cr.. near entry in name of Caleb Anderson. 14 May 1819.
31	341	20954	**William Wheeler** .. 40 acs .. dry fork of Flynn's Cr .. near Uriah Anderson. 14 May 1819.
31	341	20955	**John Brown** .. 10 acs .. dry fork of Flynn's Cr .. 14 May 1819.
31	341	20956	**Thomas Brown** .. 5 acs .. dry fork of Flynn's Cr .. to incl improvement made **by Miller Broom** .. 14 May 1819.
31	341	20957	**Thomas Brown** .. dry fork of Flynn's Cr .. ridge between Roy's branch & the Horse Hollow .. 14 May 1819.
31	341	20958	**Thomas Brown** .. 12 acs .. waters of dry fork of Flynn's Cr .. tract **on which he now lives** .. 14 May 1819.
31	344	20982	**Samuel G. Smith** .. 36 acs .. Doe Cr .. adj entry in name of James McCall .. 31 May 1819.
31	344	20983	**John C. McLemore** .. 30 acs .. Doe Cr .. Adj Nicholas Hale .. path to William Stafford's .. 31 May 1819.
31	346	20997	**Alexander Rutledge** .. 5 acs .. in the Owl Cove on head of Blackburn's Fk .. 16 June 1819.
31	347	21001	**Joseph Shaw** .. 10 acs .. waters of Martin's Cr .. adj his own. 17 June 1819.
31	358	21096	**Tandy K. Witcher & George Hutchinson** .. one ac .. Jenning's Cr .. to incl mouth of cave .. lately opened by George Hutchinson & others. 14 Sep 1819.
31	359	21105	**Ann Dudney** .. 3 acs .. on the head of Horse Br of Flynn's Cr .. adj Nathan Haggard .. 17 Sept 1819.
31	360	21106	**Ann Dudney** .. 3 acs .. 17 Sept 1817.
31	360	21109	**Tandy K. Witcher & George Hutcheson** .. Jenning's Cr .. salt petre cave found by Vansent & others .. 2 Sep 1819. Cyrus Young, Loc.
31	360	21110	**Cyrus Young** .. 4 acs .. Jennings Cr .. mouth of cave found by John Vansent .. 21 Sept 1819.

31	361	21117	**Burnell Almond** .. 26 acs .. on Williams' Mill Cr of Roaring R .. to incl **where sd Almonds now lives.** 2 Sept 1819.
31	361	21118	**Burnell Almonds** .. 4 acs .. waters of Roaring R .. to incl **where ____ Joiner now lives.** 24 Sept 1819.
31	363	21139	**Jeremiah B. Hutchison** .. one ac .. Garrison's fork of Jenning's Cr .. to incl Samuel Hutchison's old salt petre cave .. 12 Oct 1819.
31	363	21141	**Jeremiah Baily, Jeremiah Bell, and Henry Baily** .. one ac .. Ward's fork of Jenning's Cr .. to incl cave .. which Jeremiah Bell has worked at. **12 or 21 Oct 1819.**
31	364	21154	**Martin Jones** .. 7 acs .. on Big Br of Martin's Cr .. adj William Burris .. 1 Nov 1819.
31	365	21155	**Martin Jones** .. 9 acs .. on Big Br of Martin's Cr .. 1 Nov 1819.
31	365	21156	**Martin Jones** .. 7 acs .. east side of the Big Br of Martin's Cr .. adj Joseph Shaw .. 1 Nov 1819.
31	366	21165	**William Jared** .. 4-1/2 acs .. on Indian Cr of Caney Fk .. adj his own. 10 Nov 1819.
31	366	21166	**William Jared** .. 4 acs .. Indian Cr of Caney Fk .. adj his own .. 10 Nov 1819. John Lemmons, Loc.
31	366	21167	**Sampson Williams** .. 274 acs .. on Flynn's Cr .. including **where Edward Mercer now lives** .. 10 Nov 1819.
31	366	21171	**Joseph Shaw** .. 50 acs .. waters of Roaring R south of Walton's Road .. east of Harris old stand .. to incl **where Harris formerly lived.** 16 Nov 1819. (Note: That's what it says. Must mean Blackburn's fork of Roaring R.)
31	367	21177	**Sampson Williams** .. 114-1/2 .. on Martin's Cr between tract granted to **Katherine Wilson** and another granted to Stokley Donelson including **where James McKinley now lives** .. 24 Nov 1819.
31	368	21192	**John Chism** .. 10 acs .. White Co .. waters of Caney Fk .. top of the **Gum Spring Mountain** .. adj Jno Hicken's .. 13 Dec 1819.
31	369	21195	**Thomas Gann** .. 2 acs .. on Laxon's Cr of Roaring R .. adj entry in name of James McKnight .. to incl **where John Hood (Wood?) now lives.** 14 Dec 1819.
31	386	21316	**Michael Sailor** .. 18 acs .. waters of Pigeon Roost Cr .. 7 June 1820. Thomas Philips, Loc.

31	388	21330	**Simeon Putman & Joseph Chaffin** .. one ac .. Blackburn's fork .. opposite Thomas Anderson's field .. to incl a cave **now worked by Simeon Putman.** 17 June 1820.
31	388	21331	**John M. Walkins** .. 3 acs .. Ward's fork of Jenning's Cr .. adj Silas Clark .. 20 June 1820.
31	389	21334	**John Murrey** .. 4 acs .. Rockey branch of Cumberland .. 22 June 1820. Alfred Murray, Loc.
31	389	21335	**John Murry** .. 6 acs .. east fork of Doe Cr .. adj Nicholas Hale.. 22 June 1820. Alfred Murray, Loc.
31	395	21373	**Littleton Darnold** .. one and a half ac .. waters of Indian Cr .. near John Bush .. 22 Aug 1820.
31	403	21423	**William C. Walker** .. 10 acs .. north side of Cumberland .. adj John Nichols .. to incl **where Robert Price now lives.** 11 Oct 1820. Will C. Walker, Loc.
31	409	21455	**William Twitty** .. 6 acs .. Jennings Cr .. adj survey **James Short lives on** .. to incl **where Isaac Lea (?) now lives.** 17 Nov 1820.
31	409	21456	**Adam C. Hamilton** .. 5 acs .. Doe Cr .. to incl **where Luke Williams now lives** .. 20 Oct 1820.
31	412	21487	**James Pharis** .. 3 acs .. Dry fork of Martin's Cr beginning at a sugartree near **Leonard Hough's east boundary** .. to incl **where Hyram Pharis now lives.** 8 Jan 1821.
31	412	21488	**James Pharis** .. 4 acs .. the dry fork of Martin's Cr .. to incl the improvement where **Suckey Hough formerly lived.** 8 Jan 1821.
31	412	21489	**James Pharis** .. 4 acs .. waters of the Big Br .. to incl **where Mrs. Hardcastle now lives.** 8 Jan 1821.
31	412	21490	**James Pharis** .. 1/4 ac .. waters of the Big Br .. to incl a small spring .. at head of a hollow between Mrs. Hardcastle & Amon Hale. 8 Jan 1821.
31	412	21491	**James Pharis** .. 1/4 ac .. waters of Big Br .. about a half mile east of south from Mrs. Hardcastle's. 8 Jan 1821.

BK	PG	NUMBER	DESCRIPTION

31 418 21529 **Richard Allcorn** .. 2 acs .. waters of Indian Cr of Caney Fork .. south side of the Walton Road .. 3 May 1821. Richard Allcorn, Loc.

31 423 21554 **David Porter & John Burk** .. 6 acs .. on Cubb Cr .. adj James Simpson .. 27 Mar 1821.

31 424 21562 **William J. Smith** .. one ac .. Indian Cr of Caney Fork .. 16 Apr 1821. William J. Smith, Loc.

31 425 21566 **Alexander Smith** .. 8 acs .. head of Indian Cr of Caney Fork .. 23 Apr 1821. Alexander Smith, Loc.

31 425 21568 **Joseph Shaw** .. 10 acs .. Indian Cr of Caney Fork .. to incl Austin Dillard's old improvement. 25 Apr 1821. Peter Chum, Loc.

31 425 21570 **Samuel G. Smith** .. 10 acs .. waters of Doe Cr .. adj Job Glover .. to incl place **whereon sd Glover now lives.** 27 Apr 1821.

31 425 21571 **John Sadler** .. 50 acs .. west fork of Indian Cr of Cumberland .. to incl **where William Cook now lives.** 2 May 1821. John Sadler, Loc.

31 426 21572 **John McDonald** .. 25 acs .. west fork of Indian Cr of Cumberland .. to incl **where Andrew Anderson now lives.** 2 May 1821. John Sadler, Loc.

31 433 21634 **John Barr** .. Indian Cr .. to incl improvement made by Samuel Brashears. 1 Sept 1821. John Bard, Loc.

31 440 21694 **William J. Smith** .. one ac .. White Co .. Caney Fork .. 3 Nov 1821. John Trapp, Loc.

31 441 21704 **Thomas Shute** .. 10 acs .. Indian Cr .. forks of two small drains that run through William Sadler's Field .. 13 Nov 1821.

31 441 21705 **Thomas Shute** .. 10 acs .. near the head of Martin's Cr .. first fork of sd creek below the salt petre works .. 13 Nov 1821.

31 441 21706 **Thomas Shute** .. 10 acs .. on Martin's Cr .. adj his own .. 13 Nov 1821.

31 441 21707 **Thomas Shute** .. 10 acs .. on Martin's Cr .. adj his own 13 Nov 1821.

31 441 21708 **Thomas Shute** .. 10 acs on Martin's Cr .. adj his own .. 13 Nov 1821.

31	441	21709	**Thomas Shute** .. 10 acs on Martin's Cr .. adj his own. 13 Nov 1821.
31	441	21710	**Thomas Shute** .. 10 acs .. Martin's Cr .. adj his own. 13 Nov 1821.
31	441	21711	**Thomas Shute** .. 10 acs .. on Martin's Cr .. 13 Nov 1821.
31	442	21712	**Thomas Shute.** No. 21713, also for Thomas Shute on Martin's Cr .. All of these entries for Thomas Shute were on both sides of the Cr, and dated 13 Nov 1821. Locator in every case is shown as Thomas Shute.

Finding Thomas Shute on Little Indian and Martin's Crs, and on Brimstone Cr, and in Smith County on Williamson's Branch is significant. Other names associated with him, e.g. Edward Givins, Gabriel Benson and Samuel Scraggins, may be significant.

31	445	21734	**James McHutchinson** .. 5 acs .. south side of Cumberland on west fork of Indian Cr .. to incl **where John Dillard now lives.** 16 Jan 1822. James McHutchinson, Loc.
31	445	21737	**Thomas Tadlock** .. 15 acs .. Big Trace Cr .. adj his own. 19 Jan 1822. James Riddy, Loc.
31	448	21754	**James McHutcheson** .. 50 acs .. south side of Cumberland .. west fork of Indian Cr .. near John Dillard's spring .. to incl mill and house **where sd Dillard now lives.** 9 Feb 1822. J. McHutcheson, Loc.
31	453	21783	**Elizabeth Draper** ase of Hardy Pursell .. 5 acs .. N of Cumberland on Smith's Fk of Jennings Cr .. to incl Isaac Siscoe's house and improvement. 16 Mar 1822. Hardy Pursell, Loc.
31	455	21797	**Daniel (David?) Glover** .. 9 acs .. waters of Little Indian Cr .. adj Wilham Cook's line .. 26 Mar 1822. Daniel Glover, Loc.
31	455	21799	**Alfred Hardester** .. 15 acs .. west side of Pilot Knob .. to incl Dillard's improvements. 27 Mar 1822. W. B. Shephard, Loc.
31	457	21814	**Samuel G. Smith** .. 6 acs .. Doe Cr .. adj Nicholas Haile .. Simeon Putnam .. to incl improvement made by George R. Cox. 22 Apr 1822. Sam G. Smith, Loc.

Note: The name Simeon Putman is spelled, in these records, alternately "Putnam" and "Putman." I have followed the source. Let a descendant decide which is correct. We know the county is **Putnam.** We do not know which Simeon was.

31	458	21816	**James McHutcheson** .. south side of Cumberland .. Indian

			Cr .. Isaac Walton's south boundary .. to incl improvement **where George Apple now lives.** 24 Apr 1822.
31	458	21817	**James McHutcheson** .. south side of Cumberland .. 2nd fork of Indian Cr .. above spring **where David Apple now lives** .. 24 Apr 1822. John Sadler, Loc. No. 21818, same date, also for McHutcheson ref David Apple. John Sadler was Loc.
31	458	21820	**Jesse Walling** .. 20 acs .. Smith Co .. Woolf Cr .. near plantation of James Ballard .. to incl .. house **where John S. McDaniels now lives.** 30 Apr 1822. John S. McDaniels, Loc.
31	460	21834	**Mason Watts** .. 2 acs .. waters of north branch of Spring fork of Martin's Cr .. 13 May 1822. James Carter, Loc.
31	460	21835	**Mason Watts** .. 2 acs .. on a ridge that divides the two north branches of the Spring fork of Martin's Cr .. to incl **Anderson's cotton patch.** 13 May 1822.
31	461	21840	**Robert Mansell** .. 15 acs .. waters of Martin's Cr .. near Richard Mansell's. 20 May 1822. James Taylor, Loc.
31	467	21888	**William J. Smith** .. one ac. White Co .. Cane Cr .. 25 July 1822. John Trapp. Loc.
31	468	21895	**Andrew Clarke** .. 10 acs .. west fork of Indian Cr .. to incl part of John Dillard's improvement. 1 Aug 1822. Andrew Clarke, Loc.
31	468	21896	**Ditto.**
31	468	21898	**Robert P. Chester** .. 57 acs .. south side of Cumberland .. adj Aaron Lambert's 1,000-ac survey .. to incl house **where William Wilson formerly lived.** 5 Aug 1822. A. Stubblefield, Loc.
31	469	21902	**John Sadler** .. 25 acs .. Smith Co .. west fork of Indian Cr south side of Cumberland .. below house James Womack formerly lived in .. 7 Aug 1822. John Sadler, Loc.
31	469	21903	**John Somers** .. 7 acs .. Roaring R .. north side of road leading from Gainsborough to Sparta .. 7 Aug 1822. James Somers, Loc.
31	469	21905	**William Exum** .. 14 acs .. on the Big Branch .. to incl spring and peach orchard formerly claimed by Stephen Nicholas. 7 Aug 1822. Josiah Spurlock, Loc.
31	470	21906	**Josiah Spurlock** .. 6 acs .. on the Big Branch of

Cumberland adj James Pharis .. to incl lower part of field where Nicholas turnip patch used to be. 7 Aug 1822.

31	471	21920	**Ellis Kirkpatrick** .. 10 acs .. north side of Cumberland .. Nichols' corner .. 20 Aug 1822. Ellis Kirkpatrick, Loc.
31	473	21928	**John Sadler** .. 12 acs .. Smith Co .. south side of Cumberland .. west fork of Indian Cr .. a little below house formerly occupied by James Womack. 3 Sept 1822.
31	473	21929	**James Kirkpatrick** .. 20 acs .. on Brimstone Cr .. to incl William Ryal's plantation. 3 Sept 1822. John Kirkpatrick, Loc.
31	474	21934	**Dempsey Powell** .. 7 acs .. Smith Co .. waters of Caney Fork .. James Roulston's southeast corner .. 5 Sept 1822. Robert A. Lancaster, Loc.
31	478	21967	**John Sadler** .. 12 acs .. Smith Co .. south side of Cumberland and east side of west fork of Indian Cr .. 21 Sept 1822. John Sadler, Loc.
31	482	21994	**Samuel G. Smith** .. 12 acs .. north side of Cumberland .. James Young's corner .. Brimstone Cr .. to corner of improvement now occupied by William Rogol .. to incl **where sd William Rogol now lives** .. 27 Sep 1822.
31	484	22006	**Samuel G. Smith** .. 40 acs .. south side of Cumberland between Mill Cr and Sugar Cr .. **where William Williams now lives** .. 2 Oct 1822.
31	484	22007	**Samuel G. Smith** .. 20 acs .. on the ridge between Mill Cr and Sugar Cr .. 2 Oct 1822.
31	488	22038	**Josiah Copeland** .. 15 acs .. waters of Brimstone Cr .. to incl **house now occupied by William Ryal.** 16 Oct 1822. Josiah Copeland, Loc.
31	489	22042	**Wilson Gaines** .. 2 acs .. Branch of Bullerd's Cr .. near **where Allen Biby now lives** .. 21 Oct 1822. Wilson Gaines, Loc.
31	489	22043	**Leonard Keeling** .. one ac .. branch of Bullerd's Cr .. 21 Oct 1822. Wilson Gaines, Loc.
31	490	22048	**Bailey Butler** .. 2 acs .. dry fork of Mill Cr .. near fork of the creek **where James Williams now lives.** 25 Oct 1822. G. S. Butler, Loc.
31	491	22058	**Samuel Poindexter** .. 6 acs .. waters of Proctor's Cr .. 5 Nov 1822.

31	491	22059	**Samuel Poindexter** .. 10 acs .. waters of Proctor's Cr .. William Savage's west boundary .. 5 Nov 1822. Samuel Poindexter, Loc.
31	491	22060	**David Poindexter** .. waters of McFarland's Cr .. ridge between sd Cr and Proctor's Cr .. including **where Wilson Grace now lives.** 5 Nov 1822. Samuel Poindexter, Loc.
31	493	22076	**Josiah Copeland** .. 6 acs .. north side of Cumberland .. to incl George Hutchinson's house and improvement. 9 Nov 1822. Josiah Copeland, Loc.
31	494	22088	**John James** .. 6 acs .. between the two Indian Crs .. near where William Carter lived & about a mile from D. Young's .. to incl spring & improvement **where sd Carter lived.** 13 Nov 1822. Jas. Davis, Loc.
31	495	22095	**James Short** .. 6 acs .. on Brimstone Cr .. adj entry in name of Emanuel Holmes .. 18 Nov 1822.
31	497	22106	**Richard Minebry** .. 2 acs .. north side of Cumberland on a branch of Cub Cr .. 21 Nov 1822. Sam G. Smith, Loc.
31	497	22109	**Reece V. Morrall** .. 2 acs .. on a branch of Sugar Cr .. a branch formerly called Murray's mill seat .. 25 Nov 1822. Price Butler, Loc.
31	497	22110	**Reece V. Morrall** .. 2 acs .. Sugar Cr .. 25 Nov 1822. Price Butler, Loc.
31	500	22131	**William Cotton** .. 15 acs .. west side of Buffalo Valley .. 12 Dec 1822. Felix Thornton, Loc.
31	501	22135	**Simon Carlisle** .. 5 acs .. waters of Indian Cr .. Hugh Stewart's southeast corner .. 13 Dec 1822.
31	508	22192	**Thomas Guiman** .. 10 acs .. waters of Proctor's Cr .. adj Stephen Cantrell .. above where **the Widow Martin now lives** .. 20 Jan 1823.
31	509	22202	**William Woodfolk** .. 13 acs .. north side of Cumberland .. adj Thomas Woodward's preemption **on which the Widow Currey now lives** .. 30 Jan 1823. Wm. Woodfolk, Loc.
31	510	22210	**John Sadler** .. 13 acs .. waters of west fork of Indian Cr .. adj his south boundary .. 1 Feb 1823.
31	512	22227	and 22228 **Sam G. Smith** .. 10 acs .. waters of Sugar Cr .. 6 Feb 1823. Sam G. Smith, Loc.
31	512	22229	**Sam G. Smith** .. 5 acs .. on Blackburn's fork .. to incl **where Peter Richie now lives.** 6 Feb 1823. Sam G. Smith, Loc.

31	512	22230	**Reese V. Morrell** .. 10 acs .. waters of Sugar Cr .. 6 Feb 1823. Sam G. Smith, Loc.
31	512	22231	**John Osgathorp** .. 5 acs .. south side of Cumberland .. head of the branch **that Reese V. Morrell lives on** .. 6 Feb 1823.
31	517	22268	**Alexander Keith** .. 15 acs .. waters of Big Trace Cr of Big Barren .. adj James Roddy .. to incl **improvement now occupied by Samuel York.** 12 Mar 1823. Alexander Keith, Loc.
31	517	22269	**Alexander Keith** .. 11 acs .. head waters of Little Trace Cr of Big Barren .. adj land now owned by John Gess .. 12 Mar 1823. Alexander Keith, Loc.

The name "Gess" or Gist or Guess, whatever it is, is troublesome. A library table consultant tells me it was pronounced somewhere between "heist" and "Christ." Obviously, it gave earlier scribes trouble, too.

31	523	22310	**Dudley Brown** .. 2 acs .. southside of Flynn's Cr .. near Morrison's old cabin .. 1 Apr 1823. James Carter, Loc.
31	523	22311	**Thomas Watts** .. one ac .. branch of the Spring Fork of Martin's Cr .. to incl spring and house **now occupied by Mason Watts.** 1 Apr 1823. James Carter, Loc.
31	523	22316	**James W. Smith** .. 4 acs .. waters of Indian Cr of Cumberland in a hollow above Samuel Enoch's .. to incl improvement made by John Stokes. 5 Apr 1823. Jas. W. Smith, Loc.
31	524	22317	**James W. Smith** .. 8 acs .. waters of Indian Cr of Cumberland .. west side of first west fork above the Trough Spring & about 15 poles east of a high point of the hill near Capt. Cowen's southeast corner. 5 Apr 1823. Jas. W. Smith, Loc.
31	524	22318	**James W. Smith** .. 12 acs .. east fork of Indian Cr of Cumberland .. above the Trough Spring above Capt Cowen's. 5 Apr 1823.

A conference of library table consultants about where this "trough" spring might have been and why it was so-called resulted in the conclusion that wherever there was a tanyard, there had to be a washing trough for the hides. That conclusion was reinforced by the one instance when this waterway was called "The tan troft spring." Names associated with James W. Smith and this Trough Spring i.e. Samuel Enochs, John Stokes, and Capt. Cowen place it near Little Indian Cr, and is possibly what is shown on modern USGS maps as Tanyard Branch now in Smith County.

31 525 22330 **William Rowland** .. 10 acs .. waters of Indian Cr of Cumberland .. adj his own 37-ac tract **where Wm. Elrod lived in 1818** .. 11 Apr 1823. William Rowland, Loc.

31 525 22332 **William Williams** .. one ac .. on a branch of Cumberland .. adj Thomas Scantlin .. to incl improvement made by sd Williams. 12 Apr 1823. William Williams, Loc.

31 526 22338 **Robert Mansell** .. 30 acs .. waters of Martin's Cr between James McKindley's & James McBroom .. on top of a ridge .. south side of sd creek .. 14 Apr 1823. Robert Mansell, Loc.

31 526 22339 **Robert Mansell** .. 2 acs .. about a half mile from Richard Mansell's mill on sd (?) Cr .. to incl improvement made by John Temple. 14 Apr 1823. Robert Mansell, Loc. (Undoubtedly, "sd" creek is Martin's.)

31 526 22340 **Burwell Mansell** .. 2 acs .. waters of Pigeon Roost Cr .. the Long Glade .. to incl a mill seat. 14 Apr 1823. Robert Mansell, Loc.

31 535 22410 **Nicholas Haile** .. 5 acs .. north side of Doe Cr .. adj David Cox .. to incl **where Jubilee H. Bedford now lives.** 30 Apr 1823. Price Butler, Loc.

31 535 22411 **John Osgathorp** .. 15 acs .. waters of dry fork of Mill Cr .. adj his own. 30 Apr 1823. Price Butler, Loc.

31 535 22412 **Thomas Scanland, James Hogland, Robert Jennings & Daniel Hogland** .. 5 acs .. south bank of Sugar Cr .. 30 Apr 1823. Price Butler, Loc.

31 535 22413 **Josiah Copeland** .. 10 acs .. waters of dry fork of Mill Cr .. 30 Apr 1823. Price Butler, Loc.

31 535 22414 **Josiah Copeland** .. 5 acs .. north side of Cumberland on Webster's Cr .. Reuben Price's west boundary. 30 Apr 1823. Price Butler, Loc.

31 536 22415 **Thomas Mercer & William Hamilton** .. one ac .. waters of Sugar Cr .. to houses formerly occupied by John Murray. 30 Apr 1823. Price Butler, Loc.

31 536 22416 **Abiram Stacey** .. 10 acs .. head waters of Sugar Cr .. to incl sd Stacey's improvement & house. 30 Apr 1823. Price Butler, Loc.

Were Byram Stacey and Abiram Stacey the same person, or is there some ethnic significance in these names?

31 536 22420 **Jonathan Key** .. 50 acs .. waters of Barren R .. York's plantation .. 30 Apr 1823. Jonathan Key, Loc.

CONCLUSION AND APPLICATION

James Cook, Assistant to the "Martial" of West Tennessee, was the enumerator for the 1820 Census of Jackson County. He counted 7,593 persons, including 669 slaves and 190 "free colored." The so-called white citizens were:

Males -10	1,403	Females -10	1,222
Males 10-15	544	Females 10-15	614
Males 16-25	598	Females 16-25	544
Males 26-44	521	Females 26-44	623
Males 45+	387	Females 45+	278

There were, undoubtedly, some Indians and Melongeons who were not counted, and perhaps other people missed by the census taker.

Alphabetizing the census list helped in deciphering the names, if we can assume the alphabetizer made no errors. That would be a ridiculous assumption. One entry, which I believe to be in error, is the name Samuel Bruff. I believe this name should be Samuel Huff. The name "Bruff" has been encountered in other locales but not in early records for Jackson County, and Samuel **HUFF** was there.

This Samuel "Bruff" household consisted of 3 males under 10, 3 males 10-15, 2 males 16-25, 1 male 26-44, and 4 females 16-25. That's an extended family, and we have no way of knowing which of those 3 mature males was Samuel. A very easy mistake to make would be to place or fail to place the little digit "1" in an appropriate age bracket.

A further complication is that if the head of the household was considered to be Indian, he would be **named** but not counted i.e. no mark for him in the age column. This vagary exists in counting females, also. For example, if a married woman was considered to be Indian, her husband would seem to have no wife because she was not counted. The logic was very simple. The census was supposed to be a count of tax-paying and military resources (citizens) and their two-legged, unfeathered livestock i.e. slaves i.e. property. Indians were usually not citizens, tax-payers, or property.

Exactly what Mr. Cook meant by "free colored" is unclear. Extremely interesting questions arise. How did the census taker know who was Indian (or Chinese) and who was not? Did he **ask**, or did he simply look and decide? If he asked, did he get a truthful answer? And would he always believe what a person said, true or otherwise. Melungeons always insisted they were white, but certain census takers (and citizens) refused to believe it and classified them as "free colored." In some locales, that category was created specifically to take care of the Melungeons.

Twenty years is a long time. Many people moved into Jackson County and out again during those first 20 years. These land entries with their frequent references to residents help fill a gap in the information. Surely, Charles Broadwater could be considered an early settler. Even though he seems to have returned East, he stayed long enough for later entries (1836) to reference "Broadwater's Branch." And although Moses and Samuel Belar surfaced on the Smith County census near William Huff, they made their appearances in White County and on Martin's Creek in Jackson County.

Even now, in 1992, I know of no counties that erect electrified chain-link fences along the county line. People, creeks, jack rabbits, deer, and weeds meander back and forth with little attention to the political jurisdiction until tax day or court day comes around.

Prior to 1820, there were two Leonard Huffs in Jackson County. One was on Martin's Creek adjacent the Pharis families as proved by land entries and the Pharis vs Carter lawsuits. The other was on (Knob & Brimstone Creeks) the ridge between the Cumberland and Big Barren.

Although the word "speculator" is not always complimentary, we are grateful to John Christmas McLemore and the prospectors who searched for salt petre (potassium nitrate) so necessary for gun powder. To fight a war against Indians, the British in 1812, or anyone else, three elements were necessary: people, guns, gunpowder. Any one of the three was and is useless without the other two.

As I have studied the old land records including conveyances, entries, grants, surveys and assignments, I have been amazed at the mobility of these frontier people. They **moved** fast and far, and the idea that they "settled" in one place forever must be tempered. Further, their presence in the same place on two consecutive census schedules does **not** mean they did not leave during the intervening years.

At any rate, the names in these land entry abstractions are useful supplements to other extant lists for Jackson County. Find your ancestor's name, creek and neighbors. Then you can test the "cluster theory."

This is not a book for casual reading. It is a book to be studied, scribbled in, and re-visited many times. Realize the man who entered for land next door to your known ancestor may turn out to be another ancestor i.e. your great-great-great grandmother's father! Keep a sharp lookout. Happy Hunting.

The End of this Volume

BUILDING NEIGHBORHOODS
From
EARLY LAND RECORDS OF TENNESSEE

The following 1836 Map of Jackson County and accompanying Field Notes are used by courtesy of Tennessee State Library and Archives, Nashville, Tennessee. Person or persons who drew the original map are unknown.

Comments:

1. Granville, at the mouth of Martin's Creek, did not exist when this map was drawn.

2. Falling Water is in White County south of the area shown by this map.

3. Ft. Blount and Williamsburg were near the mouth of Big Branch below the mouth of Flynn's Creek at the Big Salt Lick, an island in the Cumberland.

4. Gum Spring Mountain is in White County west of Sparta.

5. Hollomon's Ferry was between Big Branch and mouth of Martin's Creek. See modern USGS maps for Hollomon's Bend.

6. Be very careful in referencing "Indian Creek." There were and are several.

7. Two land entries mention Puncheon Camp Creek of Roaring River. Where that creek may have been is unknown.

8. Many other landmarks and creeks or branches have been renamed or have disappeared. We must have patience and remember - the fun is in the hunt.

JACKSON COUNTY, TENNESSEE - 1836

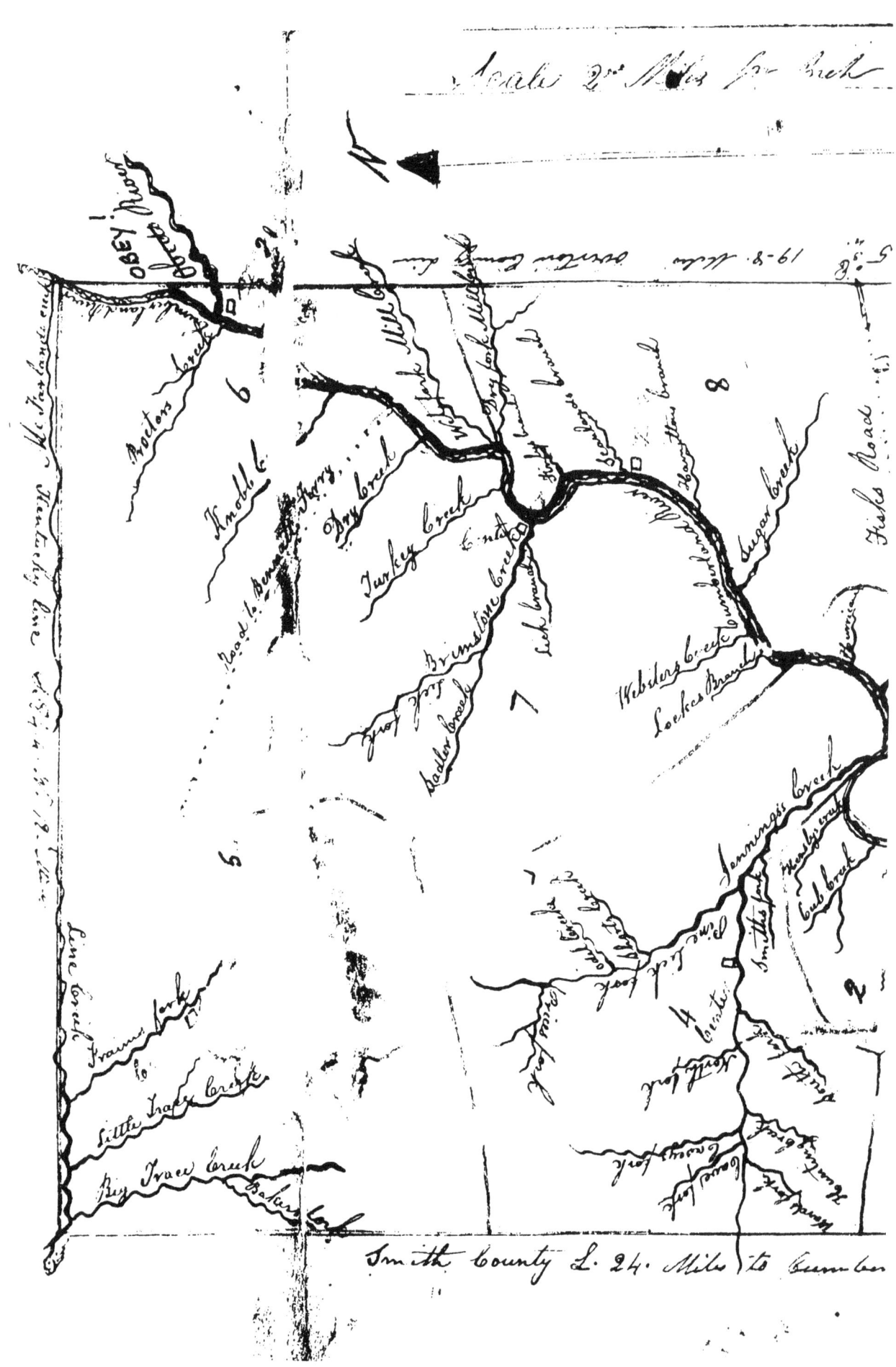

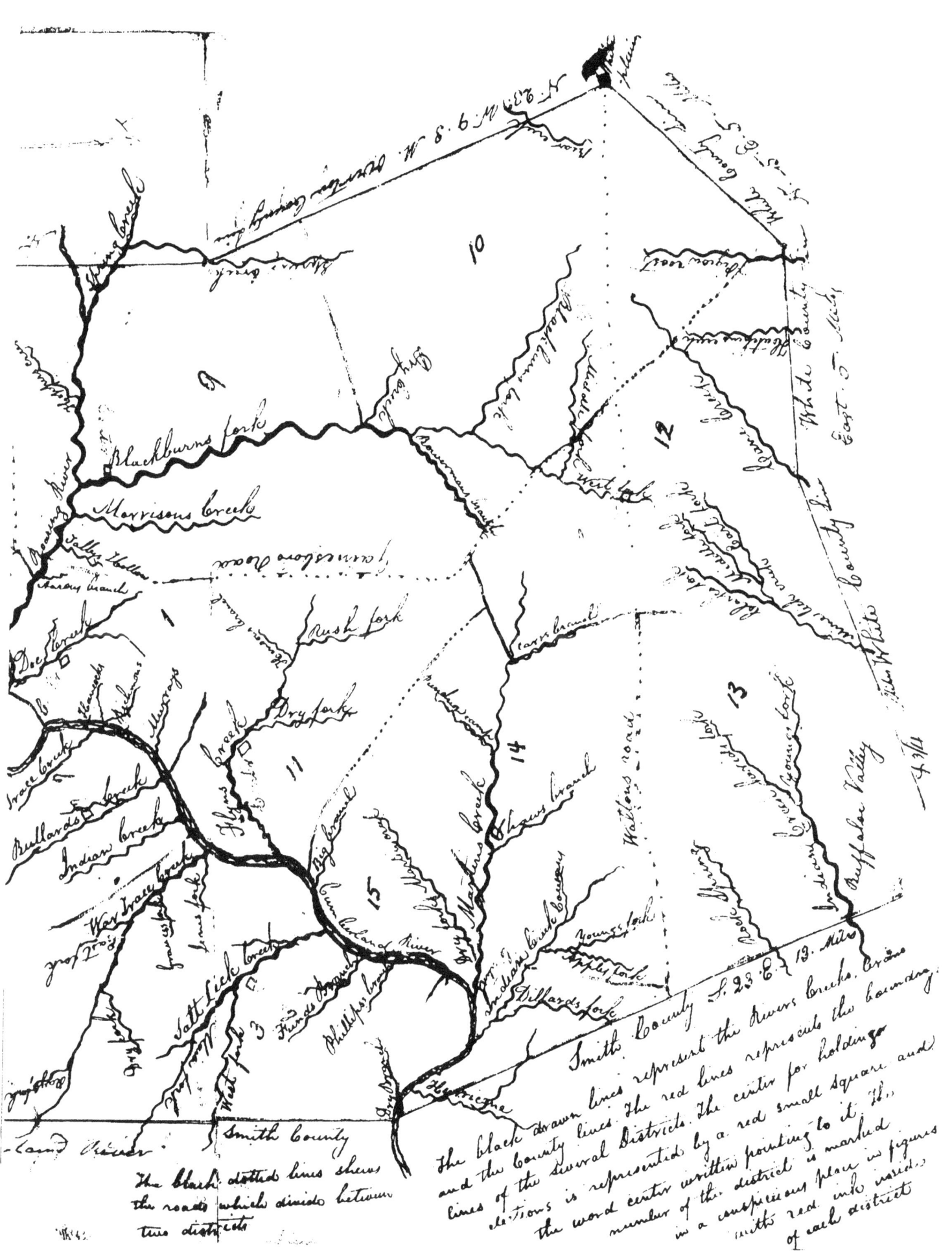

State of Tennessee } This is to certify that
Jackson County } James Young
Richd. F. Cooke, David Cox, David Griffith
& Bailey Butler Commissioners appointed by
a resolution of the General assembly adopted
the 1st. Decr 1835 to lay off the County of
Jackson into Districts of Convenient Size
within which Justices of the Peace and
Constables shall be Elected, having met
in the Town of Gainsboro on the 11th day of
January 1836 in order to proceed upon the
Duties assigned to them by act of the General
assembly passed Decr 3rd 1835 — When &
Where said Commissioners Before Me William
R. Kerr, a Justice of the Peace for said
County of Jackson did take the oath prescri-
bed by said act of assembly faithfully &
impartially to perform the Duties therein
Directed ———

William R Kerr

State of Tennessee, Jackson County
This is to Certify that we James Young
Richd. F. Cooke, David Cox, David Griffith
& Bailey Butler, having been appointed
by the General assembly of the State of
Tennessee as Commissioners to Divide said
County into Districts of Convenient Size
within which Justices of the peace &
Constables shall be Elected, after having
Taken the oath prescribed by Law,
have Executed the same in manner & form
as Directed by an act of the said General
assembly passed December the 3rd 1835
and we do hereby Report

Jackson

That the plat hereunto attached is a fair Ideal Representation of the County and Each District therein to the best of our Capasity knowledge and belief which we have laid off the Butts & Boundaries, and Ms. of & place for holding Elections in Each District — is as follows to Wit = — — — —

The first District Beginning on the South Bank of Cumberland River opposite the Mouth of Bullard Creek Running thence south to the Top of the Ridge Between Flyns Creek and the River Thence along the Extreem top of the Ridge Between the waters of Flyns Creek on the South and Murrays Branch Richmonds Branch, Hancocks Branch & doe Creek on the North to the head of Morisons Creek thence a long the Extreem top of the ridge Between the Waters of Tallys Hollow on the East and Doe Creek & Aarons Branch on the west to Roaring River at Cummins Mill thence down Roaring River With its Meanders to the first Bluff on the North side of said River thence up the bluff to the Fisk Road at the head of Hurican Creek thence Crossing the Road & along the Top of the Ridge Leaving Hurican & pigeon Roost Creek on the west down the Extreem top of the ridge Between Henry halls and Mathew Andersons Striking Cumberland River Just Below Robert Andersons thence Down the River with its Meanders to the Mouth of the Buck Branch thence up the Bucky Branch and out at the head of the same to the Top of the ridge Between the Buck Branch & Doe Creek, thence a long the Extreem top of the ridge to the head of the Rocky Branch thence down the Rocky Branch to the River thence down the River with its Meanders

to the Beginning and the Elections to be held Jackson 3
at the Court House in Jainsboro —

The 2nd District shall be Bounded as follows to wit
Beginning on the South Bank of Cumberland River
at the Mouth of the Buck Branch which is a
Corner of the first District running thence up the
Buck Branch with its Meanders and out at the
head thereof to the Top of the Ridge between said
Branch & Doe Creek thence along the Extreme Top
of the Ridge between the horse shoe bend and Doe
Creek to the head of the Rocky Branch thence down
the Rocky Branch with its Meanders to Cumberland
River thence crossing the River and Down the same
on the North side thereof with its several Meanders to the Bluff between the Mouths of Indian
and Wartrace Creeks which is a corner of the 3rd
thence with the Line of the 3rd District along the
Extreme top of the Ridge between said Creeks to the
Dividing Ridge between Indian & Linsey's Creek
another Corner of the 3rd District thence with the
line of the 4th District along the Extreme top
of the Ridge between the Waters of Linsey's
Creek and the North and Indian Bullards, Owen's
Cub, & Linsley's Creeks on the South to Cumberland
River thence across the River to the Beginning
within which Bounds the Election shall be
held at Leher Luz — — —

The third District shall be Bounded as follows
To wit Beginning on the north Bank of Cumberland
River at the Bluff between the Mouths of War-
trace & Indian Creek which is the Lower Corner
of the 2nd District running thence Down the river
with its several Meanders to a point of a hill or
Bluff just above the plantation of Col. James
Holoman and opposite the upper end of Joseph
Williamsons plantation thence up said point
to the top of the hill between the Branch that
Runs through the plantation of

4 Jackson

Col. James Solomons and the Branch that George W. Black Now lives on thence along the Extreme top of the Ridge Between the Branch that runs through the Ruffin old plantation & the Branch that runs By Thomas Burtons and Henry Solomons to the head thence along the Extreme top of the Ridge Between the Dry Branch of the South fork of the Dry Branch, and Mow-lands Branch to Cumberland River at the Mouth of the Dry Branch thence down the River with its Meanders to the Smith County line thence North with the County line to the Top of the Dividing Ridge Between War Trace & Jennings Creek which is a corner of the 4th District, thence along the Extreme Top of the Ridge between sd Creeks, to the head of Indian Creek which is a corner of the second District, thence with the line of the second District, a long the Extreme higth of the Ridge (~~between said Creeks to the head of Andersons Creek which is a corner of the 2d District, thence with the line of the second District, along the Extreme hights of the Ridge~~) Between War Trace and Indian Creeks, to the Begining within Said Bounds the Elections shall be held at the House of Mrs Elizabeth Kearby

The 4th District Beginning at the corner of the 3rd District in the County line where it Crosses the Dividing Ridge Between War Trace & Jennings Creek thence North with the County line to the Extreme Top of the Ridge Dividing the Waters of Jennings Creek and big trace creek of Barren thence along the Extreme Top of Said Ridge Leaving the Waters of Barren on the North and the Waters of Jennings Creek on the South to the head of Brimstone Creek thence along the Top of the Dividing Ridge between Brimstone and the piney fork of Jennings creek to the head of Websters creek thence along the Top of sd Ridge Leaving the waters of Websters creek and Locks Branch on the East and Jennings creek on the West to Cumberland River Just below the Mouth of Locks Branch thence down the River with its Meanders to the Lower side of the Mouth of Jennings Creek to the upper Corner of the 2nd District thence with the Top of the Ridge Between Jennings Creek & Hensleys Creek with the lines of the 2nd & 3rd Districts Leaving the waters of Hensleys Creek, Cub Creek, Bullards Creek, Indian Creek & War Trace Creeks on the South & Jennings Creek on the North to the Beginning and the Elections to be held at John Dixons —

The 5th District Beginning in the Smith County line where it Crosses the Dividing Ridge Between Jennings Creek & Big Trace Creek which is the North west Corner of the 4th District Running thence along the Extreme top of the Ridge Between the waters of Barren & Cumberland with the line of the 4th District to the head of the Lick fork the South East Corner of the 4th District thence with the dividing Ridge Between Brimstone and Little Trace Creek to intersect the Road Leading from Chinnys to William Plumbers thence with said Road through William Plumbers lane to John Plumbers and Clinton Plumbers & thence to Jarret More thence Northward down the Extreme Top of the Brushy Ridge to Kamps old Mill on McFarland Creek and on the State Line Including William Plumber John Plumber Clinton Plumber and Jarret More in the 5th District thence west with the state line to the Corner of Smith County thence with the County line South to the Beginning and the Elections to be held at James Crawfords

The 6th District Beginning in the Kentucky line at the North East Corner of the 5th District thence East with the State line to the Corner of Overton County on the South Bank of Cumberland River thence South with the County line to the Dividing Ridge between the West fork and the Dry fork of Mill Creek, so as to Include Thomas Butler in the 6th Dst thence along the Extreme top of said Ridge Between the two forks to the Mouth of Mill Creek thence up Cumberland River with its Meanders to Burnets Ferry thence Crossing Cumberland River and with the Main Road to Jarret Mores thence Northward down the Extreme top of the Brushy Ridge with the line of the 5th District to the Beginning Leaving Jarret More in the 5th District & the Election to be held at

Jackson

The 7th District Beginning on the north Bank of Cumberland River at Bennetts Ferry which is a Corner of the 6th District runs thence down the River with its Meanders to the Bluff Below the Mouth of Locks Branch which is the upper Corner of the 4th District running thence with the North Eastern line of the 4th District Leaving the Waters of Locks Branch, Websters Creek, and Brimstone creek on the East & Jennings creek on the west to the line of the 5th District at the head of the [...] lick fork of Jennings Creek & to the South East Corner of the fourth District thence with the south Boundary line of the 5th District with the Dividing Ridge Between Brimstone and Little Saw Creek to Intersect the Road Between Chinoys & William Plumlees thence with said Road through william Plumlees Lane to John Plumlees, Clinton Plumlees & thence to Garrett Mores thence with the Main Road to Bennetts Ferry at the Beginning and the Elections to be held at Baileys at the Mouth of Brimstone

The 8th District Beginning on the south Bank of Cumberland River in the fork at the Mouth of Mill Creek the Lower Corner of the 6th District runs thence with the Lower line of the 6th District with the Top of the Ridge Between the wet and the Dry fork of Mill Creek to the overton County line thence south with the County line to the fish Road Between the waters of Roaring River and the waters of Sugar Creek thence with said Road to the head of Hurricane Creek thence down a point of the Ridge with the line of the first District Leaving Hurricane Creek & pegrow Roost on the west to the River above Henry Halls thence up the River to the Beginning and the Election to be held near the Mouth of Scantlands Branch at William Hamiltons

Jackson

The 9th District Beginning in the Overton County line where it crosses the Fish Road runs thence south with the County line to a point near Peter Smiths & where the nearest road leading from said Smiths to Joseph Terrys intersects the County Line thence with sd road Westwardly to sd Smiths & up the Plumb Hollow to Liam Johnson thence with the road leading to Sherly Anderson and Garland Andersons – Leaving sd Smiths house Liam Johnson T. Sherly Anderson and Garland Andersons in the 12th District thence up Blackburns fork with its Meanders to David Richens thence up Bowmans Branch to the gainsborough Road at Elijah Prices thence with the gainsboro Road to the head of Dow Creek Near James young a corner of the first District
Thence with the Line of the first District along the Extreme Top of the Ridge Leaving the waters of Dow Creek and Aarons Branch on the West & Morgansons creek & Tallys Hollow on the East to Roaring River at Cummins Mill thence down Roaring River with the Line of the 1st District to the first Bluff thence up the point of the hill with the Line of the 1st District Leaving long Branch on the west to the Fish Road thence with said road to the Beginning – and the Election to be held at Nimrod Johnson. –

The 10th District Beginning at the south East Corner of the 9th District where the nearest road leading from Peter Smiths to Joseph Terrys Intersects the Overton County Line thence Southwardly with the County line to the corner of White County near the White plains thence with the White County line south forty five Degrees West to the corner Given the Pigeon Roost creek thence west to sd creek

8 Jackson

thence up Said Creek to Rich'd Bradford Mill thence Northwardly up the Hollow west of Bradfords house & with the Road Leading to John Huddlestons thence to John Barns Leaving D' Huddleston and Barnes in the 10th District thence with the dividing Ridge Between Pigeon Roost Creek & Hutchins Creek and with the Road Leading to Mark Mathews to Cane Creek thence up Said Creek to the Mouth of Peter Andersons Spring Branch thence up s'd Branch to Peter Andersons Leaving D' Anderson in the 2'd District thence through the Low gap of the Ridge at head of Edmunds Fins Spring Branch & with s'd Branch to the Mouth thence Down the Middle prong of Blackburns fork to Montgomery Kennards Leaving him in the 10th District thence with the Road Leading to Liberty Meeting house thence with the old Fort Blount Road to the head of Bowermans Branch at Elijah Prices thence Down s'd Branch to David Richies Mill thence Down s'd Blackburns fork to Garland Andersons thence to Shirley Andersons on the Ridge thence to Sion Johnsons in the Plumb Hollow thence Down s'd Hollow to peter Smiths thence with Said Road to the Beginning. Including s'd Garland Anderson & Shirley Anderson & s'd Said Smiths & Sion Johnson in the 10th District and the Elections to be held at John Terrys

The 11th District shall be Bounded as follows to wit

Beginning on the South Bank of Cumberland River at the Bluffs opposite the Mouth of Bullards Creek thence Down the River with its several Meanders to the Bluff Just above the Mouth of the Big Branch opposite to old Williams Burgh thence up the Bluff to the Extreme Top of the Ridge Between the Big Branch and the Branch that lies in at Williams Burgh thence along the Extreme top of the Ridge Leaving the waters of the Big Branch & Martins Creek on the West and D' Flynns Creek on the East to the head of Flyns Creek thence North with the line of the 12th Jackson District to the Main Road Leading to gains boro at wool= brights thence with said Road to the head of Doe Creek to the Corner of the first District thence with the Extreme Top of the Ridge with the Line of the first District Leaving the waters of Doe Creek, Hancocks Branch, Richmond Branch & Murrays Branch on the North and Flyns Creek on the South to the Beginning with in which Bounds. the Elections shall be held at Thompsons Mill ————

The 12th District Beginning at the South East Corner of the 10th District in the White County line at Pigeon Roost Creek Near Michael Sailors thence up the Pigeon Roost Creek to Richd Bradfords Mill thence Northward with the west Boundary line of the 10th District up the first Hollow west of sd Bradfords house and with the road to John Huddleston thence to John Barnes Leaving sd Barnes & Huddleston in the 10th District thence with the dividing Ridge Between Pigeon Roost Creek and Hickory Creek and with the road Leading on sd Ridge to Mark Mathews thence up Cane Creek to the Mouth of Peter Andersons Spring Branch thence up sd Branch to sd Andersons and thence down Edmond Lins Spring Branch thence down the Middle fork of Blackburns fork to Montgomery Kennards — thence with the road Leading to Liberty Meeting house thence to wool- Woolbrights Leaving said Kennard in the 10th District and peter Andersons in the 12th District Thence with the Extreme top of the Ridge Dividing the Waters of Flyns Creek. Bowermans Branch & Blackburns fork to Joseph Pippins leavg including sd Pippins in the 12th District thence with the Extreme top of the Ridge Dividing the waters of the two forks of Flyns Creek and James Goolsbys fork of Martins Creek to the Junction of sd Goolsby fork — and

10 Jackson

Harpers fork of Martins Creek thence up said Creek to William Cars on Wattons road Including sd Cars and all the Inhabitants East of sd Creek and Road & on sd fork in the 12th District, thence south from sd Cars with the Extreme Top of the Ridge to Craven Maddauxs Spring Branch thence down sd Branch to Benjamin Browns farm thence with the road Leading to sd Browns house Including sd Brown in the 12th District thence with the road Leading south to the Buffaloe Valley Road thence with said Road to the Road passing Sebert Odoms to Elias Greens Including all the Inhabitants of Mine Lick above where the County line Crosses said Creek in the 12th District thence East with the White County line to the Beginning —

and the Elections to be at Benjamin Kinslow

The 13th District

Beginning at William Cars on the walton road with west Boundary line of the 12th District thence south with said line with Extreme top of the Ridge Leading to Craven Maddux Spring Branch thence down said Branch to Benjamin Brown farm thence with the road Leading to Said Browns house Leaving sd Brown and Car in the 12th District thence with the road Leading from sd Browns south to the Buffaloe Valley Road thence with said Road to the Road passing Sebert Odoms place & to Elias Greens Leaving all the Inhabitants of Mine Lick above where the County line Crosses said Creek in the 12th District thence westerly with the White County line to the Smith County Corner thence with the Smith County line to the walton Road thence with said Road to the Beginning — within which the Elections shall be held at Simpsons Mill —

Jackson 11.

The 14th District Beginning at William Cass on the Walton Road which is a Corner for the 13th District Runs thence Down Harpers fork of Martins Creek to the Junction with Goolsbys fork thence up the Point with the Dividing Ridge Between the said Goolsbys fork and the Cush fork of Flyns Creek to Shepherds Road on the Ridge thence with said Road to near the head of the Dry fork of Martins Creek thence along the Extreme Top of the Ridge Between the Dry fork & Main fork of Martins Creek to the head of the Branch which Mouths into Jarvis Mill pond Between Henry Sadlers and Leonard Huffs thence a Direct Course to the Main fork of Martins Creek at the upper End of Henry Sadlers plantation thence Crossing the Creek at the upper End of Rollin Hogans plantation thence a Direct Course to the Main fork of Indian Creek at the upper End of the Widow Loffords plantation thence Crossing the Creek at the upper End of Garret Sadlers plantation thence west to the Top of the Ridge Between the Main fork & Dillards fork of Indian Creek thence along the Extreme top of the Ridges Between said forks and Apples fork & Dillards fork to the Walton Road thence with the Walton Road to the Beginning within which Bounds the Election shall be held at the house of Mrs Shaw at the Mouth of Shaws Branch

15th The Boundary of the 15th District shall Be as follows to wit Beginning on the south Bank of Cumberland River Just above the Mouth of the Big Branch opposite to old William Burgh Runs thence up the Bluff to the Top of the Ridge Between the Big Branch & the Branch which Runs in at Williams Ferry thence along the Extreme top of the Ridge Between the waters of Flyns Creek on the East side and the Big Branch on the West

12 Jackson

to the head of the Dry fork of Martins Creek thence along the Extreme top of the Ridge Between the Dry fork and the Main fork of Martins Creek to the head of the Branch which Mouths into Roberts Mill pond Between Henry Sadlers and Leonard Huffs thence a direct line to the Main Martins Creek at the upper End of Henry Sadlers plantation thence Crossing the Creek and leaving the plantation of Rawlins Hogans on the West thence a direct line to the Main fork of Indian Creek at the upper End of Edward Holfords plantation thence Crossing the Creek & leaving the plantation of Garrett Sadler on the North thence west to the Top of the Ridge Between the Main fork and the west fork of Indian Creek thence along the Extreme top of the Ridge Between said forks and Apples fork and Dillards fork to the walton road then with said Road to the Smith County line thence with the Smith County line to Cumberland River thence a Cross the River to the Point on the upper side of the Mouth of the Dry Branch thence along the Extreme hight of the Ridge between the Dry Branch & John Morelands Branch to the head of Sd Branches thence along the Extreme hight of the Ridge leaving the waters of the Branches on which Thomas Burton Henry Holoman & Col. James Holomans lives on the South and the Branches running through the old Rupp plantation & on which George W. Clark lives on the North, to Cumberland River opposite to the upper End of Joseph Williamsons plantation thence Crossing the River & up the same with its Meanders to the Beginning the Election to be held in said Bounds at Granville Given under our hands in the Town of Gainesboro the 22nd day of January 1836

James Young
Rich'd H. Cooke
Balie Butler
David Griffith
David Cox

BUILDING NEIGHBORHOODS INDEX

Refer to note on Table of Contents before using this index..

Aaron	19602
Aaron's Br	11968 11969 15269
Abner	5365 229
Aikman/Akemon	172 13720
Alexander	23 4247 4248 13019 11424 14424
Alland	12169
Allcorn	21529
Allen	44 168 170 7524 16235 16919 20670 16836
Allerd	11805 11282
Alley	190
Almond	21117 21118
Anderson	76 117 133 185 209 210 1981-2 2174 2267 2470 2475 206 215 2756 3065 3116 4198 4811 5303 5932 5917 6890 7709 8107 8247 8536 8650 8660 9363 9564 9575 10155 10335 10473 10643 10777 10814 10906 11801 12481 12493 12494 12823 13852 13853 14115 14511 14514 15283 15391 15823 16159 16381 16382 16383 16384 16386 16678 16679 16680 16864 16865 17156 17161 17162 17183 17184 17605 17606 17614 18239 18761 19691 20342 20695 20700 20953 20954 21330 21572 8585 9600 10861 17181 17182 17452 17986 21835 9126 9957 10936 16929
Anderson's Br	14485
Andrews	4262
Anthony	6606 7177 9987 13944 7458 7947
Aplin	17650 17651
Apple	21816 21817
Arant	9519
Arington	8933
Armstrong	7524 3 12 28 219 13682 5259
Attleberry	20883

Refer to note on Table of Contents before using this index..

Bailey	21141 8633 14155 14842
Baker	5921 6099 7458-9 7460 7945 8774-5 9236 9355 10108 10331 13944 19639 10328-9 10330 10333
Balch	4239
Ballard	21820
Ballon	206 trunkmaker
Ballow	20776
Banks	42 4239
Baptist	184
Bard	21634
Barge	23
Barker	7524 3116
Barr	21634
Barrens, The	78 117 594 1724 3313 14238
Barren Co, KY	7235
Barron River	153 216 1590 3228 6230 7524 8587 9303 9364 9519 9541-3 9661 9663-4 9666 9772 9774-9 9780 10557-8 10790-1 11080 11851 12949 13952 14102 14218-9 16025-6 16694 16812 22268 22269

	22420
Barry	2699 2756 3416 4198 6178 6451 7639 12823 12825 12963 13513-4 15110 15665 16851-2 19897 46 75 8100 144 7140
Bartlett	8130
Barton	7591 2789
Bates	7490
Baylor	190
Bean/Been	5482 11487
Bear Br of Jennings Cr	14252
Beason	2118 8843
Beckham	14155
Bedford	2664-5 3114-5 5198 6756 8564 10351 11282 22410 171 12282-3
Beecham	2174
Belar/Bellah	9441-2 9444 12672-5 14572 17375 18894
Bell	8628 8742 21141
Ben	62 86 215
Benjamin/Bengerman	168
Bennett	6506 9589 10348 10354 10444 10446 10502-4 11016-17 14842 15729 15730 19773 10494 16812 17338 18237 18419
Bennett's Ferry	7235 11852 12741 18237
Benson	10861 12238 12239
Biby (See Bybee)	22042

Refer to note on Table of Contents before using this index..

Bickerstaff/Biggerstaff	19773 17571 17549
Bigham	83
Big Boil	10196
Big Branch	6585 6592 7173-4 8494 10339 11817 13940 15563 16235 16237 17181-4 18683-4 18893 18895 18927 19526-7 20671 21489 21490-1 21905-6 13692 13802 10842 8678 8680
Big Spring	17635
Big Trace Cr	8140 9257 9661 9663-4 9666 9772 9847 9848-9 9881 10723-4 10790-1 16286 21727 22268 5743-4 6230 10065
Bilderback	52
Biles (See Byles)	8839
Billew	18894 19041
Billingsley	113 215
Birdwell	5679
Bisby	4766
Bishop	43
Black	154 235 2177 5379 5754 9239 10503 10540 13131 13889 15023 15024 15032-3 16943 19501-2 11000 27 71 163 165 187 211 296
Blackburn	19955 2472 4198 4541 4759 4797 4828 5267 7878 9525 10293 11807 13536 9821 70 76 92 132 175220 4027
Blackburn's Fk	92 102 161 162 6187 6482 6756 6993 7191 5143 5248 5249 8113 8573 9425 10103 10325 10452-3 10564 10777-9 10812 10994 11365 11487 11807 12051 12168-9 12495 12714 13654 13852 13853 14003-5 14402 14484 14485-6 14489 15250 16148-9 16192 16561 17506 17655 17814-15 18260 18632 18783 18995 19087-9 19099 20452 20796-7 20997 21171 21330 22229 9993 1955 2774 6991
Blackfan	14859 14860 15620
Blackmore	4147
Blackwell	16041

Blackwood	171 3114
Blair	148 4326 6811 20579 154
Blakeman	9329
Bledsoe	1321
Blount	58 83 6099 8353 10971
Bodely	10596
Bohannon	133
Bonner's line	26 194 10775 10776 10905 10454
Boon/Boone	195 197
Borden	15626
Bounds	2789 3312 11511 12627 7559
Bowdine	10993 11128
Bowen	43 58-219 594 4519 5300 5820 10778
Bowen's Mill	13654 14901
Bowerman's Br	10779 11473 20282 20452 20659 20796 20798 8113"
Bowles	14397-8
Bowman	58-206 17635 17886 5299
Boyd	2119 7643-4 10422 10426-8 18297
Boyles	16413
Bozarth	13082
Bracken	7770 13890 13892 18870
Bradcut	5288 8948-9 11686
Bradley	98 208
Brady	1598
Brannum	10933
Branson	5259
Brasel/Brassell	8665 8667-8 14238 12906
Brashears	21634
Brehan	20898 10194 20701
Brewer	1687 9522 9644 9649 9651 13269 13587 14021 14134
Briant/Bryant	8284 14004
Bridges	2122 7904 8091 11439 11675 11786-7 13659 14858

Refer to note on Table of Contents before using this index..

Brimstone Cr	5970 5971 6624 4765-7 5130 5452 7515 7516 7863 8154 8443-4 9046 9327 10342 10538-9 10770 10773 10830-1 10914 11002 11004 11005 11019 11020 11057 11060 11170-2 11229 11233 11267 11413 11681 11713 11755-7 11804 11850 11854 12242 12540 12608 12742 13129 13130 13789 13881 13952 14087 14102 14842-3 14954 15023 15025 15236 15442 15459 15691 15461-3 15465 15727 15857-8 16024 16247 17337 17459 17565-6 17900 18051 18053 18419 18735-8 18763 18778-9 20562 21929 21994 22038 114 22095 15820 15467 15727 131 140 11003 236 237 5463 9621 Brittain 111 2183
Broadwater	11418-9 11420
Brooks	5658 6759 6598 9295 12788 16038 11158
Broom	20956
Brown	1982 3073 5932 6504 7432-3 7434 7490 8369 8631 10840 10844 11438-9 11607 17155 17157-8 17185 17390-2 17986 20955-7 20958 22310 7644 232 17544
Bruington	20653
Bryan	51 11486-7 12540 12541
Bryson	3312

Buchanon	536
Buckner	19602 19643 19644
Buffalo Valley	4759 4827 4828 7286 7291 7293-4 7423-5 8523 8615 8912-4 9072 9151 9215 9218-9 9748-9 9750 10073-4 13637 13720 14529 15071 17600 17601-2 18033-4 22131 10711 13211 9451
Bullard	1984 4247 42 111 112 120 129 262 171 191
Bullard's Cr	171 191 8564 6505
Buller	7907-8 8610 8838 9802 9804 9846 10012-14 11019 11020 11890-1 13609 13610-11 13675
Buller's Cr	16036 19622 22042 22043
Buller's Mill	13837 10311
Burchett	20889
Burford	42
Burgess	10559 10560
Burke	6505 8544 8564 18870 21554
Burleson	3047 6482 17452
Burns/Byrnes	8678 8680 9179 13692 18632
Burress/Burris	114 131 1547 6560 6561 13721 17807 17820 12069 21154
Bush	1247 13761 13762 21373
Bushnell	11198 11674 11682-3 11684-5 11799 11800-02 11965 12297
Bussel	9444 12672-5
Busterton	5658
Butler	4789 5381 5443 5754 6891 7869 7870 7871 9188 9235 9236 9239 9467 9468-9 9470 9518 9625-6 9810 9863 10536 10914 11000 11125 11711-13 12406 13019 14424 14689 14690 15459 17900 19071 22048 22109 22110 22411 22412-13 7961 22414-16 11001 170 17459 22410
Button	13789
Bybee	15691
Bylor	101 104 105
Byers	14147 17243 10515
Byles	5267 8839

Refer to note on Table of Contents before using this index..

Cage	41 44 50 144 2699 2700 5192
Cagle	4180
Calf Killer	7694
Calhoon	5304
Caman/Cameron	7694 See Camron
Cameron Br	12406
Camp Branch	11065
Campbell	1590-1 3506 7277 10415 17540-3 17544 19692 17390
Camron	6499 8263 8280 17650-1 20579-80
Cane Cr	7478 8263 8402 8535 9289 9298 10012-15 10019-20 10205-6 10417-18 10515 10938 11422 11687 12067 13610-11 14021 14119 14147 14906 15010 16142-44 16176 17243 17376 18037 18208 18209 21888 7259 7264 3321 4083 5889 6499 5066 5067 5318 4324
Caney Cr	5608 12244
Caney Fork	150 5753 5929 6119 6131 4993 7640-1 8072 12645 12646 12672 12674 12917 13113 13610-1 13633 13878 14157 14572 14906 15095 15234 15498 16798 17063 17243 17281-2 17375 17985 18786 20538 20539 20540-41 20579 20580 20735 21165-6 21192 21529 21562 21566 21568 21694 21934 7255 7269 7288 7496 10161 10428 10473

	12637 2070 7641 7042 6479 13224 707 7490 7641 7642 8070-1 8090 8130 8194 8196 9444 9858 9652 9946 10009 10012-15 10020 10231 10417-18 10420 10422 10426-28 10861 11178 11476 11498 11762 11818-19 11866 11867 7694 7733 7743 219 228 229 316
Cann/Conn	10155 10718 11818
Cannady	10625
Cannon	20342
Cantrell	364 1261 1580 3114-15 5288 5290-91 5305 5499 10559 10560 13562 13869 15666 22192
Careger Cr	181
Carlisle	10830 11756-57 15489 15490 22135 11170
Carmichael	52 112
Carpender	8929 16251
Carr/Kerr	10205-6 7428 8755-56 16192 17063 17814 11092 11270-71 12917
Carter	2123 3321 3629 5066-67 6181 7289 7738 8402 8660 8692 10417 10426 11687 13998 14083-84 14261 14514 15010 15237 15268 15287 15289 14221 15288 15567 16590 17450 17569 18030 18803 19248 19414 21834 22088 22310 22311 10065 145

Refer to note on Table of Contents before using this index..

Cartwright	71
Carver	12203 16810
Casen	11964
Casey	7294 7525 7526 8615 8692 8704 8705 9154 9216 13637 15237 18803
Cassity	16373
Cave Spring Meeting House	184
Cave Spring (Rock Springs)	17 9728
Cave Spring (Williamson's Br)	10861
Cawin/Cowin	78 6181 7339 13049 15567 22317-18
Cedar Cr	4591
Chaffin	3046 21330
Chamberlain	124
Chapman	6584-5 6587 4450 6502 9297 19100
Cheatwood	7515 7863 10342 18778
Cherry	152 153 314 8668 13802 11267
Chester/Chister	120 121 122 58-206 58-209 950 2025 2480 21898
Chisholm	127 173 174 195 196 197 198
Chissum	2926 7836 9375 11018 13514 14664 17459 21192
Choat	8535
Christian	8693
Christmas	1546 1598 6428 8127
Christy	7600
Chum	21568
Clack	17605 17606
Clackston	16159
Clancy	5452
Clark	1247 3513 3917 4187 5024 7323 7343 7516 9939 11233 13031 16242-43 16249 18957 20538-9 21331 21895 21896 20541 20670 154 11128 58-316
Clary	7191 Mill 7528 8879
Clay	13651 13652-7 14403 16187-91 16439 18267
Clay Cave Fork	11198

Cleaveland	11043
Clemmons	1600 8585 8914 13602-3 15128 16864-65 17823
Clendennen	328
Cline	69
Cobb	4570 13673
Caldwell	4541 11419
Cole	15189 15190 12963
Coleman	233 318 8585-87
Colgrove	52
Collins	1547 14397 14398 19223 20679
Collom	7422 7424 11676
Combs	11562 15728
Condra/Condry	18174
Connard	16413
Conway	8650 5289 9797 9798 17441
Cook/Cooke	3125 3643 4790 5143 5359 5381 5929 5970 6187 6603 6760 8107 8111 58-215 8262-3 8563 9245 9253 9810 10335 10339 10837 10938 13263 13688 13761 103 15926 17376 17549 21571 21797 6500 6754 9441-2 8574 8578

Refer to note on Table of Contents before using this index..

Coons	179
Cope	8284 12294
Copland/Coplin	30 33 56 77 124 125 126 134 184 1908775 22076 22413-14 22038
Copperas Cr (Roaring R)	72 168
Corbin	354
Cord (Maybe Gord)	97
Cornelius	11062-65
Cosby	4824
Cotrell	10692
Cotton	8523 22131
County Lines	2789 5443 7422 8543 9518 9521 11942 11945 12012 14157 17449 19692 8915 9648 7558 13002
Cox	1643 2174 6941 20701 22410 113 55-23 58-145 16690 21814 2643
Coyle	19
Crabtree	1687 3680 7526 8785 9705 9844 9988 13641 11128
Crabtree's Cave Fork	9822 10963 15239
Craddock	2758
Craford/Crawford	142 203
Craig	15243
Crawford	13270
Crib Hollow/Branch	12297 12346 12407
Crocker	8948 11598
Crook	12627
Crosweight	13611
Crowley	80 103 176
Cub Cr	122 948 950 8544 8545 8563 10467 13802 13890 13892 14397-98 15189 15190 18870 21554 22106
Cub Run	152 314
Cubb Hollow	10565
Cumberland Mountain	8127

Refer to note on Table of Contents before using this index..

Cumberland, N side of   10 42 82 95 111 171 191 213 216 58-296 58-354 1984 2183
              3114 7770 7836 8574 12744 12745 13131 13869 13889 13890 13892
              13910 14337 14397-98 15251 15306 15467 15820 20883 21423
              22076 22106 22202 22414 9375 10456 10483 10750 11198 15024
              6329 6378 6506 6560 6997 4250 5291 5259 7961 8443 8543 8546
              8587 8944 9026 9290 9303 10026 10348 10358 10447 10448 10454
              10540 10775 10837 10905 10954 10990 11096 11168-69 11173
              11197 11228-29 11595 11685-86 11724 11964 11966 11970 12963
              13513-14 14690 15032-33 15118 16025 16812 16851 18237 18238
              18599 18601 19377 19773 19840 20407 20679 20837 21920 21994

Cumberland, South side of   9992 10194 10346 10353 12687 12825 13522 13682 13878
              14116 14774 15034 15240 15620 15926 16852 17549 17550 17571
              17658 17743 17775 20815 20898 21734 21754 21816 21817 21898
              21928 21967 22006 22231 6189 10368 2470 2570 2699 3513 3917
              3918 7339 9245 10771 10813 10814 10995 11711 11763 11942
              11945 11965 12106 12888 15110 16600 16691 16695-97 16699
              16721 18385 18427 18428 18595 18782 20513 20621 20623 8647
              10347 10428 7743 11 19 29 106 110 130 69 10497 6604-5 6762
              7167 5028-9 5031 5146 8774 9544 9984 316 223 224 225

Cummings	233
Cunningham	11918 11839
Curling	3262
Curry	22202
Curtis	13453
Dale	217
Darnald	15772 21373
Davenport	11164-65 16130 20159
Davidson	20450
Davidson Co	55-23 55-32 55-67
Davis	2835 4276 6230 8630 9663 10791 14155 15244 16242 16286 16496
	16877 17375 17573 17813 22088 7591 4591 78 58-316
DeBow	3678-79 5586 6080 5339 7122 7897-98 7900 8194
Dean	82
Defeated Cr	2758 6182 4262 10625
Dement	14087

Refer to note on Table of Contents before using this index..

Denton	1591 3125 3643 5203 5929 6119 6760 7496 9946 10161 10231
	10473 10718 11762 11818 12645 12646 13632-33 13952 14102
	14217-18 15095 15464 15465 17985 18051 18738 13224
Derosett	10352
Dick	7908 8610
Dickens	15726 18385
Dickson Co	10568
Dickson/Dixon	8100 8785 10360 11800 13721 16232-33 16550 17614 17820
Dill	6959 6599 15871-72 16837 19087 19088 19089 6479
Dillard	2475 3325 6358 7190 11476 11945 16721 18385 21568 21734 21754
	21799 21895 58-236
Dillard's Cr	1247

Dillard's Fork	13761
Dillard's Lick Log Br	1247 13761 13762
Dillard's Mill Cr	4187
Dilling	11863
Dillingham	10325 16561 18260
Dillon	228 232 585 588 594 1580 1609 3643 4253 5929 6760 12672 12673 12674 58 59 60 66 78 84 85 88 89 91 218 23 117 233 5443 9327 9441-3 9444
Dixon's Cr	8194
Dodson/Dotson	7901 10015 11422 11423 11424 13572
Doe Cr	5677-78 6045 6598 6616 6758 6759 6892 6941-43 5482 7524 8451-52 9295 9830 9989 10195 10838 10839 11158 12788 12875 12876 13233 13909 14116 16038 16690 17546 20450 20699 20700 20701 20819 20820 20899 20900 20982-83 21335 21456 21570 21814 22410 1643 2174 2643 10631 3 4 12 13 28 61 79 93 97 105 108 113 186 21 2643 20695-8
Donelson/Donaldson	1687 2926 4824 14115 21177 6189 25 43 74 151 163 55-71
Donoho/Donehues	78
Donohoe's Br	10625
Dotton/Dutton	9327 13789 15442
Double Spring	126
Double Springs	9167 9600 20644
Douglas	6308 17731 school
Dounell	58-145 3228
Dowell	8913
Doyle	6329
Draper	21783 Drake 5753 5929
Dry Cr	211 8154 9311-12 9576 10536 10750 10777 10818 10819 12714 13131 14901 15464 19688 15024
Dudley	17741
Dudney	21105 21106
Duff	14852
Duke	8543
Duncan	11804 18419
Dyal	6560
Dyer	2789 3902 10733 10936 16414 16983 16984
Dyer's Br	20794

Refer to note on Table of Contents before using this index..

Eakle	16694
Eastis/Estis	15034
Easton	7743 354
Eaton	4250 4252
Edwards	2480 13270
Elam	11597
Elk River	82 83
Eller	8100
Elliott	167 7558 8600 8915 15573
Ellis	5742 13599
Elrod	19676 school 20294-5 22330
Embry	70
Empson	7694
Enochs	20840-41 22316

Ervin	185 1590 See also Erwin & Irwin
Erwin	4980
Ethradge	10494
Evans	18240 18241 4765
Ewing	2777 4197 13281 14893 26 118 159 165 193 8573
Ewing's Hollow	16619 18223 8681 16240
Exum	21905

Refer to note on Table of Contents before using this index..

Fall Cr	44
Falling Water	8090-91 8130 8263 9362 12563 12673 15010 15469 11093 5069 5304 11819 1597 2789 2835 2790-1
Fanning	15500 17064 18407
Fanny	13219 13222
Faris/Ferris	58-145 58-219 (See also Pharis.)
Farmer	10559 13561 13562 15149 15150 18241
Farming	8755
Farr	328
Fenner	1547 5499
Ferrell	10426 10942 13049 13174-75 16148 16549
Fifer	2479
Find	10228
Findley's Tan Yard	8112 10337
Finn	3902 3905 9526 10228 10293 10733 11808 13536 13609 18405 57
Fisher Landing	3416
Fisher's Cr (Now Cub Cr)	7770 13890
Fisk	2926 6188 16561-63 16943 18261 18262 6189 24 25 26 27 43 44 45 71 72 73 74 151 154 155 156 157 158 159 160 163 164 165 166 168 169 170 187 188 189 221 222 235 227 228 229 231 232 233 223 224 225
Fitzgerald	178 5716 6941 8354 8494 8565 7490 7496 8070 10337-38 9858 3 4 5 12 13 14 19 21 39 66 106 131 138 186 209 213 214 215 58-354
Fitzpatrick	18632
Flat Cr	33 34
Fleming	14774 14775
Flynn's Cr	5658 5679 5680 5716 5932 6428 6504 7140 4811 5300 8841-42 9126 9692 9693 10336 10583 10440 10565 10585 10586 10627 10811 10827 11024 11289 11863 11864 11992 14083 14899 14900 15128 15391 15823 15965-6 16041 16159 16381-86 16590 16678 16679 16680 17155-58 17161-2 17203 17441 17448 17511-12 17741 17807 17876 17879 18001 18003 18178 19677 20672 20673 20889 20890 20953 20954 20955 20956 20957 20958 21105 21167 22310 1451 1981 1982 2758 3046 4 5 14 15 75 79 108 109 117 136 210 58-206 58-215 54-133 54-136 (2 # 136)
Flynn's Cr (Wallis Br of)	117
Forbush	8194
Ford	8273 17092 18001-03 18927 17
Forgey	58-215
Fout	58-214
Fowler	6604-06 5441 5146 7167 7946 11000-05 11763 216
Fowler's Cave Fork	7863 11233 18778 7515 7516
Fox	210 2758 11289 17203

Frame	1590
Franklin	11444 13281 13587
Franks	6123 6131
Freelock	7524
Ft. Blount	8127 58-206
Fund	10228
Fund's Br	5578 5750 20837
Fuqua	9451

Refer to note on Table of Contents before using this index..

Gaines	47 74 123 215 5932 22042 22043
Binesboro Rd	21903
Galeon	8573
Galyer	15378
Gambel/Gamble	9781 15507 17807
Gann	9520 9853 10692 12345 13082 14875 15507 16176 18037 18208-9 21195 13906
Garner	10310 10311 13837
Garrison	9542 9666
Garrison's Lick	8704 8705 18803 21139 7525 7526 8929
Garvin	9216
Gaw	8247 8536 9600
Geer	161-2
Gentry	7276 7279 7280 7432 7434 8018 8573 5889 3627 4083 10418 14021 18037 18208 15610
Gess/Gist/Guess	9306 9307 9541 10495 10496 1590 1591 14846 14951 14959 15000 15942 15940 22269
Gholston/Golston	24 74 3114 5288
Gibson	10073-74 11197 18033 20450 20451 14901
Gill	20540 20541
Gillihan	11675 17281 17282 17545
Gilpen	7041 school
Gilstrap	10963 10964
Givin	211 3228 58-296 2838 3240 3929 10645 13889 14102 14218
Glasgow	10846 11852 12741
Glenn	182 6230 7258 9257 9774
Gloster	7041
Glover	10009-10 13637 20698 21570 21797
Goad	77
Goforth	9783-84 13281 15730 16147 20451
Goodin	17282
Goodpasture	24
Goodwin	7479 7709 7866 15846
Goolsby	8933 20644 20645
Gord/Gourd	3 21 28
Gordon	7599 7961 11057 11171
Gore	30 52 2664 2776 7945 8778 9980-81 9993 13266 16238 17779
Grace	19117 22060
Gracie	3521
Graham	3073
Grant	116 133 14664
Grape Vine Flatt	2177 Graves 2757 2758 4519 4526 4260 18600 3045
Gray	209 7173 364 2025 2774-5 7174 8840 11605 11607 6449 12406

	12407 12812 13270 18224 18225 18226
Greathouse	10644 13129 15025 15033
Green	7177 5359 6579 8100 9810 9813 9985 15665
Grenade	1716
Gresham	13002
Griffey	15192
Griffith	1546 1902 5024 5742 9589 10358-9 10551 10957 12068 12069 12874 18575 18715
Grigg	167
Griggs	11005 Rock House
Grimes	39 18238
Guffey	8263 10019 10020 18033 18034
Guiman	22192
Gum Spring Mountain	5888 6119 6579 6760 6795 7407 8284 17737 21192 9861 9946 10161 12003 12294 13632 18786 3643
Gum Spring Tract	7255 8739 10139 14511
Gum Springs	6574 4239 7255 3643
Guthrie	15547
Gutrage	316 364 120
Guin	19651 17879

Refer to note on Table of Contents before using this index..

Hadley	1543 5029 9776
Haggard	7528 9957 10336 14484 16038 16039 16041 17741 21105
Hagland	5499 19509 20814 20816 22412
Haile/Hale	5658 5680 5482 6045 6823 6942 6992 8451 9991 10195 10838 11598 13233 13842 13909 14116 15235 22410 20983 21814 28 6616 6941 21335 21490
Hair	15283
Halfacre	6988 11700 16180 15031 16181 17728 6989
Hall	9664 9780 9881 16285
Halliday	2757 8945 9188 19041 8946 69
Hambleton	5366 5378 Mill
Hamby	7278 7432 7433
Hamilton	226 7135 10343 13528 13630 mill 16695 16699 17549
Hamilton	17550 17571 18237 18427 18428 22415 21456
Hamilton Ferry	224
Hampton	6482 6501 6616 6823 6830 8790 9991 10197 15232 15233 18995 18996 19480 6500 10594
Hancock	14263
Haney	17655
Hannah/Haner	10 95 107
Harbert	14 93 109 2119 9451-2 13651-57 14403 16187
Hardcastle	12675 18895 19526 21489 21490-1
Hardester	21799
Hardin	3325 5452 20698
Harling	9621
Harmon	1547
Harney	3521 4250 4252 9296 11919 18600 20674 3045
Harper	20646
Harpole	142 4250
Harris	26 61 78 85-6 123 131 138 7255 7258 7430-1 7906 Valley 6579 6795 5914 Mill 8402 9217 9773-4 10417-18 11094 14022 16040

	16141-44 16180 16985 18242 20291 20796-98 21171 Stand 18239 18242 10 95 107
Hartey/Harty	76 4198 4239
Hartfield	9648
Hartley	1451
Harvell	18355 18385
Harvey	7091 8756 school 9167 9591 10516 14153
Harwell	6762
Hatfield	15500
Hawkins	6310 6823 6734 5198 7258 6754
Haynes/Hines	63 87 100 119 137 8586 Hines 7478 13076
Hays	4764-67 9303 10643 10645 13131 15024
Haywood	1609 1723 7091 14153
Hecklin	18238
Heddy	11968-9 20819 20820
Henderson	14901 17550 15926-8
Henderson Ferry	224
Hendricks	16691
Henley	122 950 1959-60 1984 2480 2183 4449 6988 11964 18870 19223 46 111 112 120 121 58-206 58-209 58-213 58-216 58-263
Henry	2025 5146
Hensley	14022 12963 19223
Henson	109 185 6428 6997 8841 10811 15965 8944 8546 15966
Herrald	17203
Hesty	70
Hickens	21192
Hickman	11 12687 13682 14337 14338 16692
Hickory Nut Mountain	5203
Hicks/Hix	5365
Higdon	15241-2 19100

Refer to note on Table of Contents before using this index..

Hill	19504 19507 19509 11711 11727 12888 14732 16706
Hillums	9990
Hitchcock	7293
Hodge	12336 12831 13493-5 13599 13769 16694
Hofarton	2756-8
Hogan	7743 12823 14514
Hogg	19429 16877
Holcum	12650
Hollingsworth	13609 14157
Holloman's Ferry	18599 19377
Holloway	126
Home/Holmes	1981 2470 3116 5130-3 5971 6376 9311-12 9451 10539 10540 10750 10818-19 13881 13889 15459 15461-3 22095
Honnors	1600
Hood	21195 Wood?
Hooper's Cr	10595
Hopkins	1962
Hopper's Cr	13655-57 16187-91 16439 16942 18267 19505
Houser	15 108
Howard	15034
Howe	15234 (1815) 17737 (1816)

Howell	8369
Huddleston	200-3 9289 14119 17243
Hudson	8417 8418
Hueston	222
Huff/Hough	55-71 3240 5970 7946 8154 8587 10643 10645 10933 11114 11125 11854 11991 12742 14084 15287 15610 15727 21487 21488 11060 10826
Huffman	6616 13909
Hughlett	7743
Humber	6992 9940
Hunter	7879 9797 10310 12011
Hunting Cr	8631 16549
Huntsman	14774 14775
Hurricane Cr	67 1141 2700 10155 10995 11027
Hurricane Cr of Caney Fk	10009 12917 13002
Hurricane Cr of Cumberland	9218 11027 15772 1141 2700
Hurrican Hill	146
Hurricane Ridge	215
Hurt/Hust?	10560 15118
Hutcherson	6188 7458 8628 8629 8633 8929 9294 9844 13641 13993 14108 14687 16243 18753 21096 21109 21139 22076 6189 26 27 45 154 163 164 187
Hutchins	2789 4083 5889 6130 7947 18208
Hutchins Cr	3325 7558 7907 8247 8536 8650 9600 13837 9797 9838 10310-11 11821 11890-1 12627 13837 7259 7264
Hutchison's Cr (Mill Cr)	8933 10328 10329 10333 14727-8 16703 14403
Hutson	6131 7862 12132 12206 16249-50
Hyde	9692 10565

Refer to note on Table of Contents before using this index..

Indian Boundary   7722 40 54 58 69 101 134 176 181 58-314 3 31 39 152
Indian Cr (Big of Cumb)   12651-52 12744-45 15306 15846 17607 1463 4326 7527
           8417-18 10840 11015 11724 12539 21571 21634 3116 5291 8197
           15726 18307

Indian Cr (Cumb & Caney Fk)   22

Indian Cr (Little)   6178 6181 6358 7135 7190 4276 5192 5303 5359 7279 7280
           7339 7276-8 9953 10338 11043 7340-1 7343 7432-3 7639 11094
           11155-57 11438 13049 13173 13174-6 13658 15272 15468 15489
           15490 15567 15610 16369 16721 17390-92 17396 17540-44 17556
           17986 18246 18411 17396 17540-44 17556 17986 18246 19897
           20294-5 20840-1 21704 21734 21754 21797 21816-17 21895 22088
           22135 22316-18 22330 2122 2125 2475 2699 3100 65 79 115 133
           143 144 50 11942 17545 21572 11945 139 21902 9939-40 21967
           10079 22210 18436 20157 21373

Indian Cr of Caney Fk   58-238 31 39 131 4797 7430 7600 7709 7866 7905 7286
           7479 7924 8194 8195 8280 8369 8642 7906 8693 9586 9712 9713
           9715 10010 10073-74 10512-13 10711 11090-92 11942 12482 13673
           14535 15498-9 17281-2 17545 17650-1 18407 19691 19934 20538-9
           20540-1 20579-80 21165-6 21562 21566 21568 22088 1598 1599
           1600 3506

Irwin	585 588 594 1724 5608 5817 8203 14187
Isham/Isom	13 186 9946 10161
Island Cr	236 237
Islands in Cumberland	11683 14117 14943 Big Salt Lick 18782 6998 7741 20513
Jackson	5918 9957 14901 15965-6 17876 19271 19471 19274 79 82 168
James	3116 5753 22088
Jared	58-235 511 8752-4 9819 10419 10420 10422 10427 10428 11043 11044 11045 13878 16798 17062 19716-17 21165-66 15058 17063
Jarvis	113 1643 3116 13910 15467
Jee	150
Jeffers	10368
Jeffrey	20816
Jenkins	12927 15137 4355 1687
Jennings	214 1451 1462-3 1716 2125 4262 4326 4526 4811 6997-8 6592 6178 6181-2 8543 8546 7135 8944-5 9126 10625 13940 15563 17741 20814-15 22412 8946 143

Refer to note on Table of Contents before using this index..

Jennings Cr	5742 6376-7 6451 6561 6865 5022 5024 5339 7254 7323 7481 7525-6 7770 7836 7860-1 8212 8488 8627-32 8100 8633 8665 8667-8 8692 8704-5 8742-3 8779 8785 8821 8929 8934 9161 9246 9294 9396 9375 9546 9589 9705 9822 9844-45 9983-4 10070 10353 10358 10359-60 10494-96 10844-45 10846 10963 10964 11016-18 11065 11683 11753 11800 11966 11970 12041 12068-9 12541 12650 13513-14 13641 13721 13890 13907 13993 14108 14154-55 14238 14252 14358 14404 14664 14687 15237 15238 15239 15626 15665 16232-33 16242-43 16249-51 16549 16550 16701 16704 16743 16851 17614 17653 17820 18247 18575 18715 18803 18957 19247 19248 19414 21096 21109 21110 21139 21141 21331 21455 21783 8893 10065 12906 949 1543 1546-7 1959 1960 2479 3678 3679 3680 2(Bk 54) 9 82 58--216 58-354 153 178
Jethro	41
Joab/Jobe/Job	94 102 8839 17452
Johnson	58-238 2838 4449 4451 7804 13688 15270 16025 16129
Jones	1598-9 1716 2699 8679 8680 10842 12283 12788 13673 13882-3 15239 16250 16615 20695 20700 21154 7743 21155-6 42 88 143 144 7291 7293-4 7422 7426 7428-9 7430 7860-1 8111 8197 6892 6943 8779 8913 8929 8912 9072 9151 9154 9179 9216 9219 9748 9749 9750 10194
Joyner	1141 21139
Justice	10914
Keeling	22043
Keith	43 9541-3 10557-8 12949 14846 22268 22269
Kenady/Kennady	19 4180
Kendall/Kendall	1590 8154 10914 11000
Kent	5578 5750 17449
Kentling	9650
Kentucky Line	45 18228
Kettle Cr	14774

Key	18762 22420
King	7694 95 3321 5066 5069 6561 9781
Kinnard	8879 9425 11024 11598 11807 14738 16585-6 16919 19605-7
Kirby	4250 7900
Kirkendal/Kuykendahl	6181 15567 7340 143
Kirkland	7424 15489 16798
Kirkpatrick	7961 10830-1 10906 10955-7 11170-3 11229 11413 11681 11712-3 11755 11763 12242 21920 21929 14337 15251
Knob Cr	4764 4767 5379 7946 8586 9253 9574-5 9577 10348 10354 10444 10446 10502-4 10540 10643 10645 10933 11001 11114 11125 11852 12741 13528 15666 17565 9547 9245 1469 1902 2177 3240
Lacey's Br	5658 5680 12293
Lackey/Lockey	130 194
Lambert	2570 12687 13682 16600 16697 17658 17743 21898
Lancaster	2070 7641 7905
Lancaster's Ferry	8072 8092 10861 11866
Lancaster's Road	8092 8072 8753 11498 21934 7645 88
Lane	10552 12068 14958 14959 15000 15531 17573
Langford	7945 8778 9863 9864-6 9868 9963-5 13020 14425 15926-8 16692 16813 16834-5 19088
Langston	153
Lawson	16690 20699 20899 193
Lax	16590 18895 11990-1
Laxon's Cr	21195
Leach	8112
Ledbetter	100 Millwright

Refer to note on Table of Contents before using this index..

Lee	171 1469 1902 2775 4451 4764 6306 6586 6606 7254 7286 8212 8821 8912 8934 9246 9303 10364 10512 10513 10597-8 10815 11685 13234 13907 14358 171 58-354 16036 18242 21455 8893
Leighton	7173-4
Lemmons	10827 21166
Lenoir	4187
Leonard	14852 20457
Lewis	3513 4276 4791 4980 6306 7177 7254 25 27 163 165 187 189
Lick Br of Big Branch	17181
Lick Fork of Brimstone	11170
Lilis/Liles/Lyles ?	20293
Lincoln	8647 5499 10368
Line Fork of Barren	2838 9773 12336 12831 13452-3 13493-5 13599 13769 14102 14218 14859-60 16024 16026 16124 16694 16985 18174 19687 9774-6 14846
Linn's Br	11684
Little	11091
Little Bear Valley	39 131 1599
Little Island Cr	221 222
Little Trace Cr	12927 15137 12949 15940 22269 14846
Lizenby/Lizenberry	7288 9218 18033-4
Lock	6378 5022 6297 6697 7166 8821 10455-6 10483 2(Bk54) 10 11 107 117 11016-18 11196 11763 11801 11802 12106 16550 16701 20696 8893 12195 8068 10837 11673 11674 20819

Lockhart	143	Locust Hollow (Flynn's Cr)	17155

Long 16851
Long Br of Roaring R   11607 18225
Long Fork of Barren   7122 7897 7898 7900
Long Glade   9802 22340
Long Hollow, Martin's Cr   10584 13998
Longest   9661 9778 9779 9848 10723-4
Longley   11080
Looney's Br   12674
Love   25 58-354
Love's Br   7640
Lovelady   2789 3312 7559 8932 11511 12627
Lovell   9797 10934 14005
Lovin   15071
Lowry   2778 4248 7279
Luty   18405
Lynn   5198 10563 10599 17856
Lyon   1543 14022
Lytle   1902 2789 3258 5288 6795 6892 13802

Refer to note on Table of Contents before using this index..

Refer to note on Table of Contents before using this index..

Macklin	204
Magnolia Ridge	6188 6189
Mahoon/McHoon	314 152
Maize/Maze/Mays	6574 6579 7214 9861 11042 17886 7041
Manear/Menere	7174 13602 13995 16237 17184
Mann	7269
Mannen/Manning	13602 16930
Mansell	2118 4541 8838 8840-43 mill 8844 10811 12874 21840 22338-39 22340
Maraign	14154 This name is probably Marion.
Marchbanks	2756
Marion	17614
Markus	10447
Marlin	7122
Marr	17600 17601
Marshall	1687 65
Martin	42 44 83 4193 5744 7166 8871 10440 10627 10826 10827 10971 10990 11096 11197 11228 13019 13630 13940 13998 14424 15288 15726 16382 16680 16694 18002 22192 11990

Refer to note on Table of Contents before using this index..

Martin's Cr	5717 5932 6603 2118 2756 3258 7189 4541 4824 7599 7737 7738 7741 8107 8353 8585 8660 8678 8679 8680 8840 8842 8843 8844 8945 9179 9180 9451 9452 10335 10339 10441 10584 10627 10824 10825 10826 10842 10971 11418 11419 11420 11423 11444 11450 11991 12600 12601 12675 12823 12825 12874 13522 13602 13603 13692 13883 13998 14083 14084 14115 14117 14261 14514 15110 15128 15192 15268 15287 15288 15289 16150 16235 16510 16590 16864 16865 16928 16929 16930 16982 17043 17092 17173 17185 17450 17451 17823 18002 18030 18178 18179 18894 19117 19676 20156 20163 20291 20292 20293 20599 20670 20839 21001 21154 21155 21156 21177 21487 21488 21705 21706 21707 21708 21709 21710 21711 21712 21835 21840 22311 22338 22339 11992 21834 16852 41 8946 11991 20646 69 232 314 (Earliest mention) 7733 8578 9442 11990 13882 19651 19606 20646
Mason	14003 14004 20653
Massey	3
Maxfield	3256
Maxwell	3321 4519 9643
May	14102
Mayben	172 200 203
Mayberry	119 137 199 201 203 138
Mayfield	204 11721 12407 11458
Mayner	13995
Maynes	5820 6624 13995
McAlgon/McColgan	9574-7 11114 11852 12741 15032 15467 20883
McAllister	18001
McBroom	22338

McCall	6941 17546 20982 318
McCallas	16563
McCalley	17546
McCann	1141 5028 10155
McClain/McLane	24 151 156 166 6942
McCloud	8745 10724 14541 16369
McClure	6045 5259 8068 9830 9989 13909 14484
McComas	9964
McCormack	17155
McCown	189 154
McCrothers	176
McCulloch	16240 16247 88
McCutchen	128 175 176
McDaniel	2665 2774-78 5248-9 5888 6596 6597 6760 10079 10564 school 10599 12283 14488 21820 19087
McDonald	3643 21572 18436 18435 119 137 87 201 120
McFarland's Cr	5914 5916-19 5920 10364 11562 13234 14217 15728 17338 17569 17635 18228 18239 18242 18760-61 22060 10492
McGahan	5678 5482 7524 10838
McGarah	7429
McGee/Megee	2025 4570 9545 12406 14943 114 115 4193
McGibbon	13599
McGibson	11365
McGinnis/McKinnis	16373
McHutchinson	21734 21754 21816-17
McIver	6123
McKaughan/McCann	12875-76
McKinley	7340-41 13174-76 20156 17556 21177 22338

Refer to note on Table of Contents before using this index..

McKinney	5716 8912 9151 9154 9215 13211 14529 17 106 214 354178
McKnight/McNight	2480 8949 21195
McLarren/McLassen	4793 4794 18239 18761
McLaughlin	5028
McLemore	3228 3929 9026 7478 8417 8647 9290 9293-96 9544-48 9772-80 9810-12 9822 9830 9830 9980-93 9999 10195-97 10342-53 10446 10448 10452-57 10483 10563-64 10643 10645 10773-79 10812-15 10995 11114 11195 11801-2 11805 11196-7 11674 11681 11800 12297 14402-04 15236-40 15250 18778-79 18782-3 19099 19511 19840 20983 1469 3240 7177 14486 20679 23 Pg. 28 Pg. 68-69
McMillin	536
McMurtry	9564 13869
McNabb	135 141
McNairy	24
McNutty	145
McRay/McRea/McRhea	9296
Meeks	167
Meginson	102
Menable	124
Menees	8354
Mercer	5443 13909 22415 14689 20697 21167
Merchant	124

Meredith	15462
Meriday	13881
Merrell	11168-69
Merrinor	19
Merriweather	2267
Meyers/Myers	12714 13281 13842 15233 15235 17728 18996 10594
Michison	36 37
Midkiff	5817
Military Line	2789 8127 11189
Mill	146
Mill Cr	43 154 228 230 22048 22411 5754 5921 6099 6606 6890-91 7178 4253 4789 5366 5378 5380-81 8775 8778 11486 13630 13651 14403 14424 wet fk 14425 14689 14726 14727 14733 104 116 151 22006-7 22048 22411 22413 10005 7458-60 7869-70 8154 7871 7945 7947 8561 8871 9188 9235-39 9352 9355-56 9467-69 9518 9544 9625-26 9810-11 9813 9846 9863-65 9866 9985-87 9999 10006 10106-8 10199 10200 10298-99 10330-31 10328-29 10333 10343 10345 13019-20 13944 16129 16692 16703 16813 18735 19071 19501-02 19639-40 19647 19643
Mill Cr Sampson's Fk of	27 43 45 163 164 166 169 227 234
Miller	2776 7737 7947 8739 10339 10473 10539 11060 12645 13233 13269 14954 17184 18030
Mindinhall	65
Mine Lick Cr	13906 3256 9520-22 9591 9643-44 9648-49 9651 10516 10692 12345 13031 13082 13269 13587 14022 14134 14221 14534 14852 14875 15500 15507 16140-41 16496 17813 20457 8643 9167 9781 9853
Mineby	22106
Mitchell	1902 7166-67 10299 10560 12608 27 43 73 125 126 128 155 157 158 159 160
Moirs (Meyers?)	12811
Molden	14541
Mollorn	64
Montgomery	6203 10771 11168 16696 19510
Moody	7645
Moore	205 1590-91 4239 5291 5318 6008 6505 7235 7496 8535 8564 9797-98 10364 10515 10538 11001 11062 11063-65 11819 11942 12244 16812 18786 11229 11818 1469 3118 5753 9046 9298 17556 11821 11851 16036 17900

Refer to note on Table of Contents before using this index..

Mordock	9544 9865 9443
Morgan	9520 9521 9522 9881 10012-13 10015 10020 10014 10415 11422 12282-84 14022 14906 18261 154 4324 16562-3
Morrell	22109-10 22230-31
Morrison	2778 22310
Morrison's Cr	6596-97 6599 6988 6992 5289 5290 2777 2778 7804 15874 16834 16835 16836 16837 5639 6989 8948 10607 10774 11598 11700 14737 14738 15031 15378 15873
Morriss	62

Morrow	14087
Mosely	7908 8610
Moss	19687 19688 13002
Moyor	6482 5307
Muire's Fk (of Caney Fk)	7694
Mulherrin	7743 14115
Mulkey	6624 8443 8444 10770
Mundine	2758
Murray/Murrey	1547 1643 2025 2174 2664-5 2775 2779 2838 4789 4793 5914-15 7166-67 9293 9546 9574 9811 9813 10197 10443 10750 11800-02 11674 12297 14486-89 15236 15665-66 16232 16690-92 16697 16699 16700-01 167703-04 16706 16743 17857 18763 19501-10 20695 20697-99 20700-01 20898-99 20900 21334-35 14108 14403 14484 17451 18760 8161 22415 22109 mill seat 5754 5918 8574 14485
Mynes	8451 8452
Narrock	115
Nelson	8262
Nelston	123
Nevell	11753 14108 18715
Nevels	213 216
Newman	7041 20599
Newsom	511
Nicholas	9519 15563 18684 18927 21905 21906
Nichols	5463 5750 5318 7173 7269 15820 18893 20407 20562 21423 21920
Nobaway	126
Noble	97 214
Nolen	948-50 1546-47 1902 1959-60 2177 2470 2479 3114 3116 3416 58-206 58-296 58-354 6376-77 5288 5291 5499 11966 19773 5639
Norris	3312-13 5608 7259 7264 8247 9838 12067
Norrod	16721
Norton	17636
Nourse	219 230 234

Refer to note on Table of Contents before using this index..

Oakes	1591
Oar/Ore	172 173 174 179 180 181
Obed Rd	123 126
Obed's River	143 145 149 146 202
Obey River	74 192 233
Odle	205 9161 10070 17566 7481 8212
Officer	43 73 155 158 160 183 188
Ogden	195 197
Orsburn	9661 9777 9780 9847 10723 11596
Osgathorp	22231 22411
Overton	26 46
Overturf	13528 15467
Owl Cove	20997
Ownby	9352 10106-8 14733 19640
Pack	19247-48 19622

Page	17653
Paile	5639
Pain/Payne	7140 10583 14083 14261 17741
Park	19622 20513 20621 20623
Parker	3073 3114 3116 12525 12812 16240 16619 18223
Parkins	3118
Parris Spring Place	146
Parrott	11917
Parson/Person	66 84
Passons	5339 11080 14252
Patterson	316
Patton	949 6865 8543
Payton	29 110 213 354 9443-4 9445-6 9847 9985 10005-6 10199 9518 9848-9 5743 8140 9519 178 5744 10200 11528 11721 12297 12346 13907 14108
Payton's Cr	214
Pearce/Pierce	8821 12051 13651 18260 8893 16561
Pearson	6206 7091
Penitentiary Cave	6605 10353 12888
Pennington	9663-64 9666 9881 11562 15728
Perkins/Purkins	7259 7264 9838 12067
Perrin	2789
Person	6358 7188
Peters (Piles ?)	147
Peterson	5918 5920-21 8774 9782 10331 15581 15582
Petre	9443 9518 9544 9863 9188 9868
Pettijohn	9852 9853 16140
Petty	236 10824-25 11476 11817 11991 12600 14083 14261
Peyton's Cr	4355 5586
Pharis	7173-74 15563 17182-83 18030 18683-84 18893 18927 19676 20671 21487-88 21489 21490-91 21906
Phillips	2789 3506 12012 21316
Pigeon Roost Cr	7559 7879 7908 8394 8610 8838 8932 9798 9802 9804 11424 11511 11819 11821 11889 12011 12012 12563 13675 14866 15573 1962 2790 6959 22340
Piles	6992-93 8681 16619 18223 20792 6991
Pillow	42
Pilot Knob	21799
Pinckney	17775
Pine Lick Fk	11016-17 12068 14404 16851 18247 7254 7481 8212 8667 9306 10495-96 10551-52 10846 8665 8668 9161 12906
Pinsley	6451
Pippin	10103 11808 16150 19606 19651 20282 20599 16586
Plumley	4764-67 13789 14954 15442 15727-28 15857 16024-25 16247 17337 17565-66 18053 18419 18779 19688 18763

Refer to note on Table of Contents before using this index..

Plunkett's Cr	14893
Poindexter	17636 22058 22059 22060
Poiner	1451
Pond Spring	15058
Poor	139
Porter	950 4180 8544 8545 10467 21554 19

Porterfield	498 1597 5667 52 79 82 59 82 90 91 229 265
Poston	3100 3918 7339
Powell	183 11178 21934
Prater	4993
Prentis	197
Prewett/Pruart	354 178 13514
Price	1597 5305-06 6306 6308-09 6310 6502 6584 8790-91 9548 209 10070 10595-98 14238 15823 18247 19527 21423 22414 10563 10892 10892 9297
Prince	8578
Prim	5920
Proctor	6377 6997 8546 8944 11966 11970 14664
Proctor's Cr	6811 4791 4792-94 5915 9547 9564 9782-84 10492 10559 10644 13234 13561-62 13869 13922 13994 13995 15149 15150 15466 15581-82 15666 15729 15730 17636 18240-41 22058-59 22192 22060 364 1261 1580
Pryor	2123 5066 5069 15874 20659 14737-38 16 18 20 68 141 205 58-236
Puncheon Camp Cr of Roaring R	15871 16147
Purcell	8665 18247 20562 21783
Pursley	10846 13513 16232
Putman	6759 6943 5299 5300 9621 12293 17879 21330 21814
Pyburn	22 65
Pyron	8438 9329 9330 18753 18754 9331
Quary	7515
Race Grounds	16563
Radley	2118-19 2835 7042
Ragland	1981 2789 10586 10627 11889 11992 17448
Ragle	10337
Ramsey	47 48 Pg. 3
Rankin	8017-8 12092 17807
Rash	9525-26 16919
Ratliff	58-213
Rawls	7407
Ray/Rhea	12205 16130 18742 585
Raybourn/Rayburn	116 206 58-228 2125 3506 4315
Rayman/Raymond	6119 5248-49 10452 13263 18786
Razor	9772 12927 15137
Reason	3258
Red River	3925
Redick	9953 13173-74 17556
Redkins	3262
Reece	8494
Reed	7591 136
Reneau/Renno	9217 10942 11092 11094
Reynolds	7426 9866 9965 13720
Rhoades/Roads	94 212 10840 236-7 192
Rice	127 212
Rich	5916 5918-5919 6993
Richardson	1955 3521 4260 11444 20674
Richey	9945 10994 11473 17506 20792-93 20797 22229

Refer to note on Table of Contents before using this index..

Richman/Richmond	46 58-262 1463 3114 4315 6203 8879
Riddy	21737
Ridge	7709 9643-44 9648-51 9652 10512-13 10940 11821 11889 12067 12627 13675 14134 14534-35
Roaring R	10 14 15 20 22 26 30 33 34 35 36 39 40 41 43 44 46 49 50 51 52 53 54 55 56 57 58 59 61 62 63 64 65 66 67 68 69 70 72 73 76 77 78 79 80 81 83 84 85 86 87 90 91 92 93 94 95 96 98 99 100 101 103 114 118 123 124 125 129 132 142 151 157 158 160 166 173 188 193 195 204 218 209 210 105 126 134 169 175 220 1609 1723 2025 2123 2472 2570 2664-65 5820 6008 6206 6297 6306 6308-09 6449 6501-02 6584-87 6734 6823 7091 7166 4193 4197-98 4247-51 4570 4790 5143 5267 5288 5305-06 7528 7804 7846 7878 7901 8016 8018 8113 8273 8565 8681 8790 8839 8879 9026 9293 9297 9425 9526 9545 9548 9821 9830 9945 9957 9980 9981 9988 9991 9993 10195-97 10228 10293 10349 10352 10457 10563 10595-96 10597-99 10607 10733 10774 10815 10837 10892 10934-36 11282 11473 11528 11597-98 11605-07 11682 11684 11721 11754 11786 11807-08 11965 11967-69 12092 12282-84 12297 12346 12406-07 12493 12811-12 13197 13263-64 13266 13270 13281 13536 13572 13609 13688 13842 14153 14169 14488 14901 15031 15232-33 15235 15241 15242-44 15269-70 15378 15871-72 16039 16147 16180-81 16236 16238 16239 16413-14 16509 16562 16585-86 16697 16919 16983-84 17311 17452 17658 17731 17743 17779 17856 18224-26 18261 18405 18996 19100 19271 19270 19272-74 19480 19602 19605 19607 19643-44 20282 20451 20653 20792-95 21117-18 21171 21195 21903 8949 10452 9989 13852 14003-04 14487 16834 19505 2775-76 2779 2926 3047 3902 3905 4147 6500 6754 6991 8017 10594 12195 155 9424 9525 4449-50

Refer to note on Table of Contents before using this index..

Roaring R Copperas Cr of	155 157 170
Roaring R Dry Cr of	44 72
Roaring R Lamb's Cr of	33
Roaring R Lick Cr of	81 183 11458 11786
Roaring R Little Island Cr of	221 222
Roaring R Spring Cr of	69 127 128 135 174 176 212 5307-8
Roberts	8113 10779 11289 16039 16432 16414 16864-65 17043 17173 17823 17876 17879 18178-79 18405 Roberts 18595 19605 20283 20659 20794 7591 4591
Robertson	22 23 69 81 120 171 191 6187 6297 4248 7871 10935 14004 14219 17452 19270 19470 19272 19273-74 6479
Robertson Co	15286 Jacob Young
Robeson	7924
Robinson	3929 19470 19270
Rochester	6178
Rock House Lick - Jennings Cr	15238

Rock Island	4239 8070 9853 10515 10718 10940 12672
Rock Springs Cr	4180 7422 7426-29 7642-45 7904 8196 8752-53 8755-56 9361 9728 9994-96 10419 10942 10981-82 11045 11270-72 11439 11676 12405 13219 13222 13659 14858 17062 17064 18297 20735 11675 14893 8754 19 82
Rockhouse Cave	9548
Rocky Br of Cumberland	21334
Roddy	22268
Roden/Rodden/Rotten/Rhotan	8 9237 10139 10345 14727 14728 7458-59 8872 9188 13513
Rogal	21994
Rogers	3114 9819 11727 12539

Refer to note on Table of Contents before using this index..

Roland/Rowland	7269 8280 9574 9576-77 13113 20294-95 20291 22330
Rollins	6451
Rork	1321
Rose	8394 10298 10750
Roulston	7425-26 7434 7639-43 7645 8752 11045 11178 69 215Sheriff 228 229 231 232 234 235 236 237 238 265 11866 12481 13219 13222 15058 17064 21934 498 511 536 1321 1598-99 1600 1955 2118-19 2122-23 2125 2475 2700 2789-90 2835 3073 3506 3905 7042 4180 4541 4759 5028 5303 9652 9712 11945 115
Rowan	144 146 148 149 172
Roy's Br	10585 19677 10824
Roy's Br of War Trace	11062-64 10824
Royal Cave	11711 12242
Rugle's Br of Cumberland	14263
Rush	11864
Rush Fork of Flynn's Cr	17876 136 8841-2 9692-3 10811
Russell	3680
Russell	6 9 48 49 63 66 78 82 182 58-117
Russell Mill Cr	18 68 141 205
Russell's Fk of Jennings	16251 20775
Rust	11863
Rutherford	18226 12812 19643
Rutledge	2774 3047 3240 3513 3929 4253 5289-90 5305-07 6008 7901 8643 8660 9980-81 12168-69 12493 12495 12714 13263-64 13266 15244 15270 16236 16238-39 18995 19470 19270-71 19471-72 20794-95 20997 4451 6599
Rutledge's Mill Cr	6796 7041 7214 11042
Rutledge's Branch N of Cumberland	11686
Rutledge's Mill Cr of Roaring R	8949 11805
Ryal	5971 7516 12242 15691 17459 17900 20407 21929 22038

Refer to note on Table of Contents before using this index..

Sadler	144 2699 6358 8660 10914 11057 11172 11413 16681 11755 15567 17396 18411 18435 19897 20735 21571 21572 21704 21817 21902 21928 21967 22210
Sadler's Fk (Brimstone)	11004 11005 11171 12608
Sailor	21316

Salsberry	7173
Salt Cr	3521
Salt Lick Cr	6998 9221 9364 11080 14943 15283 16615 69 2757 2758 5751 4250 4252 4260 4262 4354 4526 4519
Sanders/Saunders	213 8070 8071 328 18174
Sanford	74 151 156 166 182
Santee	22 31 39 131 139
Saul/Soul	4180 19
Savage	22059
Saxton	226
Scanland	5367 8599 8600 10813-14 14732 16696 17546 19622 20814-15 22332 22412
Scanland's Br	8599 8600 8647 17775
Scantling	213
Scott	5743 8140 10557
Scurlock	55-23
Seagrave	46
Searcy	5717 8016 9546-47 9830 11450 11438-9
Seeley	8130
Seguche Valley	16192
Settles	6182 16690
Sexton's Cr	2480
Seypert	34
Shadden	18003 14022
Shankle	9293 9982 10196 10564 10599 10892 11684 13263 13688
Shanklin	4451
Shary	131
Shaw	7188-89 9180 10195 11450 11967 13197 13802 16509 16982 20156 20291-93 20839 21001 21156 21171 21568
Shelley/Chilly/Sheeley's Knob	10194 10346
Shepherd	7528 21799 60 88 89 151
Shipman	10457 10563 11458 11528 11684 11686 11802
Shoemake	5717 9180 11423 11450 20775
Shores	3312
Short	6624 7254 7481 8212 8821 9246 10773 10844-46 18736-37 21455 22095 8893
Shute	8072 8092-94 8630-34 8742-43 8745 10861 11866-67 12637 15034 16250 18910 19867-68 21704-12 12238 55-23 55-32 55-67
Shuttlesworth	11444
Simmons	1982 16384 16385-86 17161-62
Simpson	948-50 1462 4451 7804 11683 Floating Mill 21554
Simpson/Simson	110 130 122 58-213
Sims	4764-65
Sinclair	180
Siscoe	2779 21783
Skaggs	122 5291 8091 18307
Skeggs	87?? 8785 11724 12651 12811 13264 15306 16239
Skelton	234 7598-99 7600 8690 8691 8693
Skiles	7423 7425 8196 12405 15499
Slinger	11817
Sloan	3

Refer to note on Table of Contents before using this index..

Smith	1469 1687 1902 3100 5022 5024 5378 6297 6561 7289 7428 7741 8754 8755 9586 9625 9838 10013 10019 10026 10299 11027 11270 11966 12069 12674 12963 13522 13721 14888 16743 17043 17173 17185 17375 17820 17823 18595 20163 20538 20775 20839-41 20982 21562 21566 21570 21694 21814 21888 21994 22006-07 22106 22227 22229-30 22316-18 41 77 88 134 69 316 318
Smith Co	3 19 87 120 2475 3065 4993 5543 5586 7042 7122 4180 4354 5028-29 5031 7289 7422 7641 7862 7897 7898 7900 8072 8240 8295 8418 9364 9441 9650 9728 9774 9776 9994-6 9773 10861 11080 11178 11498 11676 11866-67 12637 12674 14572 14893 16798 17063 17375 18602 18754 20735 20776 21820 21902 21928 21934 21967 7269 7640 10497 11476 22 31 39 41 42 43 50 52 77 79 82 115 133 88 131 144 6479 69 316 214 236
Smith's Fk (Jennings Cr)	213 216 8488
Snow Cr	7042
Somers	21903 See Summers
Sorrell	9819
Southwest Point	1723 7091 7434 7598 8690-91 12481 15058
Southwood	18037
Sparta	10515
Spear	18228 18760
Spears	216
Spicewood Cove	7407
Spivey	9289
Spraggins	8092-94
Spring Cr	6734 6823 6310 5198 5307 11282 11682 12282-84 14487 16562-63 18261 22607 8 52 217 22607 3073 8565 10351 10596 9991 6754
Spurlock	21905-06
Stacy	8600 8647 9983 9990 10347 10350 10770 11727 16706 19506 19511 22416
Stafford	2025 2480 2779 5288 8016 8018 8573 9988 11969 12532 12812 15269 15270-71 17311 17728 17731 18226 19602 8017 209 210 20983
Stalcup	1463
Stamps	9361 9994-96 16496 9728
Stanton	8072 10441 11450 15272
Starkey	49 68
Starling	5067
Steakley	4759
Stephens	7190 10584 17450
Stephenson/Stevenson	4187 41 58-69
Sterling	2267
Stewart/Stuart	5359 22135 78 129 58-237 55-23
Stokes	22316
Stone	10026 11267 13197 20457
Stone's R (Rutherford Co)	55-71 Robert Huff
Stoner	11967
Stotgrass	17807

Stothart	4811 9126 16382-83 16678 7743
Stout	198
Stover	9356 9986 10106-07 10345 16129 7178 19639 19647
Stowell	26

Refer to note on Table of Contents before using this index..

Struthers	133
Stubblefield	1141 3256-58 3262 4180 4197 18735-38 21898 3 19 22 31 140 193 316 318 7042
Stukley	92
Sugar Camp Hollow	17203
Sugar Cr	6203 5365 5499 5367 16700 16706 17857 19503-04 19506-11 20814 20816 22006-07 22109-10 22227 22230 22412 22415-16 10368 9990 9992 10347 10350 25 26 60 219 229 231
Sugar Run	29
Suggs	7490 11818
Sullivan	2700 5028-29 5031 6762 11945 14022 15489 16369 18246 16
Sumner Co	328 7733 145 3240 3929
Sutton	6596-97 6599 5289 10607 15031 15873-74 17441 18995 19087
Swaford	10538
Swagerty	11711
Swain	140
Swearingham	20775
Sweasy	3115 5291 7527 12652 12744-45
Swift	16721
Swindle	15234
Swinney	11096-97 11228 20696 20819
Sycamore Spring	198
Tachett	13610
Tadlock	21327
Taggart	1580 4791-92 5914-17 6811 9547 9783-84 13922 13994-95 15466
Tait	145
Talley	66 108 129 206 5677 10774
Talley's Hollow	16619 16834 17728 18223 8681 16240
Tate	14572
Tatum	154 230 236 87 120 1247 3065 3917 10861 143 55-71
Taylor	588 594 1723-24 3902 3905 4147 4980 6206 7091 7188-9 7191 8578 9852-53 10417 12041 14737 16143 16509-10 16982 19934 21840 39 133 16 18 35 36 39 40 50 52 53 55 67 77 83 96 97 100 101 102 103 104 105 106 113 116 118 125 127 134 135 175 176 190 206 212
Taylor's Cr	4980 14187 13076 8203 39 5817 14187
Teal	5751 9221 16615 18601 11164-65
Teffteller	7460 8561 9811 9987 10106
Temples	16235 16237 16929-30 19526-27 20670-73 22339
Templeton	7407 12003 12132 12206
Terman/Turman	9940 17545
Terrell	585

Terry	8273 16919 4355
Thackston/Thaxton	3680 9294 9845 16251
Thomas	107 5543 9692-93 11918 7733
Thompson	10343 10348 10440 16381 16680 20889 20890 42 11863-64 206 209
Thompson's Br	11864 11863 10336
Thorn	6574 7214
Thornton	7897-98 9822 11839 13452-53 13494-95 14859 22131
Tilford	20513 20621 20623

Refer to note on Table of Contents before using this index..

Tilghman	57
Tillery	17185
Timmons	133
Tinsley	2470 5146
Totten	143
Town Cr	3313 8915 18742
Townsend	3627 3629 3902 4083 5888-89 6119
Trace Cr	42 120 15942 18762 11596 14541 14951 14958-9 15000 10557-8 18174
Trace Cr of Big Barren	9519 9541-43 9777-80 15547 15942 18762
Trace Cr of Cumberland	8354 8745 14541 14951 14958-59 15000 16285 17573 17653
Trap	8262 17813 18742 21694 21888
Trough/Tan Troft Spring	15272 20840 22317-18 7280
Trousdale	5543 4993 8240
Turkey Cr N of Cumberland	10443 10354 9470 14690 8574
Turney	5381 16942-43 52 77 39 8194
Twitty	8488-89 10456 11015 11173 12650-52 13907 14108 15306 21455
Tyler	70
Tyre	5543
Tyrell	3513 13802 43 350
Usery/Usury	10733 11003 14843
Vaden	5028 5031
Vallance	9712-13 15498-99
Van Hooser	6865
Vance	7286 7288-89 7291 7905-6 8642 9311 9362 11090-93 12482 14866 18407 39 131 139 1598-99 1600 4759 4797 9586 9715 10849 234 238 354
Vaney	7733
Vaulx	9026 9290 9293-96 9544-48 9705 13641 13993-95 14687 15251 19840
Vettito	14083 14261
Vinson/Vincent/Vansent	328 9364 10584-5 10790 12600-01 16928 19676-77 10568 21109-10
Waddle/Waddal	536 5366 5380 6099 7945 8778 13630
Wade	16233
Wade's Br (Jennings Cr)	16232-33 16743
Wakefield	5743 6230 8140
Waldrop	10933

Waldson	94
Walker	17775 20540-41 21423 3257 11282
Walkins	21331
Wallace	7423-27 8523 4828 8756 9361 9072 10711 17600-02 18030 10942 10981-82
Waller	2926
Walling	8739 10139 21820
Wallis Br (of Flynn's Cr)	117
Walnut Ridge	11044
Walters	12195
Walton	2122 2125 8240 21816
Walton Road	3 152 1321 2119 3257-58 3262 7434 7598 7862 8111 8690-91 314 10515 12481 14153 15058 16982 19716-17 20342 21171 19691 19934 21529 11439 18632 10338 9526 22 65 79 82 115 133
Walton's Ferry	7434 7598 8690-91 12481 15058
Walton's Br	35

Refer to note on Table of Contents before using this index..

War Trace	8438 9296 9329-31 11062-64 11164 11839 11917-19 12203 12205 12525 16130 16373 16810 16877 18753-54 18910 19041 19429 19867-68 20159 20674 3118 8161
Ward	3100 4187 5069 7276 7279 15610
Ward's Fk (Jennings Cr)	14155 16242 18957 21141 21331 8632 8742-43 8634 8628 8627 8630 8633
Warmack/Wommack	18 41 8195 9649 11155 11945 14157 14534-35 21902 21928
Warren	120 10497
Warren Co	6131
Warthen	99
Waters	114
Watkins	8628 8632 8742 19934
Watson	36 102 129 11851 14169 15547
Watts	8563 21834 21835 22311
Weaver	76 4198 11727
Webb	11486 17281
Webster	3678 3679
Webster's Cr	6697 9363 10344 10454-56 10906 10955-57 10990 6697 10954 11096 11168-69 11173 11195-98 11228 11674 11712 11799 11801-02 22414
Welch	16025-26 18051
Well's Cr	15034
West	8586 11850 13129-30 14843 15023 15025 15462 16464 16834 17337school 17506 18053 20450 20452 20794
Whartner	80
Wheaton	4180
Wheeler	7924 9652 14899 14900 17156 17511-12 17448 20672 20953-54
Whitaker	8130
White	1321 11673 12525 18893-95 55-71
White Co	5304 9444 9858 12012 5667 5753 5817 5888 5929 6119 6123 6130 6574 6579 6760 6795-96 7041 7214 4239 4253 4980 5069 5203-4 7407 7478 8070-71 8090-91 8203 8262

```
                        8284  8402  8739  9861  9946 10139 10161 10231 10718 10849
                       10940 11042 11762 11818 12003 12067 12132 12206 12294
                       12563 12627 12645-46 12672-73 13076 13632-33 13675
                       14187 14511 15010 15095 15234 15469 15573 17737 17813
                       17886 18742 18786 21192 21694 21888 7255 7258 7490
                       7496 10473 11093 17985 9362 13224 585 588 594 1597
                       2789 3643 117 219 228 229 237
```

White Co (Elk River?)	55-82 55-83
White Plains	10940 12672
Whitecox	1598
Whiteside	5198
Whitley	10228
Whitney	10492 11852 11854 12741-42 15727 16247 17569 19688
Whitson	3629 5067 11687 15010 16142 16176
Whortner	80
Wiggins	55-71
Wilbourn	7733
Wilburn	1247 2475 4187 5359 11945 18436
Wiles/Willis	5586 8871 9237-38
Wilkeson/Wilkerson	3228 6297 8929 8934 9425 10993 14842 15858 16036 11128 6991
Wilkinson	4993 16549 117 15857

Refer to note on Table of Contents before using this index..

Williams	1984 5679 5750 5578 5677-80 6188 6758 6892 4824 5381 5482 7190 9235 16703 3045 2070 2125 2756-59 3046-47 3114-15 5290 7478 8872 9355 9468 10106 10497 10627 10826 10838-39 10905 10955 10971 11096 11170-73 11754-59 12876 12888-9 13675 14115-17 14726 15192 15288 17449-52 18002 18735-38 19640 20163 21167 21177 22048 22006 22332 11271-72 12875 13076 13944 13998 15192 15620 16510 18601 21456 69 7323 7737-38 7878 7901 8353 7694 8127 25 42 43 45 46 79 133 144 161 162 220
Williamsburg	6592 6603 15620 17182 18595 18683-84 18927 15240 18782 20513
Williamson	6796 8072 10861 20837 Pg. 3
Williamson's Branch	3065 9441 10861 (Note: Shown on present-day maps as St. Mary's.)
Willoby/Willoughby	15128 17092
Wills	3513
Wilson	4083 5742 5339 6297 6890 8631 8647 9161 9375 9424 9964-65 10359 11419 11685 13853 13993 14252 14358 14687 15846 15857 16147-50 16187 16549 16983 17655 20679 20793 20795 21177 21898 354 hors slew bottom 149 354
Wilson Co	9080
Winchester	7722 58-145
Windsoor	5339
Winfrey	4248
Winwright	2838

Wisdom	5291 10631
Witcher	3678-80 4354 9294 14154-55 21096 21109 4355
Wolf River	119 137 138 139 144 199
Wolf River (Caney Fk of)	148 150
Wolf River (Spring Fork of)	147
Womack	See Warmack
Wood's Br (Spring Cr)	14487
Wood/Woods	5915 7846 7878 9167 10536 11804 12336 13452 13493 14951 14958-9 17338 9547 9591 9644 9782 9821 10336 13561-2 13572 13599 14846 15149 15272 15940 15942 16124
Woolfolk	115 4519 8273 3521 4250 4252 8091 15287 15610 18599 18600-02 19377 20837 22202 8161 8194
Woodward	18600 22202 3045
Woolf Cr (Caney Fork)	7289 7641 13720 15071 21820 7288
Woolf Pen Br (Martin's Cr)	12675
Woolfolk	115 4519 8273
Work	33 34 51 54 98 99 100
Wornell	12297
Wright/Right	12539 13761 20157

Refer to note on Table of Contents before using this index..

Yarber	8871
Yarborough	10328-30 10333
York	9775-6 10790 11595 16985 22268 22420
Young	2790 2791 8642-3 4276 5303-4 5667 7279 7559 8090 8091 8194-5 8932-3 9362 9712 9953 10311 10849 11094 11155-57 11596 11917-19 12012 12203 12205 12563 13658 13837 14022 15286 15468-69 15573 15610 17605-07 18736-38 21110 11511 18735 21109 22088 16690 21994 50 79
Youngblood	10103 16192 17814 17815